Allied Looting
in World War II

ALSO BY
KENNETH D. ALFORD

*Civil War Museum Treasures:
Outstanding Artifacts and the Stories Behind Them*
(McFarland, 2008)

Allied Looting in World War II

Thefts of Art, Manuscripts, Stamps and Jewelry in Europe

Kenneth D. Alford

Foreword by Sidney D. Kirkpatrick

McFarland & Company, Inc., Publishers
Jefferson, North Carolina, and London

LIBRARY OF CONGRESS CATALOGUING-IN-PUBLICATION DATA

Alford, Kenneth D.
   Allied looting in World War II : thefts of art, manuscripts, stamps and jewelry in Europe / Kenneth D. Alford ; foreword by Sidney D. Kirkpatrick.
      p.   cm.
   Includes bibliographical references and index.

   ISBN 978-0-7864-6053-3
   softcover : 50# alkaline paper ∞

   1. World War, 1939–1945 — Destruction and pillage. 2. Allied Forces — History. 3. Pillage — Europe — History — 20th century. 4. Theft — Europe — History — 20th century. 5. Art thefts — Europe — History — 20th century. 5. Art thefts — Europe — History — 20th century. 6. Art treasures in war — Europe — History — 20th century. 7. Jewelry theft — Europe — History — 20th century. 8. Manuscripts — Europe — History — 20th century. 9. Postage stamps — Europe — History — 20th century. 10. Lost articles — Europe — History — 20th century. I. Title.
D810.D6A44   2011
940.54'12 — dc22   2011004828

BRITISH LIBRARY CATALOGUING DATA ARE AVAILABLE

© 2011 Kenneth D. Alford. All rights reserved

No part of this book may be reproduced or transmitted in any form or by any means, electronic or mechanical, including photocopying or recording, or by any information storage and retrieval system, without permission in writing from the publisher.

Front cover: The most valuable painting stolen by American soldiers from the Schwarzburg Castle was Caspar David Frederich's *Landscape with Rainbow on the Island of Rügen*. The oil painting on canvas was cut from the frame. It is still missing (Wikimedia Commons); frame © 2011 Shutterstock.com; Schwarzburg Castle, 1900 (Wikimedia Commons)

Manufactured in the United States of America

McFarland & Company, Inc., Publishers
  Box 611, Jefferson, North Carolina 28640
    www.mcfarlandpub.com

To my wife, Edda,
who has filled my life with happiness

Acknowledgments

I am thankful to the many people and institutions that have helped with this research and writing of this book.

Thanks are due to the following individuals: Arthur W. Bergeron Jr., PhD, Carlisle, PA; Dr. Rolf Bothe, Kunst zu Weimar Sammlungen, Weimar, Germany; Dr. Barbara Eschenburg, Städtische Galerie im Lenbachhaus, Munich, Germany; Professor G. H. Hertling, Lake Forest Park, WA; Robert Kudelski, Warsaw, Poland; Opritsa D. Popa, librarian, Shields Library, University of California, Davis (most fortunately, she linked Berman's name with the *Hildebrandslied*); Al Regensberg, senior archivist, Records Center and Archives, Santa Fe, NM; Dr. Thomas Seibel, Bad Wildungen, Germany; and Dr. Konrad Wiedemann, Bibliothek University Kassel, Germany.

Special thanks to Kate Chavez, for reading and correcting my work; also the continued help of my dear friend Thomas Sharp is much appreciated.

I would also like to offer my gratitude to Perseus Book Group for permission to use material from *Great Treasure Stories of World War II*, one of my earlier books.

Last but not least, I pay tribute to my wife, Edda. Without her support the tasks that I have undertaken would have proved impossible.

Table of Contents

Acknowledgments   vi
Foreword by Sidney D. Kirkpatrick   1
Introduction   3

Part I
STEALING A TROVE OF STAMPS

1. The 273rd Infantry Regiment   7
2. The Looting of Anton Wiede   13
3. The Investigation   19

Part II
A PASSION FOR LUCAS CRANACH PAINTINGS

4. Donovan Senter's Early Days   33
5. The Counter Intelligence Corps   40
6. The Quest for Lucas Cranach Paintings   47
7. The Charade Continues   59
8. Unanswered Questions   71

Part III
PLUNDERING PRICELESS MANUSCRIPTS

9. The Capture of Bad Wildungen   79
10. Lieutenant Bud Berman   85
11. The Rare Book Dealer   91
12. The Papal Countess   96
13. Other Bad Wildungen Robberies   102

Part IV
THE SCHWARZBURG CASTLE

14. The Robbery — 109
15. A Break in the Case — 117
16. Churchill "Chuck" Jones Brazelton — 122
17. The Nun and the Poster — 135

Part V
VIGNETTES OF LOOTING

18. The Gravediggers Pillage Reutti, Germany — 141
19. The U.N. Red Cross Robbery — 146
20. The Rabbi's Egyptian Ring — 149
21. Frederick the Great's Handwritten Manuscript — 153
22. Berlin Central Archives — 157
23. The Golden Book of Saarbrücken — 162
24. The Priceless Mainz Psalter — 166
25. Raphael's *Portrait of a Young Man* — 170
26. Clara Elisabeth Hertling — 180

Part VI
LOOTING FROM HUNGARY IN WORLD WAR II

27. Hungary — 189
28. The Hungarian National Bank's Gold and Silver Reserves — 191
29. The Acquisition of the Hungarian Crown Treasure — 201
30. The Gold Treasure of Kremsmünster — 211
31. Cardinal Mindszenty — 214
32. The Return of Saint Stephen's Crown — 221
33. The Hungarian Gold Train — 227
34. The American Army Takes Custody — 232
35. The General's Kingdom — 235
36. The End of the Gold Train Property — 239

Appendix A: Anton Wiede's Missing Stamps and Paintings — 245
Appendix B: The Missing Kaltenbrunner Treasure — 248

Appendix C: Thefts from the Weimar National Art Collections   251
Appendix D: Otto v. Falke's Description of the Crown of
   Saint Stephen   254
Chapter Notes   259
Bibliography   269
Index   271

Foreword
by Sidney D. Kirkpatrick

If the National Archives in College Park, Maryland, were to issue private detective badges to writers chronicling the chaotic and explosive final days of World War II, Kenneth D. Alford would be wearing the gold medal. Alford doesn't rewrite the work of others; he advances, through careful and painstaking scholarship, the pool of information that rank-and-file researchers use as their road map. He is a first-class detective, operating with his own global positioning system, uncovering lost documents and ferreting out the truth in the National Archives, as he does in archival repositories worldwide. Over the last three decades, his work has been used to inform government policy, hunt down criminals, and track the rat-line movement of plundered gold, silver, diamonds, artwork, and rare manuscripts. He has shared his provocative and always valuable research with heads of state, international police agencies, museum officials, and the many others who follow in his footsteps.

The results speak for themselves: file cabinets of his original research can be found in such disparate locations as the Hungarian Ministry of Culture, the Clinton Presidential Library in Arkansas, and in *Hitler's Holy Relics*, my own latest book. *Allied Looting in World War II*, his new book, is like a Pandora's box. There are those who will be offended by what he has discovered and those who will champion the conclusions he has drawn, but no one can question that he knows what he is writing about: vanished treasure and the greed, fraud, deceit, and treachery that did not end on the battlefields of war-torn Europe.

Sidney D. Kirkpatrick is a prizewinning filmmaker and international best-selling author. His documentary film *My Father the President*, about Theodore Roosevelt, was a winner at the American Film Festival. Kirkpatrick's work has been featured on HBO, the History Channel, the Discovery Channel, and A&E. He has been profiled in the *New York Times*, *Time*, *The New Yorker*, and *Playboy*.

Introduction

"After all, society is divided into two classes — the fleecers and the fleeced — and assuredly it is better to belong to the fleecers."
— *Ursula Countess von Eppinghoven, 1893*

Every conscripted army reflects the society from which it is drawn, and the American army at the end of World War II was no exception. It had fought bravely and furiously in the most destructive war in history, and by the time American soldiers drove into the heartland of Germany, they were in no mood to "go easy" on the defeated enemy, especially in light of German atrocities during the Battle of the Bulge and the unimaginable horrors of the extermination camps.

Most American military men and women, however, still followed American military protocol and American rules and regulations. Some 295,000 had fallen in combat, and 200,000 more had died as a result of accidents, friendly fire, and illness. They are our heroes. There were those, however, who reflected the less admirable elements in the broad spectrum of American society by exhibiting a larcenous bent and even, in some cases, raping, murdering, and plundering the great treasures that the Nazis before them had seized in their rush to dominate Europe and North Africa. The glitter of so much treasure was just too tempting for some, and in this time of enormous disorder, widespread ordinary looting — justified in most minds by a universal hatred of German brutality — was, in practical terms, not considered stealing. What makes this book, *Allied Looting in World War II*, unique is that it focuses not on the soldier who stuffed the occasional Nazi flag or *S.S.* Luger into his pack but on those others who "appropriated" priceless hoards of paintings, sculptures, rare books, gold, platinum, and silver, and other items of great value.

The following is but a taste of the escapades of the main characters in this volume, those who took the biggest bites out of the fruits of victory following the conquest of the "thousand-year Reich."

Lt. Donovan Senter was "awarded" paintings by Lucas Cranach the Elder by a German industrialist's wife with whom he had carried on a torrid love affair; it ended only when he began romancing the wife's teenage daughter. He organized black market activities in France, Belgium, and Luxembourg while cheating his collaborators. Eventually, however, he came to an ignominious end in a Volkswagen camper in a Reno parking lot.

Maj. Charles A. Owens was a medical corps officer who, along with his fellow officers, seized Germany's largest private stamp collection, a huge coin collection, valuable paintings, and other treasures, all from the same family. Owens sold the stamps to a Chicago dealer and eventually became an award-winning physician at the Mayo Clinic.

Lt. Bud Berman stole two ancient books, one of which contained the oldest known writing in German — the priceless *Hildebrandslied*, a two-page poem. The stolen items' journey to a respected New York rare book dealer and then to the Doheny Museum in Los Angeles is a tale of greed, intrigue, and shady dealings until the U.S. government stepped in.

In 1945, Churchill Brazelton coerced the director of the Weimar Museum into handing over a treasure trove of art; he then opened a lucrative antique and art dealership on Madison Avenue in New York City.

This book also describes the journey of the sacred Hungarian crown treasure and how it was moved from a muddy oil drum to Fort Knox and eventually back to its rightful owners, the Hungarian nation, over the objections of Senator Bob Dole. Players in this drama included two cardinals and a pope.

Allied Looting in World War II also contains hitherto unpublished information about such items as the still missing *Portrait of a Young Man* by Raphael, stolen manuscripts written by Frederick the Great, the *Golden Book of Saarbrucken*, the *Mainz Psalter*, the earliest dated printed work of the Gutenberg press, the Giuseppi Ferlini *Egyptian Ring*, and a host of other treasures.

In all, this book portrays what happened when some liberators were driven by dreams of great wealth to "liberate" treasures that they were, by military law and American morality, not supposed to touch.

Part I
Stealing a Trove of Stamps

"Whenever requisitioning was done legally or with a show of legality in the proceedings, the population accepted it submissively and without serious complaint. On the whole, requisitioning, legal or otherwise, was accepted as the lot of the conquered."

History of the Fifteenth United States Army (1945)

Chapter 1

The 273rd Infantry Regiment

On the morning of April 16, 1945, the 2nd Battalion, 723rd Infantry Regiment, acting as the advance guard of the 9th Armored Division, spearheaded the First Army's drive to the Elbe River, receiving heavy direct fire as it rolled into Trebsen, Germany. Because of the fast and furious Allied advance at the unheard of pace of 60 miles per day, the retreating German Army did not have time to blow up the long bridge covering a marsh and the Mulde River. Martin Conner and his buddy Fran Dionne were ordered to look under the bridge for explosives but not to cross the bridge, as anyone on the other side would be German. As Conner was looking for explosives, some of the men in the 273rd began to run over the bridge; Conner yelled at them to stop. The advancing soldiers told Conner that army intelligence had changed the order and they had to cross and hold the bridge before the Germans returned to defend it. Conner and Dionne then started running across the bridge. As they reached the part over the Mulde River, they heard lots of noise and, turning around, saw a plane firing at them and flying so low that they thought it would crash into the bridge. The plane made repeated passes firing at the soldiers. On the third pass, Conner was hit in the shoulder and Dionne was hit in the leg. The plane was a U.S. Army Air Corps P-47. Tanks of the 9th Armored Division made radio contact with the P-47 and called it off. When Connor and Dionne made it to the end of the bridge, the P-47 flew over and, in a repentant manner, dipped its wing to the soldiers. This signal did not help the two men, who were not happy campers, but the pilot's action did get them out of the war.[1]

Anton Wiede, a German civilian, together with a group of foreign workers stood in the street and watched the battle as American tanks entered Trebsen. Wiede was co-owner of the firm Wiede & Söhne, which owned textile and paper manufacturing plants, as well as coal-producing facilities, including the development of synthetic diamonds using laser technology, quite an advanced scientific development at that time. The Wiede enterprises included a large paper mill in Trebsen, the second largest paper factory in Germany.

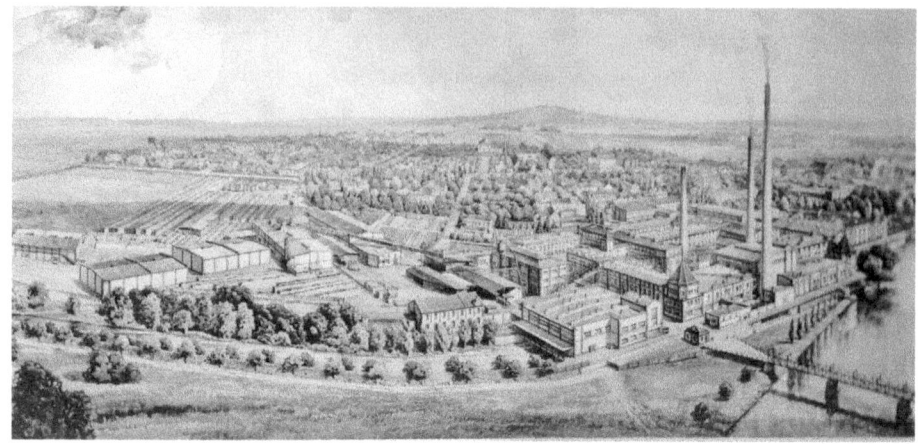

The German village of Trebsen, captured by the 273rd Infantry Regiment. The three chimneys are attached to the paper factory of Wiede & Sons. A safe in this factory contained some of the stamps acquired by U.S. Army medical officer Charles Owen (courtesy Stephan Wiede).

Anton J. Wiede, a well-educated engineer, inherited this industrial complex from his father, who had died in 1937. Born on May 3, 1911, the 34-year-old Wiede was indeed a very rich young man, married but in the process of a divorce. An American officer asked Wiede about the town and paper mill, and he gave them the required information regarding German troop activity in Trebsen. As was customary, the American troops took over the homes of the Germans and used them for housing and headquarters. They had learned early to take only occupied homes, as the empty homes were often booby trapped. One of Wiede's workers told him that the Americans were occupying his house. Wiede then went to his house, at 6 Ostmark Strasse, and found at the entrance a guard who asked him what he wanted. Wiede responded that this was his house and that his personal property was still inside. The guards asked how much time it would take to get his property out, and Wiede replied, "Approximately two hours."[2] The guard pointed to his watch and said that Wiede had 20 minutes to remove his property.

Wiede was quite nervous as he removed his clothing, linen, food, and some suitcases from the basement. In his haste, he forgot to remove a suitcase containing a box of jewelry — rings with sapphires and diamonds — valued at $2,500 (in 1945 dollars). He noticed that in the main room of his house the drawers had already been emptied and that his watches, camera, and other valuables were missing. He asked about these items, and the American soldier in the room merely laughed. With the help of a foreign laborer, Wiede relocated as much as he could to a nearby labor camp. He returned three days

The Wiede family's house in Trebsen, scene of the looting of the valuable paintings and a large coin collection (courtesy Stephan Wiede).

later and noticed that the suitcase with the jewelry was gone and a steel safe in the basement had been blown open; the 80,000 Reichsmarks it had contained were missing.

The following day the 273rd Infantry Regiment, with the support of attached armored and tank destroyer units, received the order to move back from Trebsen to an assembly area in the town of Lieberwolkevitz for an attack into Leipzig. That afternoon the task force moved directly into the city, riding on the armored vehicles; despite strong opposition, they reached the city hall by early evening. At the same time, the First and Second Battalions were advancing in their designated sectors. The First Battalion met stiff resistance while approaching Holzhausen; the Second Battalion advanced into Leipzig and was engaged in fighting near the Sports Palace against an entrenched enemy.

By 8 o'clock that night the Second Battalion was fighting against heavy opposition around the monument of the Battle of Nations. This encounter was the most difficult confrontation during the battle for Leipzig. At this highly symbolic monument, the Germans, with a force estimated at several hundred storm troopers, made their final stand. When the initial assault of the regiment's Second Battalion was made, resistance was so fierce that the monument was bypassed and subjected to a constant artillery barrage. By midnight, the First and Second Battalions had fulfilled their missions, and reorganization was effected in order to capture the city hall, against which previous assaults had failed. The city hall was taken early the second morning; inside, the men of the 273rd found that the mayor, his wife, their 18-year-old daughter, and a number of city officials had committed suicide rather than surrender to the Americans. Shortly after noon, all resistance in Leipzig had ceased except for the still well-defended force in the monument. Efforts to take the stronghold were repulsed during the afternoon, so surrender negotiations were attempted. The fanatical Nazis still inside refused to give up, although evacuation of the wounded was allowed by the Americans. As night wore on, it was decided to leave a guard outside and abandon all attempts to seize the monument, inasmuch as orders to move to the east had been received. At 2 o'clock on the afternoon of April 20, the German commander agreed to surrender so as to avoid further bloodshed.

When the regiment moved out of Leipzig by motor on the morning of the 20th, little remained of the once proud city. American air and ground forces had combined to reduce most of the city to little more than rubble. With the conquest of Leipzig completed, the regiment moved out to take up defensive positions along the Mulde River. Excitement ran high as rumors of a possible meeting with the oncoming Russians spread throughout the area. Patrols were constantly crossing the Mulde in hopes of making contact, while positions were established across the river from Trebsen to hold the only remaining bridge, all others bridges having been blown by the retreating Germans.

A fever of expectation ran through the soldiers, as contact with the Russians was imminent and hopes of it had begun to grip the Allied troops and commanders, particularly those of the First and Ninth U.S. Armies holding the line of the Elbe and Mulde Rivers. Eager to go down in history as the unit that first established contact, divisions vied with each other in devising stratagems to secure this honor for themselves. What would happen when Allied and Russian troops came together had been on many minds on the Allied side for a long time. Strict orders were given that patrols would venture no more than five miles beyond the Mulde River, so that serious clashes with the Red Army would not ensue. Previously U.S. fighter pilots had thought they were attacking German columns and had killed several Soviet soldiers, including a general.

Frustrated with waiting, the commander of the 273rd Infantry Regiment directed Lt. Albert Kotzebue to go look for the Soviets in a village four miles beyond the Mulde River. Encountering dispirited German soldiers, jubilant American and Allied prisoners, apprehensive German civilians, and exuberant, sometimes intoxicated foreign laborers, Lt. Kotzebue and his men advanced almost due east toward the Elbe. It was almost noon as the jeeps slowed to enter the farming village of Leckwitz, less than two miles from the Elbe and well beyond the restricted five-mile limit.

Far down the main street, the men spotted a horseman just as he turned his mount into a courtyard and passed from view. At a glance, the man's costume seemed unusual. Could it be? Was this it? Spinning forward, the jeeps came to a halt at the entrance to the courtyard. Inside, among a crowd of foreign laborers, was the horseman. There could be no doubt. He was a Soviet soldier; Kotzebue and his team had spotted him.

The time was 11:30 A.M., April 25, and the setting inauspicious, but the moment was historic: it marked the first contact between Allied armies from the west and Soviet armies from the east. Through Russian-speaking Tec/5 Stephen A. Kowalski, Lt. Kotzebue asked directions to the soldier's commander; but the Russian was suspicious and reserved. Waving his arm to the east, he suggested that one of the foreign laborers, a Pole, could lead them better than he. With that, he galloped away.

Taking the Pole as a guide, the patrol continued to the Elbe, a few hundred yards. Seeing uniformed figures on the east bank milling about the wreckage of a column of vehicles close to the remains of a bridge, Lt. Kotzebue raised his binoculars. Again there could be no doubt. They were Russians. The rays of the sun reflecting off medals on their chests convinced him.

At the lieutenant's direction, his driver fired two green signal flares. Although the figures on the far bank gave no answering signal, they began to walk toward the edge of the river. As Kotzebue's driver fired another flare for good measure, the Polish laborer shouted their identity across the water. Then Kotzebue made a mistake that he would regret for the remainder of his life. He radioed the wrong map coordinates for his location.

Using a hand grenade, Lt. Kotzebue blasted the moorings of a sailboat and, with five of his men, rowed across the Elbe. A major and two other Russians, one a photographer, met them. The meeting was at first restrained, but as Kotzebue explained who he was, the Russians relaxed. Minutes later, Russian Col. Alexander T. Gardiev, commander of the 175th Rifle Regiment, arrived. Making clear that he intended to take the Americans to meet his division commander, he suggested that the men return to the west bank of the Elbe and proceed northward to a hand-operated cable ferry opposite the village of Kreinitz. There the Russians would meet them again, presumably at the pleasure of two motion-picture cameramen who by that time had also arrived on the scene. But owing to Kotzebue's mistake in sending the wrong map coordinates, there were no American reporters or high-ranking military generals at the gathering.

Forty-five minutes later, Lt. William D. Robertson and his men made contact with the Russians at Torgau, a village of 13,000 inhabitants, on the Elbe River. He returned to the 1st Battalion Command Post and telephoned the 273rd Infantry Regiment Headquarters with the news. As those at HQ were skeptical, Robertson then drove there with four Russians. By the time he arrived, the place was inundated with war correspondents and photographers. With this amount of publicity, Robertson for the most part was credited with making the initial contact with the Russians.

A bit later on the east bank, Americans and Russians pounded each other on the back, everybody wearing a perpetual grin. Then they drank a series of toasts in wine and brandy provided by the Russians.[3]

Chapter 2

The Looting of Anton Wiede

On April 20, 1945, the 273rd Infantry Regiment had returned to the village of Trebsen, 16 miles east of Leipzig. The large home of Anton J. Wiede and his mother, Else Wiede (born April 6, 1885), had initially been taken over by the troops of the 9th Armored Division, but now the 273rd retained Wiede's home as its headquarters. The house, known as Villa Wiede, was quite large, containing 16 rooms. Frau Wiede was given one hour to remove a few things such as bed linen, food, and other basic items, which were taken to a country home belonging to the Wiede family. Remaining in the house were precious rugs, paintings, jewelry, Meissen porcelain, and cash. The officers' room for headquarters was on the first floor; the second floor was use for sleeping, with one room set aside as a medical dispensary. Anton Wiede could not help but notice the name Tryhard, on the vehicles as well as buildings. This was their code name and was placed there by the soldiers of the 273rd Infantry Regiment headquarters.

During this time valuable paintings and etchings by well-known artists, a collection of German postage stamps, a large collection of Meissen china, and the entire Wiede family's jewelry and cash were taken by U.S. occupation forces. The stolen objects included four valuable paintings: *Rumanian Head* by Franz von Lenbach, *Even Mood on the Lower Main River* by Hans Thoma, *Falconer on a White Horse* by C. van Valena, and *Council* by Wilhelm Löwith.

Of the missing valuables, Anton Wiede wrote:

> The jewelry of my mother principally consisted of lady's jewelry; however, I am not able to state details. Among other things, she had a very precious chain made of exquisite, genuine pearls. The jewelry was in a safe, which she only could open. Americans took the jewelry. I cannot state a value of her jewelry. It probably had a value of more than 10,000 Deutschmarks.
>
> My mother's porcelain was very old; partly originating from the first production of Meissen and having the mark of Boettcher. She also had precious services from the time when Saxony was governed by kings. The porcelain was in very large cupboards in the ground floor of the house. My mother observed military trucks picked up the porcelain. Also precious rugs were

taken out from the house by means of jeeps. I cannot state the value of these stolen items.

A part of the precious paintings in the house was on the walls, among them the two precious paintings *Falconer on a White Horse* by C. van Valens and *Conzilium* by Löwith. These two paintings were in the hall that served the Americans as an office. A part of the paintings, among the two most precious pictures, *Rumanian Woman* by Franz von Lenbach and *Evening Mood on the Lower Main River* by Hans Thoma were in the basement packed in nailed-up crates. The pictures disappeared when the Americans moved out at approximately the end of June 1945.[1]

Anton Wiede's mother, Else, was allowed to remain in the house but was not allowed into the basement or other areas. She did notice that large shipping boxes were made in the paper mill's carpenter shop and delivered to her home. Later she saw the same boxes shipped from her home under the supervision of U.S. Army officers.

In the middle of May, a major in a medical detachment of the 273rd Infantry Regiment and his adjutant went to the school building where Anton Wiede had taken up temporary residence and asked him whether he had a stamp collection. By accident the soldiers had discovered a deposit receipt from the Deutsche Bank in Leipzig for a stamp collection that had been in the paper mill's safe. The collection had been placed in the bank in 1943 to protect it from Allied bombing attacks. These two men, who were staying nearby in the home of Anton Wiede, asked Wiede to go with them in a jeep to the bank since, as the adjutant (speaking flawless German) put it, "the major only wanted to see the collection."[2] Wiede objected that it was probably impossible to obtain access to the bank or to the vault. His objection was of no use and the major and adjutant said they would pick Wiede up at 10 A.M. the next morning. Wiede thought that this was only an inspection — that the officers only wanted to check on whether the collection had been stolen during the war from territory occupied by German troops. As his father had acquired the collection legally, Wiede was not worried, but he was somewhat surprised that a medical corps officer was investigating the stamp collection.

The following morning the medical officer, the adjutant, and a driver picked up Wiede as agreed. The jeep had military police markings. They asked Wiede the way to Leipzig and he told them the usual way was through the town of Wurzen, which was north. One of the Americans responded, "no, that's impossible." Wiede responded that there was another way, and then they drove south to Grimma and then northwest directly to the ruins of the Deutsche Bank at number 2 Martin Luther Ring, Leipzig. There were still plenty of dead bodies about, and smoke was rising from the cellars of many of the city's destroyed buildings. Bombs had destroyed the building of the Deutsche Bank all the way down to the ground floor.

On arrival at the bank, the two Americans drew their revolvers and hurriedly entered with Wiede in tow. In the basement of the building, which, owing to heavy bombing, was the only usable office space, were five or six German employees. When the two Americans asked to see the person in charge of the vault, an elderly employee appeared; with a sideways look at Wiede, whom he knew very well, he stated that unfortunately the vault was not accessible, since the key had been misplaced. Because of the drawn guns, the bank employee assumed that the stamp collection would be taken away by force. One of the soldiers rapped his revolver on a table and demanded immediate access to the vault, saying that otherwise "something would happen."[3] The bank official, sensing that resistance would be useless or even dangerous, guided the two Americans and Wiede to the elevator, which descended into a vault cut into granite. The medical major did not enter the elevator but remained at the entrance while the bank official, Wiede, and the adjutant went down into the vault. In addition to other valuables of prominent Leipzig families and museums, the vault contained the five albums of Wiede's stamp collection. The adjutant removed the albums and the three men left the bank. Wiede asked for a receipt, but the Americans refused to give him one.

The three men left the bank in a southeasterly direction and drove along a street renamed Lenin Street by the Russians. From that main road they drove to a solitary farm where U.S. troops were garrisoned. The adjutant remained in the jeep with the stamp collection while the major went inside the farmhouse, where he remained for more than an hour. Wiede had no idea why they had stopped, as his understanding of English was limited and he could not follow the conversation at the farm.

Then, without another stop, the men returned to Trebsen, arriving in the afternoon. They dropped Wiede off near the school and told him to report to them the next day. "They wanted to talk the matter over with me, after they had inspected the collection."[4] They then drove off and took the stamp collection to Wiede's house. Wiede was not concerned, as he expected the major to check out the collection and return it to him the next day.

The next morning Wiede went to the quarters of the two Americans and the guard let him in without any questions. He entered the main room of his home and found, present in the room, the red-haired medical corps major and his adjutant. The doors were open and six or seven military officers were moving into the house. The five large albums were displayed on a table in front of Wiede. The adjutant placed himself in front of Wiede and said "Dass dem Major die Sammlung gut gefalle; er sei Expert und versteht Briefmarken.

Der Herr Major wünsche die Sammlung zu übernehmen."[5] (That the major had taken a fancy to the collection; he was an expert who understood postage stamps and therefore wanted to take over the collection.)

At first Wiede did not understand the meaning of the words, though they were spoken in German. He thought the stamps were being requisitioned temporarily and asked for a receipt. The adjutant repeated his words and said that a receipt was entirely out of the question. Without mentioning the value of the collection, Wiede stated that he did not want to give away the collection, since it was an inheritance from his deceased father, who had collected it for all of his life. After a short discussion in English between the two soldiers, the adjutant told Wiede in a sharp and cynical manner: "Well, you have your plant as an inheritance and do not need the collection. However you can have your choice, either a carton of cigarettes or nothing." Again Wiede stated that under no circumstances would he part with the stamp collection. At that point the adjutant stated, "then it is nothing."[6] Again Wiede requested a receipt as he was pushed out the door of his own home. He recognized that any resistance would be useless and left.

During the next few days Wiede repeatedly went to the office of the military government located in the district of Grimm, requesting their help in the return of his stamp collection, stolen by the U.S. Army Medical Corps major. An officer took his written statement requesting assistance, stating that the matter would be considered. At the same time the officer told Wiede that it was unlawful for an officer to take possession of a valuable collection after the end of hostilities.

In mid-June, Wiede called again at the office of the military government and was told that it had been impossible to consider his case. Meanwhile, Wiede went to Maj. John O. Towers, the U.S. Military town commander of Trebsen. Towers was shocked at the unjustified and unlawful misappropriations and promised to help as far as it was within his power. Towers stated, of course, that he was unable to take any disciplinary action against the medical corps major, whom he knew well. Wiede had described the two men. The medical corps major was 1.85 meters tall and of slim build, with red hair. His adjutant, who spoke fluent German, was small and square with dark hair. Wiede wrote, "The competencies of the individual officers appeared to be very limited."

Despite his persistence, Wiede's attempts to recover the stamp collection and his missing valuables were unsuccessful. The collection of five large albums contained stamps of the German Reich, complete from the first prints in whole sheets and blocks of four and a large number of misprints. Also in complete sheets were all the early stamps of Saxony, Prussia, and Bavaria and finally stamps from all the former German colonies. The collection was so extensive that a full-time philatelist had been assigned to care for it. (See Appendix A for complete description.)

At the end of June, as Wiede was pursuing this matter with the U.S. Office of Military Government, he was told that the Soviets, who had already moved west to the other side of the Mulde River, would advance still further to the west, and that the entire area of Thüringen and Saxony would be in the Soviet Zone of Occupation. In his capacity of an entrepreneur and engineer, Wiede knew he would be imprisoned in Siberia by the Russian authorities. At his request, Maj. Tower, the town manager, issued travel papers allowing Wiede to go to Bavaria.

Before fleeing the Russian occupation, Anton Wiede met with his longtime employee and friend Hans Unger and at 4:15 on the morning of June 18, 1945, bade him farewell; they parted with tears in their eyes. Wiede told Unger to inform his mother if he, Unger, heard anything about the stamp collection. Wiede gave Unger a written goodbye note to distribute to the more than 1,000 employees of his firm. The staff of Wiede & Söhne was deeply grieved by the news of Wiede's departure and the arrival of the Soviet troops. The mill was placed under Soviet control and then dismantled and shipped to Russia.[7]

After Wiede left Trebsen, Capt. F. K. Siegfried John Ohringer, the officer in charge of Prisoner of War Interrogation Team 145, told Wiede's mother, Else, that the Russians would arrive in a few days. He wanted to help her and suggested that she send her coin collection to western Germany or the American Occupation Zone. She agreed to give the collection to Capt. Ohringer, who would take it to Otto Duerbech, a friend and owner of the paper sack factory in Lauterbach. She then handed her coin collection over to Ohringer on trust, with the oral and written understanding that it would be placed in safe custody or that she would be compensated for its value. The receipt reads as follows:

> 20 June 1945. This will certify that I have received from Mrs. Else Wiede of Trebsen a collection of coins for safekeeping and future disposal to a recognized museum or to a person of Mrs. Wiede's designation.
> John Ohringer
> Capt. FA.[8]

However Mrs. Wiede was never reimbursed for the collection, as it disappeared. After the occupying troops left her home, she went into the basement and discovered that the paintings, too, had been taken away.[9]

Thus, on July 4, 1945, the Americans vacated the provinces of Thüringen and Saxony. The Russians received 16,400 square miles of this rich and fertile land in exchange for 185 square miles of bombed-out rubble in the western sector of Berlin. Wiede traveled to Munich, while his mother remained in the Soviet-occupied zone of Germany.

In Munich, Wiede was employed as an expert in paper production by the U.S. military government. During this time he discussed the theft of his property with several high-ranking officials and was told that such a misappropriation by U.S. officers of valuables owned by unimpeachable Germans was in conflict with the laws and ordinances in force in May/June 1945. He was further told that such cases involving military personnel would be prosecuted.

In this connection he was referred to a judgment delivered in Frankfurt, Germany, in a similar case against Col. Jack Durant and Capt. Kathleen Nash. The two had been convicted in one of the greatest robberies of World War II — theft of the Hesse crown jewels. (For the complete story on this, read my book *The Spoils of World War II*.)

After nine years of frustration with the U.S. Army, Wiede acquired the services of Dr. Brückner of the German Federal Ministry of Foreign Affairs in an effort to recover his missing valuables. This was now possible, as the occupational status had changed on May 26, 1952, with a contractual agreement that gave the western German government (the Bonn government) almost complete sovereignty. On July 15, 1954, Brückner presented George Scott, secretary of the Allied High Commission, with a two-page letter and five testimonial annexes regarding the theft of Anton Wiede's property. The letter began with the words "I would be grateful for your good offices in the following matter." Most importantly, the letter contained a description of the red-haired medical major and two names: Maj. John O. Towers and Capt. Siegfried John Ohringer. Wiede fixed the value of the paintings as DM 70,000, the stamp collection at DM 500,000, and the numismatic collection at a minimum of DM 5,000. This came to a total in U.S. dollars of $143,750, which was a fortune in 1954, when the average U.S. family was earning $2,500 a year.

Chapter 3

The Investigation

Brückner's letter, with the accompanying annexes, was forwarded to the inspector general, Department of Army, Washington, D.C., reporting the alleged wrongful removal of certain paintings, coins, and stamp collections from the home of Mr. and Mrs. Anton J. Wiede during April/May 1945. With this information the army began an investigation of the matter. The central point of this inquiry was the Office of the Provost in Munich, Germany, but it also included the Central Intelligence Divisions of the First Army, Governor's Island, New York; Second Army, Fort Meade, Maryland; Third Army, Fort McPherson, Georgia; Fifth Army, Chicago, Illinois; and Sixth Army, Presidio of San Francisco, California.

On October 21, 1954, at the Terminal Building in Idlewild Airfield, New York, Criminal Investigator Michael Janetis interviewed Claude E. Post. The former major stated that, while assigned to the 69th Infantry Division, he usually dealt with regimental commanders and that he was unaware of the Wiede theft. He also stated: "I was never assigned to the 273rd Infantry Regiment." A week later, in the Trenton Trust Building in Trenton, New Jersey, an army investigator interviewed former Col. Edward J. Leary. Leary stated, "I have no knowledge of the alleged loss of oil paintings, coin or stamp collections, but do remember seeing at the Villa Wiede many oil paintings, which I cannot describe. To the best of my knowledge the contents of this beautiful home were intact when the staff of the 69th Division moved out 24 hours prior to occupancy by the Russians."[1]

During October, Maxwell A. Snead, in Denver, Colorado, gave the following statement: "I Maxwell A. Snead, hereby verify that I was assistant chief of staff G-2 (intelligence) of the 69th Infantry Division during the period mentioned in this communication. I did not know about the incident described in the communication shown to me by M. E. Stouffer, of the Criminal Intelligence Division. I also do not recall the name of the medical corps officer described. I also do not recall the name or description of the medical officer of the 273rd Infantry Regiment during this period."[2]

In a letter of November 24, 1954, retired Brig. Gen. Robert V. Maraist wrote that he had read the letter signed by Brückner. As division artillery commander of the 69th Infantry Division, he did not recall Major Tower or Captain Obringer [*sic*] and furthermore did not recall hearing about the alleged incident in Trebsen. Harold Pengelly made the following statement:

> I was adjutant general, 69th Infantry Division from its activation in May, 1953 [he meant 1943] until my transfer to Seventh Army Headquarters in August, 1945.... I do not know the Captain Obringer [*sic*] mentioned; however, an old roster of mine showed him as a member of G-2 Section.... The statement made that American officers forced Herr Wiede to accompany them to Leipzig to the bank and there took away a stamp collection, etc., I consider entirely without basis for the reason that of my personal knowledge, the city of Leipzig was declared off limits to all American troops as soon as it was captured and before the junction of American and Russian troops at Torgau, Germany....
>
> I do not know of any major of the Medical Corps of the description stated. To the best of my knowledge there was no regimental medical detachment commanded by a major.[3]

But Pengelly did have an old roster in his possession and it contained the names and addresses of Joachim Ohringer, 1418 Jonquil Terrace, Chicago; John O. Tower, Cedar Springs, Michigan; and Lt. Col. Robert S. Anderson, 281 Washington Street, Wilkes-Barre, Pennsylvania.

On December 13, John O. Tower was interviewed; he stated that during the short period he was in Trebsen, he did not specifically remember a Frau Wiede making any complaints and he did not remember a Captain Ohringer. "The Medical Corps major I don't remember either or any red-haired officer."[4]

Thus the investigation continued in an effort to identify John Ohringer and the red-haired medical corps major, but it was met with negative results, including a "certificate" from the commanding officer of the 369th Medical Battalion, 69th Infantry Division, who stated, "It is suggested that the medical officer in question was probably the regimental surgeon of the 273rd Infantry regiment, whose name I do not recall."[5] With an abundance of "I do not recall" or "I do not know," the cover-up continued. These men of the former 173rd even denied knowing the term *Tryhard*, though it was the code name of their headquarters. After many interviews, an army investigator wrote:

> From the foregoing investigation, it is concluded:
> a. That this investigation has failed to disclose any information, which would aid in the establishing the identity or location of Ohringer, the medical corps major, or the adjutant.
> b. That this investigation has failed to disclose any information which would aid in establishing the present location of the oil paintings, coin or stamp collection.[6]

This would normally stop an investigation, but because of its broad scope it continued with an interview on December 15, 1954, with Dr. Charles A. Owen, Jr., in his office at the prestigious Mayo Clinic. Owen was a man of many interests and an avid collector of stamps and coins. His statement follows:

> During World War II, I was a captain and major of the 69th Division, 273rd Infantry Regiment, Medical Detachment. Our official headquarters was at Trebsen on the Mulde [River], Germany. I was stationed here in the later part of April, all of May, and the first part of June 1945. The later part of the time we spent at Villa Wiede.
>
> I first met Mr. Wiede when he had a large slave camp of British laborers at his paper mill. At my personal order, we made Mr. Wiede sweep and mop out the barracks where the slave laborers were. The second time that I remember when we met Mr. Wiede was when we moved into his home. I recall this incident, as he told us to be careful of the windows, walls and other things, like the owner of a home would do. I have limited knowledge of the German language but do not remember if Mr. Wiede spoke any English or not. I also saw Mr. Wiede many other times when he came to check the house. At last Mr. Wiede departed, as the rumor was that he was running away from our military government. I wish to state at this time, that at no time did Mr. Wiede ever complain to me of anyone stealing any pictures, coins, or stamp collection from his home or from his possession as he so stated in a statement prepared by him, which was read to me in part by Mr. Geschwind of the Criminal Investigation Department of the U.S. Army. At the time we stayed at the Villa Wiede I was a captain and later on, just before I left, I was promoted to major.
>
> During the last part of my stay at the Villa Wiede there was a second major there. His name is Harry Underwood, M.D., presently residing at Easton, Pennsylvania. As far as the pictures go, I have no knowledge of anyone taking these. We had one signed C.A.O. painting of a nude woman in the villa and had kept this on the wall. Every time the chaplain would visit the villa, he would take it down. The name of this chaplain I do not recall, but he was Catholic and was with the 273rd Infantry Regiment.
>
> I was a stamp collector, and have a collection of stamps at the present time. This was known through the regiment that I collected stamps. During my tour of duty with the American forces, I collected stamps from wherever I was. Many of the stamps were cancelled while others were unused. When first entering the plant in Trebsen, I found a large number of stamps and added these to my collection. I still have these stamps at the present time. The total of these stamps, which I collected in Europe, would not exceed a few hundred dollars. I have no knowledge on any major and captain taking stamps (albums) from Mr. Wiede at gunpoint. I do not know the whereabouts of a Captain or Major Towers. I have nothing to add to this statement at the present time.

A week later Graham S. McConnell was interviewed at his home in Republic, Washington, by Investigator Robert R. Musselman of the U.S.

Army's Criminal Investigation Division (CID). McConnell stated that he was assigned to the 273rd Infantry Regiment on or about April 25, 1945. He was stationed at an ammunition depot located near the town of Altenheim, three miles west of Trebsen. On the average of two to three nights a week he would visit the 273rd Regimental Headquarters building for the purpose of playing bridge. McConnell further stated he had no knowledge of a large and valuable stamp collection being missing, but he had observed Maj. Charles Owen to be in possession of a large number of sheets of Hitler stamps. When McConnell commented about them, the major replied that he had lots more. McConnell went on to tell the investigator that Maj. Owen was the only red-haired medical officer on duty with the 273rd and that he was often accompanied about the countryside by a small sergeant or Tec/3 who spoke fluent German.

McConnell went on to say:

> I received numerous reports from various members of my detachment alleging that Lieutenant Colonel Anderson, the 69th Division surgeon, was sending a great number of boxes and packages to the United States. As near as I can recall the above information had originated with the 69th Division APO [Army Post Office] personnel. I made no direct observation of Anderson's activities but the story of his many shipments was told and retold by so many different persons during this period that I was with the 3rd battalion, 273rd Infantry Regiment, that I am sure the stories are true. I was informed by unidentified personnel of my detachment that Anderson had obtained some of the articles from the Villa Wiede, but I am unable to describe the property.[7]

At last, a newly arrived member of the 273rd could remember the days in question with a clear and concise memory and told his story to the U.S. Army investigators.

During Owen's interview, he could remember only one name, Harry Underwood. Owen also knew his address. Was Owen throwing out the name of this major to take suspicion away from himself? If it was, then it was a mistake, for on January 2, 1955, Dr. Harry B. Underwood, in the Easton Medical Arts Building, gave the following statement:

> I was in service with the United States Army during World War II and served with the Medical Detachment, 273rd Infantry, 69th Division. At that time Captain Charles Owen replaced me as regimental surgeon and was promoted to major during my absence. You have asked me about a medical adjutant who spoke fluent German. The only person that I recall was Edward Schlag, Tec/3, 273rd Infantry Medical Detachment, who spoke fluent German; however he was not an adjutant but a surgical technician. I believe at present he resides in New York City.
>
> You have asked me about the missing stamp collection from Germany. I wish to state that I did not take them. At that time when I returned to Trebsen I heard that Major Charles Owen had a collection of stamps.... I last saw Dr.

Charles Owen in Atlantic City on November 14, 1954, at the convention of the American College of Surgeons, at which time I casually asked about the stamp collection which he had picked up in Germany, and was told that he and Edward Schlag had taken care of the collection. I had heard that Major Owen and Schlag had gone to Leipzig to procure these stamps....

You have given me a description of a medical major who was tall, slim built and red-haired and this would be a description of Major Owen. The other person you described to me who spoke flawless German and was small and square built and had dark hair would be the description of Edward Schlag, who worked for Major Owen.[8]

After this detrimental interview of Underwood regarding Owen, the CID on January 5, 1955, reinterviewed Owen, who had now obtained legal counsel. Owen verbally stated that although he answers the description of the major referred to by Wiede, he was never at the Deutsche Bank in Leipzig and that Wiede had a personal grudge against him for having forced Wiede to perform manual labor in his own plant. Owen further stated the accusation of the larceny of Wiede's private property was "Utterly false." On the advice of his lawyer, Owen allowed the CID investigator to view his stamp collection and compare it with the inventory supplied by Wiede. The collection Owen provided did not match up with the missing collection's description.

Owen stated he had started his collection when he was seven years old and had continually built up his collection to what it was at the present time. He had many stamps given to him by patients from foreign countries who were treated at the Mayo Clinic. Owen further told the CID investigator that he had many stamps from Germany from 1938 through May 1945 and that these stamps came from the plant of Anton Wiede.

Was this checkmate for Owen?

It might have been except that the CID found Edward A. Schlag living in Westbury. Long Island, New York. On March 2, 1955, he was subject to the following short interview:

Q: Who was your immediate commanding officer?
A: Major Owen.
Q: Do you remember the occasion when Major Owen obtained a stamp collection?
A: Yes. While we were billeted at this country house in Trebsen, and as far as I can remember, I was called out on a detail to accompany Major Owen, his driver and the owner of the building in which we were billeted and a saw mill, and we all got into a jeep. We drove to Leipzig to a building, which I found out later was a bank. When we arrived at this building, the owner, Major Owen, and myself went into the basement, where the owner received several books. We then proceeded back to headquarters in Trebsen. At this time I knew the books contained stamps but I cannot

remember how many stamps were in the books or what the value of them was. To my knowledge, this individual was paid for the stamps with cigarettes, which at that time was the value of legal tender. I do not know how many cartons of cigarettes he received.[9]

Anton Wiede's story and Edward A. Schlag's statement agreed. There is a bit of confusion regarding a sawmill; maybe Schlag was thinking about a paper mill during this time 10 years later. Regardless, it was time to talk with Owen once more.

On May 3, 1955, five months after asking for an official statement from Owen, the army requested another one from the red-headed doctor. This time the interview was not in Owen's office at the Mayo Clinic but in his lawyer's office in the First National Bank Building in Rochester, Minnesota. Indignantly, Owen asked William R. Canton, the investigator, why it was necessary to make this second statement. Owen had to have been tipped off by his former comrades about the investigation and made a lengthy statement regarding his arrival in Trebsen, Germany, and his duties in taking care of the sick and wounded in the paper factory that had been converted into a hospital. He told of moving into Anton Wiede's home, and now his story changed from the original. It continues:

> One entire floor of this factory was utilized as a large ward, and the business offices were utilized to house the doctors and nurses. One of these rooms I utilized as my personnel [personal] office. In the desk of the office I occupied I found a large number of loose stamps. Upon examining these stamps, I found they were of more interest to a collector, and not the type that would normally be kept in a business office for daily postal requirements. Most of these stamps I took and held at the time to become a possible portion of my collection. Some of them are presently a portion of my collection and others I have disposed of by trading them or giving them away. About this time we moved into the Wiede home.
>
> Shortly after the time we moved into the Wiede home, I recall one time that Mr. Wiede came to me extremely frightened and informed me that he had information that Russian troops were going to occupy the area that we were in at that time. It was at this time that Mr. Wiede had something of value that he would be glad to give me for consideration. To the best of my recollection I believe he told me that he rather I have the stamp collection than to have them fall into Russian hands. It was a short time later that accompanied by my jeep driver whose name I cannot recall, Sergeant Schlag, and Mr. Wiede and I went into one of the banks in Leipzig. When we arrived there, Mr. Wiede approached a man in the bank and spoke to him, but I did not understand what he said. At this time I do not recall who went down to the bank vault to obtain the stamp collection, but I remember that I remained upstairs while they were gone. When the stamp collection was bought upstairs, I saw that it was wrapped in individual packages in waterproof paper.

We returned to Trebsen and went to Wiede's home, where Wiede gave me the stamps, and I satisfied our agreement. At the time of this transaction, Wiede seemed perfectly happy and was in town for several days afterwards, during which time he did not even come to see me. I opened one package to check and see if it contained a stamp collection as alleged by Wiede. After ascertaining that it did contain stamps, I put all of the packages in a footlocker along with some personal items and had it bound. The footlocker remained with me unopened until I returned home. It was approximately one day after my return home that I first examined the stamp collection and it was at that time that I discovered that it was considerably more valuable than I first thought it to be when Wiede first approached me. Some of the stamps are a part of my collection and the others were disposed of.

Q: Dr. Owen, when you referred to payment of Wiede for the stamp collection, you said it was for considerations. To what do you allude by using this term?

A: As far as I am concerned it was a mutually satisfactory agreement.[10]

Owen, according to his statement, acquired a stamp collection of unknown value and paid for it "with consideration." Then, after he "paid" for the collection and before he packed it into a footlocker, he opened one package to see if it actually contained stamps! This does not seem logical.

This was Dr. Owen's final statement to the army. After all, he was a former army officer and now a prominent doctor on the staff of the Mayo Clinic. Wiede was only a German and in 1955, Germans were not highly regarded. Owen had stated that he had taken the valuable stamp collection; the army had his written confession. What were they going to do about it? The army had no authority regarding a U.S. civilian.

At the time of the investigation in the United States the military authorities in Munich located and interviewed Maria Milatovic in Yugoslavia. Her sister had been the wife of Anton Wiede between 1939 and 1946. Milatovic had seen the missing paintings in the Villa Wiede and was there during the American occupation. She told the investigators that Wiede's wife, Julia, lived in Icking, Germany, from December 1942 until 1945, and that Wiede met her there in 1945 but did not live with her. Both Julia and her sister, Maria, lived in Icking, which was in the U.S. Army Zone of Occupation; therefore Wiede visited his wife after he left Trebsen. Wiede told Maria and Julia that he had guided members of the U.S. Army over the Mulde River Bridge. Julia had remarried and was now Mrs. Julia Fahrenkamp and, ironically enough, lived at 171 East Providence in Milwaukee, Wisconsin, 250 miles from the Mayo Clinic. There is no indication that she ever knew Dr. Charles A. Owen.

Now the paper trail goes cold on the subject of Owen and the stamp collection. Owen told army authorities that he gave Wiede a medical certificate in return for the stamp collection and that this certificate allowed him to travel to the American Occupation Zone. Apparently Owen knew that the cigarette story was inappropriate and therefore invented this story. When informed of the tale of the medical certificate, Wiede's mother, Else, said she did not know anything about such a certificate and doubted that the story was true. She further stated her son had obtained a travel document to go to the west on the pretense of attempting of purchasing lumber and therefore would not need a medical pass. Owen also refused to identify the person to whom he had sold the stamp collection.[11]

Then the army conducted a survey among all known art dealers and stamp and coin dealers in the Chicago area to determined whether the stolen paintings and stamp collections were in that vicinity. The army's search was negative, but an investigation in the same area by the Bureau of Customs determined that part of the Wiede stamp collection had been sold in 1946 by Charles A. Owen through Henry Kuhlmann, owner of Stamp Auction Services in Chicago for $35,000, a fortune, considering that Owen was then earning approximately $2,600 a year. A large part of the Wiede stamp collection was in the possession of J. Schroeder, also of Chicago. Could Schroeder have purchased the stamps from Stamp Auction Services?

In February 1956, former Capt. Joachim Ohringer was located and a lengthy legal discussions took place regarding the coin collection that he had acquired. He had been the officer in charge of Prisoner of War Interrogation Team Number 145, attached to the 69th Infantry Division, and had signed for the coin collection belonging to Else Wiede. Ohringer did not submit to an interview; instead, all correspondence with the military was through the law office of Burton Hugh Young, located at 7 South Dearborn Street, Chicago. The communication was primarily legalese: "establishment of the claim of the lawful owner and facilitate its presentation ... doubtful, incomplete, and fragmentary ... save Mr. Ohringer harmless and indemnify him against any and all claims."[12] Regardless and fortunately for all, on October 1, 1957, Joachim Ohringer, upon the advice of his attorney gave 1,228 coins to U.S. Treasury officials. He did not give any details of the circumstances under which he came into possession of the coins but did say that a member of the Wiede family in Trebsen, Germany, gave them to him.

Because of the interviews with Graham S. McConnell on December 21, 1954, and February 14, 1956, stating that surgeon Anderson had shipped boxes home with articles from the Villa Wiede, the CID interviewed Col. Robert S. Anderson. On July 5, 1956, Anderson was interviewed at Walter Reed Army Hospital in Washington D.C.

When questioned about the closing days of the war in Germany, Anderson was most vague and stated he was stationed within a 20- to 25-mile radius of Halle and lived in small duplex-type homes, but he did remember living

3. The Investigation 27

? Are You Interested in Buying at Auction? ?

- The finest collections are built up thru this method of obtaining stamps and other philatelic material.

- Thousands of satisfied collectors and dealers, here and abroad, buy thru our auctions which are held regularly thruout the year.

We would be pleased to place your name on our mailing list. Just drop us a request.

! We Can Handle Your Stamps to Your Perfect Satisfaction !

- General or specialized collections of any size, accumulation of worthwhile material, exceptional single items, in fact anything, except ordinary junk, will be either purchased outright or handled on consignment.

- Thru our mail auctions and over the counter sales, to DEALERS as well as COLLECTORS, we handle a tremendous volume of fine Philatelic material.

We can handle YOURS to YOUR complete satisfaction.

Henry Kuhlmann

Stamp Auction Service

"The House of Philatelic Service"

127 N. Dearborn St., Chicago 2, Ill.

Phone: Franklin 2-6726

432   S. P. A. JOURNAL

An advertisement from Henry Kuhlmann's Stamp Auction Service. The stamps taken by Dr. Charles A. Owen were sold through this service in 1946.

in a two-story home. He continued with "I don't believe we stabilized our location.... They were just temporary setups as they were assigned by headquarters command."

When questioned specifically about sending packages home, Anderson continued:

> Yes, I think I can recall, generally, but not specifically. Some of the items that I picked up along the way from the remnants of the German Army — trinkets, perhaps, and items of that nature, that were discovered or found and were of no value to the individual. I did not go into homes and steal anything. I did not break any door down.... If I have any items they are in my home in Pennsylvania, but I seriously doubt if I have any of them as they are destroyed or broken through usage, or as gifts to members of the family.
>
> Q: will you voluntary submit yourself to a lie detector examination?
>
> A: I have no fear of a lie detector examination but I can't understand why I should have to be subjected to such because this is degrading to me. I don't know what a lie detector test is about, and think it is entirely unnecessary. This is 1956, over eleven years, and someone is digging up something like this. I think this is like a straw in the wind.[13]

According to Anderson, a 46-year-old medical doctor, he shipped numerous boxes of war souvenirs of little or no value to his home at 281 Washington Street, Wilkes-Barre, Pennsylvania, from Europe during World War II. Anderson was still in the army and the army could continue to investigate him, but they didn't. On August 6, 1956, the Office of the Provost Marshal in Munich wrote its final report:

> Conclusions: Based on the foregoing investigation, it is concluded:
> 1. That Owen did, at Trebsen on the Mulde, Germany, on or about May 1945, unlawfully take a stamp collection of an alleged value of $125,000.00 (DM 500,000.00), property of A. Wiede.
> 2. That Ohringer is in possession of a coin collection, consisting of 1,228 coins, of an alleged value of about $1,250.00 (DM 5,000.00) property of E. Wiede.
> 3. That insufficient evidence exists to establish that Anderson has any knowledge concerning the missing paintings.

This ended the army's investigation.

On January 29, 1958, in Washington D.C., an accredited representative of the German government signed for the delivery of 88 stamps and 1,228 coins, which were claimed by Mrs. Else Wiede and Mr. Anton Wiede. On May 20, 1958, the 88 stamps were returned to Wiede in Munich.

Charles A. Owen continued with his medical practice at the Mayo Clinic. He was born on December 3, 1915, in Assiut, Egypt. He received his associate degree from Monmouth College in New Jersey and a medical degree from the University of Iowa in 1941. On June 8, 1939, he married Edna Stonter in Conrad, Iowa. His internship was at Harper Hospital, Detroit, and he served in the U.S. Army from 1942 to 1946. In 1946 he moved to Rochester, Minnesota, to enter the Mayo Graduate School of Medicine. He received a doctorate in medicine from the University of Minnesota in 1950. Appointed as a Mayo consultant in clinical pathology in 1950, he served as chairman of Medical Sciences Biochemistry as well as the Department of Clinical Pathology in 1958. He was a member of Mayo's Board of Governors from 1965 to 1970 and Mayo's board of trustees from 1970 to 1971.

The author of six books and more than 400 publications, he contributed extensively to the literature of hematology, clinical pathology, and biochemistry. He was a professor in the Mayo Graduate School of Medicine and a visiting professor at medical institutes in the United States, Canada, Argentina, Venezuela, Japan, Russia, Iran, and Egypt. He was active and received honors in numerous professional associations. Other honors included being named the Edman A. and Marion F. Guggenheim Professor in 1978 and receiving the Mayo Clinic Distinguished Professor Lectureship Award in 1980. He also received the Mayo Clinic Distinguished Alumnus Award. Owen was president of the Minnesota Society of Clinical Pathologists and served as chairman of the National Red Cross's blood bank committee. He retired from the Mayo Clinic in June 1981. Owen died at the age of 85 on March 3, 2001.[14]

Part II

A Passion for Lucas Cranach Paintings

Chapter 4
Donovan Senter's Early Days

Donovan Senter was born in 1909 in the town of Estancia, New Mexico, the center of the state, 40 miles southeast of Albuquerque. His father was, 30-year-old Martin Hale Senter; his mother, Florence, was a year older than her husband. Martin and two of his brothers had homesteaded from Alvarado, Texas, having come to Estancia as part of the 1891 Homestead Act. This act allowed any citizen 21 years of age or older to live on 160 acres of land and, after 18 months, to purchase the land for $1.25 an acre. After five years, the homesteader could have the acreage free. Martin met his wife in Estancia; her family had settled there from Carthage, Missouri. Previously Florence had attended the University of Chicago.[1]

Donovan was the oldest of three brothers, the middle brother, Cedric Hale, was born in 1918 and Albert, the youngest, was born a year later. The family struggled to make a living by dry farming pinto beans, carting ties for the new railroad, working in construction and operating the first telephone system in Estancia. When Donovan was nine years old his father invested in a large herd of cattle. During a harsh blizzard, the cattle starved to death, and Martin had a hard time recovering from this loss. During the Depression years, Donovan and his brothers remained in Estancia, and Donovan finished high school in 1927. Florence earned extra income by teaching school locally, including schools attended by Cedric and Albert. Like many young men at that time, Donovan joined the New Mexico National Guard (Troop A, 111th Cavalry) for three years.

After a year-long absence, Donovan rejoined the same unit in the medical detachment. This duty consisted of one night a week training and a two-week summer camp. It supplied much-needed pocket money and, in the late 1920s, the chance of active duty was totally remote. In 1929 Donovan entered the University of New Mexico and seven years later received his bachelor's degree. In 1937 the family moved to Albuquerque, and at about the same time Donovan left the National Guard. Martin, his father, did construction contracting, well digging, and house moving. Florence, Cedric, and Albert all attended the University of New Mexico and Florence received her degree just before her early death in 1940.² During an interview, Albert told the author: "My mother always liked Donovan best."

During his seven years in college Donovan worked for the Mutual Life Insurance Company of New York and was a car salesman for the Packard distributorship, both located in Albuquerque. In 1936 Senter obtained a master's degree in anthropology from the University of New Mexico. While obtaining this degree, he helped with the 1934 restoration of the Old Quarai Spanish Mission.

As a young man, Senter explored the nearby ruins of the Old Quarai Mission. He must surely have stared up at the towering walls and thought, "How did they build this?" "Why is this here?" "What happened here?" After all, these ruins were only a few miles from his birthplace of Estancia.

In the 1580s, when the first Spanish explorers marched through this area, the Salinas pueblos were already large villages. The Spanish incorporated the Salinas area into their existing social and administrative structures: the Roman Catholic Church and the civil government. This authority ultimately derived from the king of Spain, who ruled by "divine right."

In 1626, Fray Alonso de Benavides, the new custodian of the missionary effort in New Mexico, decided to send a mission to a pueblo called Quarai in the Salinas basin. Fray Benavides had been in New Mexico only a short time, having just arrived from Mexico City on the supply train that reached New Mexico in December 1625. To help with the job of establishing the new mission, he selected another newcomer to New Mexico, Fray Juan Gutiérrez, one of the missionaries who had traveled north with Benavides. Gutiérrez rode

A young, handsome Donovan Senter attended the University of New Mexico in the late 1930s. During World War II, his life, like many others, was turned upside down by the war.

into Quarai a few months later with his wagon load of starting tools, equipment, and supplies. The leaders of the pueblo apparently approved of his intent to convert the Indians of Quarai, because he encountered few of the problems of opposition or harassment so common to the first efforts of conversion in a new pueblo. Gutiérrez purchased several rooms in the pueblo and added to them to make a residence for himself. After an examination of the pueblo and the surrounding land, he selected a mound of ruins left near the northeast corner of the pueblo as the site of his church and monastery. During the remainder of 1626–1627 Gutiérrez designed and built the new church and convent of Quarai with the help of Indian work crews.

The trade to and from a mission was an important part of its life. It influenced the planning, construction, activities in, and changes to the monastery. Throughout the existence of the mission, wagon trains provided the vital 1,800-mile link between the missions and civil settlements of New Mexico and the supply and trade centers of New Spain.

In 1669, Fray Juan Bernal remarked on the twin misfortunes that had caused so much difficulty in the province of New Mexico for the previous three years and threatened to "put it out of existence." These were the war with the Apache Indians, which had escalated since the mid–1660s, and crop failure, which had been causing problems in one part or another of the province of New Mexico since 1667. Bernal was prophetic: he was observing the beginning of the process that put an end to the province of New Mexico. The twin stresses of famine and Indian insurrection eventually caused the abandonment of the Salinas jurisdiction in the late 1670s and contributed to the loss of the entire province in 1680, barely 100 years after its inception.[3]

During the 1934 excavation of the Old Quarai Mission, which at the time was under the management of the University of New Mexico, Senter spent a great deal time learning the German language from one of the professors working on this project. The work of shoring up and reinforcing the walls to the church was done using 20 men which ran from the Civilian Conservation Corps (CCC) camp at nearby Manzano. The CCC was a public work relief program for unemployed men which ran from 1933 to 1942. As part of President Franklin D. Roosevelt's New Deal, the CCC carried out a broad conservation program involving natural resources on national, state and municipal lands. Donovan Senter was the student archaeologist on the job at Quarai.

The mission was located on the side of a bluff with a view of the so-called Accursed Salt Lakes about 25 miles east. A dry stream bed with large cottonwoods stood nearby, and these majestic fiery-gold giant trees still remain today. Just south of the ruins there was a large outcrop of red sandstone, its walls covered with petroglyphs pointing to an ancient shrine outlined by a

On May 26, 1936, Donovan Senter and Florence Hawley were married in these ruins of the Old Quarai Spanish Mission, New Mexico. The author stands by the main entrance of the church, which is today administered by the National Park Service.

great circle of stone slabs farther up on a hill.[4] It was while working on this project that Donovan Senter met and married Florence Hawley, who had a doctorate in archaeology. Their marriage took place on May 25, 1936, in the roofless, partially restored Old Quarai Mission, which had walls four feet thick built in the form of a Latin cross; the original stood 60 feet tall. Unusual for the time, Hawley retained her maiden name; probably because Senter was a student and his wife was addressed as Dr. Hawley, he was often addressed as Mr. Hawley. This did not sit well with the sensitive Senter. It is of interest to note that she had the same first name as Donovan's mother.[5]

Florence Hawley had been born in Cananea, Mexico, on September 17, 1906. During the Mexican Revolution, in 1913, her family moved to Miami, Arizona. Hawley's education began at the University of Arizona. She graduated in 1927, completing a major in English and a minor in anthropology. During the Depression she decided to use her savings to attend the University of Chicago. In 1934, she received her Ph.D., using her excavations of Chetro Ketl, one of the largest pueblos in Chaco Canyon, New Mexico, as the basis for her dissertation. After graduating from the University of Arizona, she was hired as a professor at the University of New Mexico.[6]

Donovan and Florence studied archaeology together. One of their more famous studies was about Hopi and Navajo child burials. In 1937, they dug up Hopi and Navajo burial sites. The Hopi burial contained a young infant that did not have any clothes. The grave was covered with stones, and sticks were sticking out of the mound, which signified the Hopi's "ladder for the soul." The Hopi also believed that they needed to have earthly possessions buried with them when they died. This Hopi infant had an empty Post Toasties box, some rubber baby pants, and modern glass beads. The Navajo site contained two Navajo children, both dressed in traditional Navajo clothing. There was a large stone with a cross engraved on it at the head of the grave, showing the influence of Christianity. One child was buried with a Crackerjacks box and a tin cup, while the other was buried with a piece of candy and a spoon. The study concluded by Senter and Hawley showed that these Native American tribes still used some of the rituals of their ancestors. Hawley said, "There were no rules in those days covering how things should be excavated."[7] Fortunately, after protest from Native Americans, this type of "grave robbing" was outlawed by the state of New Mexico.

After receiving his master's degree, Senter was granted a fellowship at Harvard University, where he commenced working toward his doctoral degree in the field of physical anthropology. After one year at Harvard, he transferred to the University of Chicago, where he remained for five years. It was here, on February 26, 1939, that their daughter, Florence Anita Senter, was born. She was affectionately nicknamed DonAnita, a combination of her and her father's names. In 1940 Senter returned to Albuquerque as a research sociologist to continue working toward his Ph.D. He was supported by the Indian Health Service, an agency within the Department of Health and Human Services, which had provided the University of Chicago with a grant for a study of the cultural, nutritional, and environmental factors in the lives of American Indians. Senter decided to make this a lengthy project, working from Canyon, Taos, 125 miles north of Albuquerque. The town of Taos lies in the north central region of New Mexico; it is seated on the high desert mesa at the foot of the Sangre de Cristo Mountains. The word *Taos* means "red willow" in the Tiwa (Taos) language.

In a requested report to the University of Chicago regarding his now two-year project, Senter wrote:

> I may be able to fill them out nearly completely, with a little more effort for the villages of Canyon, Canyada, Ranchos, Manzano and Trampas. Of course, I couldn't give you detailed family studies and such. The people are pretty [in touch with] what people think about what they eat here in the canyon. They "know" what they should eat like the Americanos, but can't afford it. White flour and canned milk, etc., dominate. Frijoles without the expensive chili still remain favorites despite the fact they are not "anglo."

Canyon is about as good as I know to show the mess that American store food has made to their diet.

Florence has considerable information on foods for Zia [Zia Pueblo]. She even has quantitative data from store. In fact, one of her largest field expenses is buying groceries and clothing for her informant.

Senter and his wife were planning to spend the month of December 1941 in Taos. On Easter Day, 1942, Senter was to be initiated into the Brothers of the Pious Fraternity of Our Father Jesus the Nazarene, a lay confraternity of Roman Catholic men active in Northern New Mexico and Southern Colorado. These men came together in the absence of a priest for the purpose of prayer and to offer spiritual and social aid to the community.[8]

On December 7, 1941, then 32-year-old Donovan Senter found his academic career ending with the bombing of Pearl Harbor by the Japanese. After that day, whole armies of soldiers and fresh-faced young women converged on Washington and transformed a sleepy old-style southern town into the energetic world center of action and power. Eighteen months later, in September 1943, Senter arrived amid a government that produced nothing but paper — in the form of laws, currency, regulations, and reports. This government of paper shufflers had recruited an entirely new government to be piled on top of the old one in order to get tanks and airplanes built; uniforms made; soldiers assembled, trained, and shipped overseas; and battles fought. Like many during that time, Senter went into this lucrative job market and soon got a job with the Office of War Information (OWI).

Just prior to Senter's employment, the OWI had created images that remain among the most famous documentary photographs ever produced. Created by a group of U.S. government photographers, the images show Americans in every part of the nation. The project initially emphasized rural life and the impact of the Great Depression, farm mechanization, and the Dust Bowl. Ansel Adams was commissioned to create a photo mural for the Department of the Interior, from photos taken at the Grand Canyon, Grand Teton, Kings Canyon, Mesa Verde, Rocky Mountain, Yellowstone, Yosemite, Carlsbad Caverns, Glacier, and Zion National Parks; Death Valley, Saguaro, and Canyon de Chelly. Many of the latter locations, which were well-known by Senter, show Navajo and Pueblo Indians, their homes and activities.

The core of the OWI collection is made up of about 164,000 black-and-white photographs. The photographers in time turned their attention to the mobilization effort for World War II. In addition to patriotic works or photos playing up a wholesome image of America, OWI photographers covered less happy occasions. The OWI also documented social change, including the massive movement of women into the workforce and the advancement of African Americans in the military.

During his early months in this job, Senter traveled the border states as a farm labor organizer to recruit, transport, and established camps for Mexican nationals to grow agricultural products. He was responsible for administration, pay, and food for the immigrant workers. Six months later, Senter held the position of regional intelligence officer and conducted intensive interviews on different studies for the OWI, such as attitude surveys among all classes of people. One of the studies was a survey of racial opinions. On a train trip in 1943 from Dallas, Texas, to the Florida panhandle Senter reported: "Just two ears listening." What he heard was a rising din of racial hatred. Whites on the train expressed raging anger that African Americans had obtained defense jobs, were receiving decent salaries, and refused to bow to white supremacy. While working as a civilian with the OWI, Senter earned $420 a month, an excellent salary during the war years of 1942–1943.[9]

Senter remained with this job until he joined the army on September 22, 1943, as a 6-foot, 175-pound, 34-year-old first lieutenant. His enlistment papers indicated that he had a doctor's degree from the University of Chicago with credentials in nutrition, both claims being false. But this gave the impression that he was a medical doctor. He remained in Washington as director of personnel training for the coordinator of Inter-American affairs because of his fluent command of Spanish and extensive knowledge of Latin American affairs. A particular concern of the coordinator was the elimination of German influence in South America, as well as that of other Axis powers. Trade routes to Europe were disrupted following the fall of France in June 1940, presenting opportunities to both Germany and the United States, for at that time many agents or affiliates of U.S. firms operating in Latin America were sympathetic to the Axis powers. The office encouraged a voluntary program of noncooperation with companies and individuals perceived to be anti–American and, in the process, established a blacklist of companies and individuals. It engaged in counterintelligence activities and the collection of intelligence, controlling subordinate field offices in the Canal Zone and in Brazil and operating its own intercept system to locate possible enemy-agent transmitters throughout Latin America.

Chapter 5

The Counter Intelligence Corps

Senter asserted that he requested a transfer to get into the thick of things and obtain an assignment with the Counter Intelligence Corps (CIC). Senter could speak and write English, French, German, Spanish, and Portuguese; as a result, in April 1944 he was transferred to Camp Barkeley, near Abilene, Texas, where the 45th and 90th Infantry Divisions and the 11th and 12th Armored were training. Camp Barkeley eventually grew to be a complete city, twice the size of Abilene. It had a 2,300-bed hospital, two cold storage plants, a bakery, four theaters, two service clubs for enlisted men, 15 chapels, and 35 post exchange buildings. Here Senter went through some basic training that included a class titled "Infiltration Course — Day and Night." Three months later, on July 21, 1944, he was assigned to the CIC.[1]

It is interesting to note that the principal task of the CIC was to investigate and observe Communist activity in the United States. It is also questionable that Senter requested an assignment with the CIC considering that he knew about the general criticism of the corps, brought on by the most ill-advised act any intelligence unit could ever commit. That is, in their pursuit of Communism, the CIC agents had installed a listening device under the bed of Eleanor Roosevelt in the Blackstone Hotel in Chicago. Mrs. Roosevelt had a young male acquaintance, Joseph P. Lash, with whom she was deeply involved. Lash's friendship with Mrs. Roosevelt began in 1939 and lasted until her death in 1962. Lask was a 1931 graduate of City College in New York who earned a master's degree in philosophy and literature at Columbia University; he later became an officer of a socialist youth organization.

Mrs. Roosevelt had long had an abiding interest in politically idealistic young people, and Mr. Lash was then a prominent radical leader. The CIC justifiably suspected Lash of being a member of the Communist Party. As he was believed to be sharing Mrs. Roosevelt's room at the Blackstone Hotel, they wanted evidence that she was discussing war-related information with her young friend. During the night, the agents listened and recorded all the intimate sounds of their lovemaking. Even more preposterously, the CIC agents allowed her husband, the president, to listen to this recording. The watered down story was that Mrs. Roosevelt had loaned her room to Lash to share with Mrs. Trude Pratt, who later became Lash's second wife. The Federal Bureau of Investigation (FBI) obtained the story from CIC Agent G. C. Burton and they wrote it up as sexual intercourse between 29-year-old Joseph Lash and 63-year-old Eleanor Roosevelt. President Roosevelt was so furious over this single act that he demanded the disbandment of the CIC and ordered all of its members to be immediately shipped overseas.[2]

Historians will differ over this story for years. Nevertheless, Lt. Gen. James J. McNarney, the army deputy chief of staff, directed the army's inspector general to launch an investigation. As a result, all CIC agents were without delay ordered out of Washington, D.C. The devastating critique charged that many CIC investigations were "superficial and unproductive of positive results except in rare instances." The inspector general's report, as already noted, led to the immediate unraveling of the CIC, so that in 1944 the CIC virtually went out of business in the continental United States. The CIC agents were merged with the agents of the provost marshall's Criminal Investigation Division (CID). All CIC schools were abolished. The principal reason given was the need to eliminate duplication and conserve manpower. The army had decided to practically abandon the field of domestic counterintelligence, limiting the CIC to a tactical support role overseas. J. Edgar Hoover was euphoric over this decision, as it gave the FBI complete control over all wartime activities within the United States. Colonel Harold R. Kibler, the former chief of the CIC, blamed the fall of the CIC on the hostility of the White House, specifically Harry Hopkins, President Roosevelt's personal advisor. As a result of this single act, even today the Central Intelligence Agency (CIA) is not entitled to arrest or interrogate an American citizen or conduct activities within the United States.[3] (This may have changed after the 9/11 destruction of the World Trade Center in New York City.)

Overseas the CIC was greatly diminished, with only six men assigned to a division; therefore, generally speaking, the 28th Infantry Division, Counter Intelligence Corps, was not a corps at all but one officer and five enlisted men. The corps themselves consisted of three divisions with a staff of 2 CIC officers, 11 enlisted men, and a field army of approximately 5 officers and 45 CIC enlisted men. Thus the total number of CIC agents in the European Theater of Operations would be less than 1,000 men. The CIC agent wore a simple United States insignia reflecting no rank. If asked their rank, the men were instructed to respond "Just slightly more than yours." The net result was that they all pretended to be officers.

Thus, under this gloomy cloud, Donovan Senter was sent packing from Washington, D.C., to Camp Barkeley, Texas. Here, on July 24, 1944, Senter began classes in security intelligence that included infiltration and map and aerial photography analysis. From here Senter was sent to Chicago for counterintelligence training and then assigned to the XXI Corps at Camp Polk, Louisiana. The XXI Corps was activated on December 6, 1943, and was responsible for training an estimated 200,000 men and 70 units of varying sizes before it embarked for the European Theater on the *Queen Mary* in November of 1944. There were only two ports large enough for the ship to dock, Southampton and Glasgow, Scotland. Therefore for the duration of the war both the *Queen Mary* and her sister ship *Queen Elizabeth* docked in Scotland, as Southampton on the English Channel was too dangerous owing to German submarines. After a short stay in England, the corps landed in LeHavre, France, and became operational on January 13, 1945, after being assigned to the Seventh Army.

From LeHavre the XXI Corps' CIC detachment was transported to the town of Morhange, France, 15 miles from the German border, where they set up their interrogation center. As the American troops advanced through Europe during the preceding six months, many French refugees had fled toward Germany. Now, with their backs to the wall, they had no place to go but back home. To obtain a release to return to France, they had to travel to Morhange for screening by a CIC agent and thus to acquire a travel document. The CIC was looking for Nazi agents who were trying to infiltrate the American lines. Several men wearing Free French armbands strolled into the interrogation center, but their German combat boots gave them away. For the present, the battle line here was static, but a ferocious battle known as the Battle of the Bulge was being fought a bit north in the frozen Ardennes. While working at the interrogation center, Donovan Senter and several CIC agents occupied rooms at the home of Albert Menger in nearby St. Avold, France. This 52-year-old electrical engineer and his 38-year-old wife, Amelie, and their two children, ages 10 and 13, occupied the upstairs apartment and the CIC agents had the ground floor, complete with bath and kitchen. The large dwelling consisted of seven rooms, two kitchens, a cellar, and an attic. The CIC agents remained with the Menger family for several weeks and then, in January, the detachment left for Germany. Apparently Senter developed a friendly relationship with the Menger family, as we shall see later.[4]

This German offensive at Ardennes, which Hitler had hoped would catch the Allies off guard, included a second offensive attacking southward toward the Seventh Army. This was the battle of the Colmar Pocket. The fighting was hard, in bitter cold and snow, and resulted in 16,000 Allied casualties; but the Germans lost 25,000 men whom they could not replace. From January 25 until February 16, 1945, XXI Corps took part in this bitter winter combat, which ultimately collapsed the Colmar Pocket. During the confusion of the fighting there, as the Germans were being driven out of Alsace, a U.S. Army truck carrying the Sigaba, an encryption and decryption machine, the most important piece of equipment assigned to the XXI Corps' 28th Infantry Division, went missing. This was a horrendous, inexcusable security lapse. The Sigaba was the main communication system for the U.S. Armed Forces in Germany in that most messages and all classified messages were sent through this system. The Sigaba was the only machine system used during World War II whose codes remained unbroken by the enemy.

On this particular night, the crew responsible for the Sigaba, in moving from one area to the other to establish a new command, pulled into a French tavern and parked the truck outside; then all went in. No one was left to guard the Sigaba or the other equipment. After they had a few bottles of wine, they came out to find the truck gone.

The theft of this truck and the Sigaba caused an unbelievable degree of concern and anxiety on the part of the entire military establishment, including the CIC and General Eisenhower's headquarters, for if the Sigaba fell into the hands of the Germans, it would compromise all Allied communications. On February 25, 1945, a Sunday, and a particularly cold and sunless one, Allen Dulles, the Office of Strategic Services (OSS) chief from Switzerland, was summoned to XXI Corps headquarters at Hegenheim, France, as a consultant, and a thorough investigation began. After a day or so, the truck was found in French hands, but it was empty. Two young French soldiers had been ordered by their commander to go find some wood for the camp stove. So they "borrowed" the truck in question without having any idea of what was in it. On the way to their camp, they crossed a small river, Le Bruche. Stopping on the bridge, they threw everything, including the Sigaba, into the water. Upon learning of its location, a special detail from Seventh Army Headquarters went into the river and pulled the Sigaba out.[5]

On March 20, 1945, as the German defenses crumbled, the XXI Corps gained momentum and broke through the West Wall defenses and captured Saarbrücken. The Corps then advanced toward Wurzburg against light resistance, and captured that city. After assisting in the seizure of Schweinfurt, elements of the Corps raced to the Danube River, taking the bridge at Dillingen before the Nazis could demolish it. The Corps spearheaded the U.S. Seventh Army drive, securing Landsberg, and on May 3 crossed the Inn River and the Austrian border.

After VE (Victory in Europe) Day, May 8, 1945, while the 221st CIC detachment was located at Degerndorf, John G. Hammond and Dale Shughart received a call from William Mark, the commanding officer of the 36th CIC detachment, asking them to visit him some 50 kilometers farther west. A man of few words, Mark lost no time in displaying to them four footlockers, which they soon discovered were filled with obviously stolen loot. The contents of the lockers were not organized, but each contained an assortment of jewelry, diamonds, watches, American currency, gold coins, and other items.

Mark advised them that he wanted to be relieved of his cache and forthwith turned it over to Hammond and Shughart for removal to corps headquarters. He told them that each of his agents might remove one $20 gold piece as a souvenir, but other than that the contents were to remain exactly as he received them. The valuables, containing thousands of gold coins, including 475 U.S. $20 gold pieces, had been dumped in haste. The chests were found by members of the 36th Infantry Division in the sewer of a cement factory in Eiberg. Shughart recalled that he was told the possessor of the valuables was Nazi Ernst Kaltenbrunner.

Indeed, the treasure was the large foreign exchange fund that had been kept in Ernst Kaltenbrunner's office for purchasing gifts and personal items for the chief of the Reich's Main Security Office. The fund contained $500,000 worth of foreign currency, including $100,000 in U.S. currency. The fund also contained several small bags of gold coins weighing about 20 pounds each.

The money was kept in boxes about 3 feet long, 18 inches wide, and 2 feet high. In April 1945, these boxes were loaded onto a train in Berlin. Later, in Bavaria, U.S. planes strafed the slow-moving train and it was destroyed. Off loaded from smashed boxcars into two trucks were the boxes of treasure, whiskey, and office files that were then transported by two trucks to Gmunden, Austria. The gold treasure was then to be transported approximately 15 miles south to Alt Aussee. The files and whiskey were to be transported to the Castle Glanegg, near Salzburg. In Gmunden, where the cargo was to be divided for its separate destinations, a mistake, either deliberate or unintentional, was made. The files and whiskey were sent to Kaltenbrunner and the gold was sent to the Glanegg Castle; from there it was further transported to Imst. These valuables destined for Kaltenbrunner contained six sacks of gold weighing 66 pounds each and 600,000 units of U.S. dollars, Swiss francs, and English pounds.[6]

How this treasure ended up 50 miles from Imst in a sewer of the Alpine village of Eiberg is unknown, but now Shughart and Hammond had these heavy boxes loaded into their jeep and headed back to XXI Corps headquarters. With that much loot, they should have been escorted by an armed guard but were not.

At headquarters, the lockers were unloaded and a receipt taken. Neither Shughart nor Hammond took any of the loot for souvenirs. The four boxes were turned over to the Seventh Army Interrogation Center in Augsburg and, on May 19, 1945, were delivered to the U.S. Foreign Exchange Depository in

Frankfurt, Germany. The depository, under the command of Colonel Bernard Bernstein, contained more gold than any place in the world except Fort Knox. These valuables, along with tons of others, were later turned over to the Intergovernmental Committee for Refugees, where they served to aid many European victims of the war. (See Appendix B: The Missing Kaltenbrunner Treasure.)

A few days later, agents of the 221st CIC detachment apprehended a group of high-ranking German officials in Bad Gastein, Austria. Many among them were later tried as war criminals, including Baron Huroshi Ōshima and his three aides. Ōshima was a general in the Imperial Japanese Army and Japanese ambassador to Nazi Germany during World War II. In 1934, Ōshima became the Japanese military attaché in Berlin, with the rank of colonel. He spoke perfect German.

After their arrest, the German officials were transported to 221st CIC headquarters in Nussdorf in their own vehicles driven by German chauffeurs. On arriving at headquarters, the vehicles were confiscated and the chauffeurs released. The officials were then taken on to the Seventh Army Interrogation Center in Augsburg, Germany, in command and staff cars with drivers from the U.S. Transportation Corps.

Dale F. Shughart was in charge of the convoy of eight to ten cars, and was accompanied by a CIC interpreter. Shughart rode in the front seat of the lead vehicle; another agent occupied the rear seat of the last vehicle. Both were armed with .38- or .45-caliber pistols; each driver had a carbine or similar weapon.

One of the uniformed aides gave Shughart's fellow agent a German pistol as he left the vehicle to be interned; this concerned them because they had assumed that all prisoners had been searched. Otherwise, the trip was uneventful.

The Seventh Army detention officials advised that the Japanese ambassador could not be interned and had to be returned to the hotel from whence he had come. By the time they returned to Nussdorf it was dark, so they could not continue on to their headquarters in Bad Gastein to spend the night. But there was another problem at Nussdorf: Shughart's men were directed to return the ambassador's vehicle. It had been confiscated along with the others, and Shughart had to retrieve it.

Most of the CIC agents were away from headquarters, leaving no one to guard Baron Ōshima and his aides. The latter were each assigned a room in the small Nussdorf hotel and told that the corridors would be closely patrolled. The CIC agents crossed their fingers as all went to bed. Fortunately all were present and accounted for in the morning.

Locating the ambassador's car was not difficult — a colonel in the ordnance corps attached to the XXI had it. To put it mildly, he was greatly displeased with the turn of events. Although he outranked Shughart slightly, he grudgingly removed his gear from the car.

As Shughart leaned over to recover some of his baggage, the colonel removed Shughart's .38 revolver from its holster and said, "I'll give the ambassador a present." Grasping the revolver barrel, he struck the rear window a mighty blow with the butt. The window, obviously bulletproof, was undamaged. But not so Shughart's revolver—the wooden grips of the handle were shattered into matchsticks.

The colonel's anger quickly turned into an apology to Shughart. He made good on his promise to replace the grips, which he did, with Plexiglas. Now General Patton was not the only one with a pearl-handled pistol, albeit Shughart's was less gaudy.

With the car retrieved, Shughart returned to headquarters with the ambassador, along with his driver and an aide (who could barely peer over the dashboard), and was safely returned under escort to his hotel.[7]

The bewildered CIC agents of the XXI Corps had no idea that the arrest had brought to a halt a valuable flow of information for U.S. intelligence. Ōshima, being a meticulous military officer, wrote detailed reports of information provided to him by the Nazis and then promptly reported by radio to Tokyo in diplomatic cipher. Unknown to the Japanese, the code was broken by the Americans in 1940; thus Ōshima's reports were being read almost simultaneously by both the Japanese and the Americans. Often, the Americans were able to read them before the Japanese, as transmission problems between Germany and Japan frequently held up the cables for hours. The war with Japan was continuing, and Shughart and his fellow agents had suppressed a valuable source of information that might have had a bearing on the war against Japan. Ōshima was therefore released so that this flow of information might be reinstated.

Chapter 6

The Quest for Lucas Cranach Paintings

The CIC detachment of the XXI Corps had entered Austria and advanced along the Inn River until German forces in the area unconditionally surrendered on May 6, 1945. It was near here that Lt. Donovan Senter personally arrested Willy Sachs.

Willy Sachs, a wealthy industrialist, was the sole owner of Fichtel & Sachs AG in Schweinfurt, with 7,000 employees. Sachs was known as a playboy and spent much of his time hunting, womanizing, and drinking. The roaring feasts at Mainberg Castle and his mountain estate at Rechenau were legendary. Reichsmarschall Hermann Göring was a preferred guest of Sachs during his many hunts at Mainberg Castle and on the Rechenau. From 1925 to 1935, Sachs was married to Elinor Opel, daughter of the founder of the Opel Automotive Company. In 1937 he married the youthful Ursula Meyer.

Sachs did not inherit his father's business management skills, but fortunately the company was in the hands of loyal directors Heinrich Kaiser and Dr. Rudolf Diessel, who successfully controlled the enterprise. During World War II, thousands of art treasures were stolen by the Nazis. From these, the Nazi and top industrial leaders formed their private collections. Sachs was no exception and greatly expanded his collection.[1]

The most important paintings of the Nazi era were those of Lucas Cranach, and Göring dominated the market for Cranach paintings. Thus anyone of importance in the Nazi Party had to own one of Cranach's paintings. Lucas Cranach (1472–1553) was a German painter, engraver and designer of woodcuts. He was a lifelong friend of Martin Luther and painted the first Protestant paintings under Luther's guidance. He was well known in academic circles in the Province of Saxon and highly regarded as an artist and political celebrity. His works of art included landscapes, religious subjects and works on mythology, often in the form of nudes.

In the early days of the war, Willy Sachs' large art collection was located in his home, at Mainberg Castle, Schweinfurt. Whether his collection came in part from theft or entirely from legitimate acquisition is unknown.[2]

However, Schweinfurt was a principal target for Allied bombers, since it was the site of Sachs' ball-bearing plant, and ball bearings were essential for the production of military hardware of all types. Accordingly Schweinfurt was attacked first on August 17, 1943, with 230 B-17s from England sent to bomb the city. However, the Luftwaffe had over 300 fighters available to oppose them. Only 184 B-17s bombed Schweinfurt, and 36 did not return to England. After rebuilding its strength, the U.S. 8th Army Air Force again attacked Schweinfurt on October 14, 1943 — a day that would go down in history as "Black Thursday," since 291 B-17s left England, 229 bombed the target, and 60 bombers were lost. Crew casualties were 639 men, a loss the 8th Air Force could not afford.[3]

Because of these heavy Allied bombing raids, Sachs moved most of his art collection from his castle to a safer location, his estate at Rechenau, Oberaudorf, Bavaria. This picturesque Alpine location was on the Austrian border. His wife, Ursula, and stepdaughter, Jolanda, lived there in the nearby hunting lodge, while the paintings, in crates, were stored in the main mansion on the estate. Sachs, like most Germans, kept accurate records of the valuables he owned.

On May 5, 1945, Lt. Donovan Senter, commanding officer of the CIC detachment from the XXI Corps, arrived at the Rechenau estate and arrested Willy Sachs as a potential war criminal because of his rank as a senior officer in the Schutz-Staffel (SS), or secret police. Upon Sachs' arrest, the U.S. Army under Military Law 52 took control of all of his property. This basic authority for taking custody of property in Germany is noted in Joint Chiefs of Staff Directive 1067/6, which directed the U.S. Zone commander to "impound or block" certain specified categories of property, including those of the German Reich, the Nazi Party and affiliated organizations and their prominent members, and absentee owners. The American Zone commander was also required to impound all property that was transferred under duress or through wrongful acts of confiscation, disposition, or spoliation and to block the relocation of works of art and cultural material of value or importance regardless of its ownership. Thus the military made it easy for an American soldier to acquire Germany property.[4]

At this time the CIC liberated a prisoner-of-war camp consisting of mostly French soldiers. They were quickly turned over to the French liaison except for one individual who had nowhere to go and offered his services to the CIC as a cook. This person, called René, explained that he had been a chef in Paris. Therefore René joined the 221st CIC detachment. He requisitioned villas, went "shopping," and was masterly in obtaining fresh meat, vegetables, and, most importantly, thirst quenchers from generous wine cellars.⁵

Shortly after this, Senter was assigned to an Interrogation of Prisoners of War detachment at Seventh Army Headquarters in Augsburg. Senter could not have picked an assignment more suited to his talents. His fluent German served him well here, since Augsburg was the most likely spot in Germany in which to steal a fortune. Such activity involved the unethical confiscation of personal property of surrendered high-ranking German officers. Prisoners arrived daily in numbers of 25 or more. After each group was processed, a large box of confiscated material was delivered to Maj. Paul Kubala, the commanding officer. In addition to large quantities of foodstuffs, and liquor, the box contained cameras, field glasses, watches, silver and gold cigarette cases, jewelry, and large sums of money, including gold coins and American currency. The highest-ranking officer to arrive at the Seventh Army Interrogation Center was Reichsmarschall Herman Göring. Kubala took it upon himself to personally conduct the search of Göring's baggage. Kubala removed several gold watches from Göring's belongings and gave them to his clique of officers. And Senter was quickly absorbed into Kubala's inner circle. This group did as little work as possible, spending most of their days writing letters, taking sunbaths, or making trips.⁶

During this assignment, Senter drove the 125 miles from Augsburg to visit Ursula Sachs at the hunting lodge of the Rechenau estate. It was later reported that Senter spent 56 nights with Sachs' wife, Ursula, at the hunting lodge in Rechenau between May 5 and September 1, 1945.⁷

Sachs' extensive art collection at Rechenau included several crates of paintings; a few of these, executed on wood, were by Lucas Cranach. For some time, Senter had been particularly interested in such paintings, having written a thesis on painting on wood while obtaining his doctoral degree as a research sociologist from Harvard University. Because of his interest in the Cranachs, three of them came into his possession on or about June 15, 1945. They were *The Blessing of Christ, John the Constant,* and *Frederick the Magnanimous.* Ursula Sachs told many stories about the paintings. First she said that she had given them to Senter as souvenirs of Europe, without any obligations. Later she claimed that Senter had "wangled them out of her" with the statement that the CIC could take anything it wanted. Ursula said "I hoped of course that if I gave these paintings to Senter, I would receive protection for the critical time I gave them to him out of gratitude for that protection."⁸ The property was not Mrs. Sachs' to give away. It was official property of the United States, all the more so since, as the second wife of Willy Sachs, she had signed a marriage contract renouncing her legal right to common and inheritance property. According to her daughter, Jolanda, Ursula and Senter agreed to sell *The Blessing of Christ* and *John the Constant*. *Frederick the Magnanimous* was to remain with Senter as a commission for the sale.

Another cohort at the Rechenau hunting lodge was a German, Otto Simpendörfer, and his small son, Michel. Simpendörfer owned a Paillard 16-mm camera with a three-part lens system. The camera was very expensive, valued in 1945 at $1,250. Senter became enamored of the camera and seized it as a gift. Simpendörfer was attached as an informant to the CIC team headed by Senter and had been instrumental in the location and arrest in their mountain hideouts of high-ranking Nazi officials. In this position he could do very little to oppose any theft. Simpendörfer was a frequent guest at the Rechenau estate's hunting lodge and listened to many table conversations regarding Ursula's marriages and other family-related matters. When it came to items of great value, it is most obvious that Senter had very "sticky fingers." The hunting lodge quickly became a weekend and holiday haven for Senter's friends in military intelligence, including George Mandler and his girlfriend Anneliese Gustke, who helped him spend 100,000 Reichsmarks. Mandler, the youngest member of the XXI Corps' CIC detachment, had, on a patrol, uncovered a few documents and a locked box. After checking for booby traps, his team carefully opened the box, which contained more than 100,000 Reichsmarks. Mandler wrote: "Never was there a thought that this money should be turned over to anybody at all — we were refugees from the SS and considered the money justifiable restitution."[9]

At the end of May, Senter returned to Albert Menger's home in St. Avold, France, where he had spent the previous January. He was driving a large Mercedes, wearing a magnificent woman's ring set with a big diamond, and on his watch chain were proudly displayed four other women's rings in gold set with diamonds. Senter then showed Mrs. Menger a pure gold cigarette case bearing a dedication to Hermann Göring. He was doing quite well stealing the property of German officers at the Seventh Army Interrogation Center. She asked him what he intended to do with the rings, and Senter responded, "I shall sell them to make money." He spent the night and told the Mengers that he would be going to Paris on duty. Two days later, unexpectedly, he returned, spent the night, and told the Mengers that he was to be stationed in the Munich area. The following morning he left. They certainly did not expect to see him again.[10]

By now Senter's choice assignment in Augsburg had ended with the arrest of Maj. Paul Kubala, who was charged with taking unauthorized articles from prisoners-of-war luggage, sexual intercourse with female internees, and other charges of immorality. He was incarcerated, but being an "old timer," received only a "slap on the wrist" and the offer of a transfer to the highly secretive OSS. But without President Roosevelt's protection, the OSS had already been

6. The Quest for Lucas Cranach Paintings 51

disbanded by President Harry Truman. This action made it clear that Gen. William Donovan had put little time into cultivating a relationship with anyone other than his friend President Roosevelt. With strings pulled by Gen. Alexander Patch and Col. William Quinn, Kubala settled into a job with the U.S. Army Air Corps at Wright-Patterson Field, Dayton, Ohio.[11]

Senter was transferred from the CIC to the Third Reinforcement Depot in Munich. This large depot was a holding area for military personnel without an assignment. This was most fortunate for him, as his habit of sleeping at the hunting lodge had ended when he met and moved in with Jolanda Mayer-Caputo, Ursula Sachs' daughter from a previous marriage. According to Senter, she was a strikingly beautiful young girl. Her apartment was conveniently located nearby at 36 Feilitzsch Street in Munich.

In mid–June, Senter, like a bad penny, driving his big Mercedes, showed up again at Albert Menger's home in St. Avold, France. With Albert's help, he brought three paintings—*Frederick the Magnanimous*, *The Blessing of Christ*, and *John the Constant*—into the house from his Mercedes. Senter told Menger that the three paintings had been given to him by the daughter of the industrialist Willy Sachs. Senter further stated that the paintings were given in complete agreement with the mother, as her husband had been committed to an insane asylum. He had a document written in German stating that the paintings were a gift for services rendered. Senter further said that he intended to marry Jolanda. He then asked Menger to go with him to Paris, where they could sell two of the paintings. Senter said that he intended to keep one of them and take it back to America with him. Menger said that he did not know anyone in Paris but knew someone in Luxembourg who could connect them with an art expert.

They took the paintings to Aloys Biever, a Luxembourg real estate agent, who had worked with Menger previously on several real estate ventures. They had known each other for several years and were working on a deal to make Menger a shareholder in Biever's company. In the course of these visits, Senter and Biever made an agreement that the paintings should be appraised and then restored. Biever then went to the city of Luxembourg and had an art dealer named Michels appraise the paintings. Michels stated that two of the three paintings were mere copies but that *The Blessing of Christ* was an original. Senter told Menger that he needed money and would leave *The Blessing of Christ* in his custody. Menger then lent Senter 100,000 francs ($2,300) and held onto the painting while Senter returned to Germany with the reported fakes.[12]

On June 25, a very hot day, Ursula Sachs and Senter traveled to the bombed out town of Nuremberg with four of Willy Sachs' Cranach paintings: two more from Rechenau (*The Holy Virgin* and *Young Christ and Saint John*) plus the two (supposed) Cranach paintings *Frederick the Magnanimous* and *John the Constant* that had been taken to Luxembourg. They took the four paintings to the art specialist Dr. Fritz T. Schulz for authentication. Dr. Schulz validated the works as Cranach originals and furnished written certificates of authenticity for all four paintings. Senter told Schulz that he had previously had the paintings authenticated in Luxembourg and that the specialist there had stated that *John the Constant* was an overpainted print; he showed Schulz a French certificate to this effect, but Schulz just laughed it off.[13]

Senter had previously promised to help Mrs. Sachs negotiate a power of attorney so that she would be able to handle her husband's finances. Therefore, after this stop in Nuremberg, they continued on to Schweinfurt. Senter was aware that prior to her marriage to Willy Sachs, Ursula had signed a statement renouncing her legal rights to the couple's common and inherited property. They arrived in Schweinfurt later that evening at 8 P.M. and proceeded immediately to the local city jail, where Heinrich Kaiser was incarcerated. Kaiser had been a director of Fichtel & Sachs AG as well as the private administrator of the personal property of the Sachs family since 1912; he was jailed primarily because of this relation. Senter and Mrs. Sachs, accompanied by Lt. Flank, the property control officer, entered Kaiser's jail cell.

Mrs. Sachs told Kaiser, "My husband's property is all going to be confiscated. I should like to rescue for him as much as I can. I want you to transfer to me from my husband account 1 million Reichsmarks. With this money I plan to buy the Rechenau estate."

Kaiser replied, "I have no power of attorney that would entitle me to sell to you any part of your husband's property. I have spent the last three weeks in jail and have not the faintest idea as to whether a transfer is possible under the present military government regulations. Moreover, I do not have any cash at my disposal. Whether stock can be sold I would have to enquire with the bank."[14]

To this statement Senter replied, in German, "Der Lieutenant Flank ist ja der Bank" or "Lieutenant Flank *is* the Bank." Whereupon Flank made an evasive remark.

"Had I been alone and free," Kaiser later said, "I would have answered Mrs. Sachs' request by simply asking her 'Are you nuts?' But confronted by two American officers who supported her claim with their presence and an intermittent nodding of the head, I did not dare to give her the proper reply. The less so since, during the conversation, Mrs. Sachs at various instances remarked: 'Remember, the length of your stay in jail depends on us.' These remarks were made in Lt. Senter's presence, who followed the conversation from beginning to end."[15]

Senter and Mrs. Sachs spent that night in Schweinfurt with Kaiser's wife.

The following morning they returned to the jail and again applied more pressure on Kaiser for a transfer of cash. At that time only Senter and Mrs. Sachs appeared. When they entered his cell, Kaiser later said, Senter tried to get rid of the accompanying German guard. The guard, however, was stubborn and claimed to be under orders to remain. Senter got rid of him as a witness by leaving the cell with him. After a while Senter returned alone and participated in the second half of the conversation. A summary of this conversation follows:

> MRS. SACHS: "I have taken cognition of the fact that there is no cash available, but I think I could buy the Rechenau estate anyhow. I could have the estate simply transferred to me and remain indebted for the money to my husband."
>
> MR. KAISER: "I have already told you that I have no power of attorney to arrange such a transfer. You must procure an authorization from your husband."[16]

After Senter returned without the guard, Kaiser continued, the possibility of contacting Willy Sachs was discussed. Sachs at this time was interned at a civilian internment enclosure near the city of Heilbronn. Senter declared that the trip to Heilbronn was too far and could not be undertaken at that moment. Thus their attempt to obtain 1 million Reichsmarks (equivalent to $100,000 in 1945) failed. But they were determined.

The previous April, the 101st Airborne Infantry Division had discovered an underground bunker containing Reichsmarschall Hermann Göring's extensive art collection. In a hotel at Unterstein, a Bavarian village near Berchtesgaden, they placed on display the world's most valuable private art collection. Göring's collection included paintings by Rubens, Rembrandt, Van Dyck, Velásquez, Boucher, and an incredible 49 works by Lucas Cranach. Of course Senter had to view this $200-million treasure. Therefore on July 2, Mrs. Sachs and Senter drove to Berchtesgaden and from there continued on a little back road. Ten minutes later they arrived at Uterstein. In a clearing on the left side of the road was a low rambling structure of whitewashed stucco in the familiar farmhouse style. It had been a rest and recreation center for the German Air Force. The center section, three stories high, had a gabled roof with wide overhanging eaves. On either side were long wings each two stories high. Inside was the Göring collection, open only to military personnel; therefore Mrs. Sachs remained outside the building while Senter reviewed the art works. On that very day, Cranach's *Philip Melanchton and Dagon*, a 20- by 14-centimeter wood panel, disappeared.

From Berchtesgaden Senter and Mrs. Sachs continued on toward a second attempt to obtain the means with which to purchase the Rechenau estate — that is, by contacting another former employee of Fichtel and Sachs AG. They called on Dr. Rudolf Diessel in the village of Urfahrn on Lake Chiem. Dr. Diessel was one of the legal advisors of Fichtel and Sachs AG. The date of the visit was established through an entry in Diessel's diary that reads "Impertinent visit by Mrs. Sachs."

In Diessel's words:

> Mrs. Sachs asked me to transfer to her from the funds of Willy Sachs an amount of Reichsmarks, 300,000 for the liquidation of bills of the Rechenau estate. I knew that the management of the Rechenau estate could never require funds of that size and when, somewhat later in the conversation, Mrs. Sachs declared her intention to buy the Rechenau estate, I understood what purpose this money was to serve.
>
> I pointed out to Mrs. Sachs that I had no authority to honor her request and that I could not make use of such authority even if I had it, since the transfer of funds of interned Germans was prohibited by military government laws.
>
> Mrs. Sachs expressed the opinion that means and ways to affect such a transfer could be found nevertheless.
>
> Lieutenant Senter was present during the entire conversation and was well aware of its content and its purpose, as I could gather from occasional remarks of his. He did not exercise any verbal pressure upon me in this matter, but from his presence and his general attitude I had to infer that he approved of Mrs. Sachs' request.[17]

Nevertheless, on June 30, 1945, Mrs. Sachs opened an account at Kiefersfelden in her name with an initial deposit of 100,000 Reichsmarks ($10,000). This village included a bank near the Rechenau estate. The amount was deposited in 100 notes of 1,000 Reichsmarks each. On July 11, 1945, at the same branch office, Mrs. Sachs deposited 100,000 Reichsmarks in a second account in the name of her daughter Jolanda Mayer-Caputo. This amount was deposited in 100 notes of 1,000 Reichsmarks each.

Kaiser was later asked, "Do you know the property status of Ursula Sachs well enough as to be able to judge whether she had available to herself an amount of Reichsmark 200,000?" Kaiser's answer was: "I know the property status of Mrs. Ursula Sachs well enough to ascertain that she did not have such an amount at her disposal."[18]

Senter and Ursula Sachs had failed to obtain the $100,000 they were trying to extort, but they had raised the equivalent of U.S. $20,000 in Reichsmarks, a fortune in 1945, equaling nine years of Senter's current salary. He was earning $190.01 a month, with an allotment of $100 sent to his wife and a government insurance deduction of $7.70. This netted Senter $82.31 a month. What was the source of the additional money? Did Senter sell some valuable paintings, or had he taken money during a patrol looking for SS fugitives, as George Mandler had? Did Mandler recover more than 100,000 Reichsmarks and split it with Senter, his commanding officer?

A few days later, Senter drove to St. Avold and showed Menger the detailed authentication of the Cranach paintings written by Dr. Fritz T. Schulz. Then the two men continued on to the city of Luxembourg and again asked Biever to help in selling the paintings *The Blessing of Christ* and *Frederick the Magnanimous*. Senter told Biever how he had obtained the paintings and also said that he was going to marry the daughter of their former owner. Senter even produced a photograph of Jolanda Mayer-Caputo. Biever ask for a statement of origin and Senter produced the certifications from Dr. Schulz as well as a statement in German certifying that the painting were gifts to Senter and that he was authorized to sell them. Ursula Sachs and Jolanda Mayer-Caputo had signed the certification. Senter told the two men that Ursula's husband was insane, had been sent to a mental asylum, that he, and Senter, was helping the women with their financial transactions. Once Biever's interest in the paintings was aroused, Senter told him that he would have to have an advance on the paintings. Menger then immediately told Biever of his loan to Senter. Biever gave him an advance of 15,000 Belgian francs ($2,550) and requested a receipt. Senter answered, "Between us everything has to be dealt with honestly or else," as he pulled his pistol from his holster and pointed it at Biever. Senter left *John the Constant* and the certification with Biever; he took the other painting to Menger's home.[19]

Biever took the painting to Brussels and had it appraised by art expert Louis Manteau, who declared the picture to be a valuable original oil painting. Senter then asked Manteau to clean and restore the painting, which had some damage. Manteau informed him that it would take three months to complete the task. Knowing that there was money to be made, Biever and Menger went to Brussels several times to check on the painting.

In the following month, Senter removed *Frederick the Magnanimous* from Menger's home and left it with Biever. On this occasion he requested more money and received 15,000 in Belgian currency from Biever. From Menger and Biever, Senter had received more money than he could make at that time in two years as a first lieutenant.

Mrs. Amelie Menger was concerned about the loan to Senter and wrote Elmer Teply, an officer with the 221 CIC. They had become friends the previous January. Teply's reply of August 4, 1945, read:

> I will only drop you a few lines in order to notify you that I have succeeded in finding out Mr. Senter's full name and address. In case he does not come back in a short time you can send him a letter. Lieutenant Donovan Senter, Mil. Govt. Det. Augmentation, ECAD, APO 658, U.S. Army. With regards to this concern, stick to the plan we talked over. If he won't call on you or write you at all, you have at least his last address in case you want to call the police.[20]

During this time Heinrich Kaiser had managed to obtain his release from the Schweinfurt city jail and returned to his former residence, Mainberg Castle, property of Willy Sachs. The castle at this time was headquarters of the 79th Division Artillery and under the command of Col. R. C. Gott. Kaiser, not wanting to miss an opportunity while working with Military Government Detachment G-221, began to sell that part of Sachs' art collection that had remained at the castle. Officers of the U.S. Army purchased these art objects illegally. The valuable collection of armor and weapons disappeared completely. Capt. E. G. Deming purchased two 17th-century paintings, *The Temptation of St. Anthony* by David Teniers and *The Goldweigher* by Ferdinand Bol. He paid $405 for the two paintings, which were priceless. The remaining items were sold for an average price of $50 each. Kaiser apparently pocked the money. These works were not recovered and remain missing.[21]

The story would have ended here and no questions asked except for the fact that on September 11, 1945, a large cache of valuable art objects was found hidden in an old farmhouse called the Trojer Hof atop a mountain south of Munich and near the Austrian border in the small village of Oberaudorf. The CIC Border Control Detachment had uncovered the valuables and sent a report to the attention of the Bavarian Monuments, Fine Arts and Archives (MFAA) unit. The report, read by Capt. Edwin C. Rae, stated that the valuables belonged to Willy Sachs. It also stated that Ursula Sachs had placed the items there in the middle of July. Under further questioning, Mrs. Sachs wrote a statement that she had given Lt. Donovan Senter two Cranach paintings prior to moving the valuables to the mountaintop barn. Capt. Rae immediately linked Senter's name to the missing Cranach from the Göring collection. Senter had been a suspect in the theft because the guards had remembered him and the strangeness of Ursula Sachs waiting outside the building for Senter. During these proceedings, Mrs. Sachs was jailed in Oberaudorf for violating Military Law 52, which was a U.S. military law requiring any German transaction of any nature valued at more than a few dollars to be reported to local authorities. This included art transactions before the year 1938.[22]

During the following week Mrs. Sachs was interrogated by Lt. William E. Frye, at which time she reconfirmed her gift of art to Senter but denied any knowledge of the disappearance of Cranach's *Philip Melanchton and Dagon* from Berchtesgaden. Frye wrote that "she lied so much that I would hesitate to repeat anything she said."[23]

Captain Rae ordered a search for Lt. Senter, who had since been transferred from the Third Reinforcement Depot to the 132nd Evacuation Hospital as nutrition officer serving under the command of Col. Henry W. Daine. Unable to locate him there, the Criminal Investigation Division (CID) agents learned that he was staying with Jolanda Mayer-Caputo, Mrs. Sachs' daughter. CID agents obtained Jolanda's apartment address in Munich, and Senter was finally located there on October 1. There the CID agents closely questioned Senter for approximately two hours. He denied any knowledge of the missing Göring painting but did admit that he had visited the exhibition on July 2 at Berchtesgaden. He further flatly denied that he had been given any Cranach paintings or any other paintings by Mrs. Sachs. He did state that he had taken two Cranach paintings to Nuremberg to check their authenticity with an art expert. Upon their return to the Rechenau estate in Oberaudorf, however, the paintings were restored to Mrs. Sachs. Senter told the CID agents that Mrs. Sachs had offered him a Cranach as a souvenir, but he had refused the offer since he knew it was against army regulations for him to accept or take such property. Senter's girlfriend, Jolanda Mayer-Caputo, was also questioned, but she denied any knowledge of this matter. From the apartment the agents went to Senter's quarters and thoroughly searched his personal effects and baggage.[24]

Based on the search and investigations, the agents did not find any wrongdoing. After all, it was only the word of a German woman against the honor of an American army officer. The CID dropped the case and turned their findings over to Capt. Edwin C. Rae.

On October 24, 1945, Capt. Rae turned over his findings to Lt. Walter W. Horn, an MFAA intelligence officer, and requested that he reinvestigate the case. Born in Germany in 1908, Horn came to the United States in 1938 and joined the faculty of the University of California at Berkeley. He published extensively, including a three-volume study of monastic community life in the ninth century; he was also influential in the establishment of the University Art Museum.

Horn joined the U.S. Army and served in Europe as a prisoner-of-war interrogator. During the occupation of Germany, he worked as a military investigator of stolen art treasures and even secured the recovery of the coronation regalia of the Holy Roman Empire from Nazi treasure troves. After the war, he had a distinguished career as the first professor of art history in the University of California system.

Horn's first action was to have Jolanda Mayer-Caputo arrested and held in solitary confinement at the Munich City Jail. After three days in her lonely cell, Horn visited Jolanda, who at first stated that her affection for her mother and love for Lieutenant Senter might induce her to withhold information that she was being asked to reveal. After Horn explained that she would remain in jail until the truth was told, she wrote and signed a statement to the effect that Lt. Senter intended to help her mother in the sale of the Cranach paintings titled *The Blessing of Christ* and *John the Constant*. She further stated that the paintings had disappeared.

Jolanda and her mother were released from jail and placed under house arrest at their respective homes. Informed of her daughter's confession, Mrs. Sachs stated, "I did not really present Senter with these paintings, he wrangled them out of me. The CIC said they could take from here whatever they wanted. I had hoped of course that if I gave the paintings to Senter, I would, in recompense, receive protection for the critical time. I gave to him out of gratitude for that protection."[25]

Based on this written confession, Horn and Rae interrogated Senter again on November 3, 1945. He was informed of his right to remain silent in accord with the 24th article of war. While holding the original statement in his hand, the stunned Senter began a long tirade of self-accusation by stating, "My father made the same kind of mistakes. He was perfect on the small details and wrong on the big stakes. I could get hold of the paintings, produce them and then say take all the account for them; that would be fine."[26] He then hinted that the three Cranach paintings — *The Blessing of Christ, John the Constant,* and *Frederick the Magnanimous* — had been subject to a sale and that money had been received for them. Senter further stated that the paintings were still in Europe. By now the investigators were positive that Senter had received three paintings from Mrs. Sachs as compensation for his help to her in her efforts to obtain control over her husband's property.

Chapter 7

The Charade Continues

Because of Willy Sachs' role in the Nazi Party, the Cranach paintings seized under Military Law 52 were considered to be the property of the United States. Therefore Senter's offer to retrieve the paintings was accepted. On November 23, 1945, he and Captain William G. O'Brien began to track the paintings. O'Brien followed Senter into the black market art world on a trip that is definitely stranger than fiction.

On November 6, 1945, or shortly thereafter, Lt. Horn came to O'Brien's office and enlisted him in the task of recovering the stolen paintings. About a week or two later, Maj. Bancel La Farge of the MFAA sent orders for Capt. O'Brien from the Third Military Government Regiment to assist Senter in the search. O'Brien was a small black-haired individual with an excellent command of the French language. The order authorized O'Brien to travel to any country in Europe. The trip was not made in the comfort of Senter's big Mercedes but with an assigned driver in a ¾-ton command car built by Dodge; it was made famous as General George Patton's vehicle of choice. O'Brien had been given a copy of the investigative reports on the matter and photocopies of the paintings. Of course the investigative report did not contain any information regarding Senter's previous trips to Belgium, Luxembourg, and France to sell the paintings, as he had continued to lie to the military investigators. Therefore O'Brien was completely in the dark regarding, the art dealings between Senter, Albert Menger, and Aloyse Biever.[1]

O'Brien learned that Senter was temporarily assigned as mess officer at the medical detachment of the local evacuation hospital in Munich. This may have been because of the background in nutrition that he had fraudulently reported on his enlistment papers. In any case, he had agreed to accompany someone and attempt to recover the three paintings. O'Brien was uneasy about this from the start, since Senter, facing a general court-martial, might well be looking for a means of escape.

O'Brien went to the hospital that morning to meet Senter and make arrangements for the trip. He found a young man of about his own age, midthirties, who was pleasant and cooperative and offered him breakfast at his mess. He was quite relaxed. O'Brien remembered that he spent some time asking officers in the mess how they liked the eggs Benedict, which he had prepared that morning.

Senter was an enigmatic person, good-looking, affable, and personable, but there was also a dark side, a depressive, self-denigrating quality. He spoke often of *Schicksal*, or fate, as determining his failures. Whether it was because of the circumstances of their meeting or not, O'Brien also had the feeling of being in the presence of an intelligent con man who, with verbal sleight of hand, could make black look like white.

As they started off on the search, O'Brien mistrusted Senter and was unsure of what criminal elements they might meet on the trip. For these reasons he wore a .45 automatic in a holster, loaded, with a round in the chamber the entire time. This was not that unusual, as most officers frequently wore weapons; Europe was in a chaotic state and there were many individuals and small groups roaming around and living off the land, so to speak.

They started the search in Bavaria, Senter proposing that they visit different addresses and people who were possibly involved in the art black market. Their first trip was to the village of Herrsching, where the two men met with 65-year-old Ferencz Graf, a former wine dealer from Hungary. A large part of their conversation centered on Gustav Albrecht and other members of the Bavarian royal family. Graf disclaimed any interest in politics, but he did discuss the recent return of Albrecht from Italy and the possibility of his return to the Bavarian throne. Graf further stated that Albrecht had recently been in Rome and Florence. At this point Senter stated that he and O'Brien were about to leave on a pleasure trip and wanted to purchase various art objects to take home; he asked Graf if he knew the names of some art dealers. During the conversation Senter said that they were interested in primitives, particularly paintings on wood. Graf then mentioned several art dealers in Paris.

After leaving Graf, Senter and O'Brien visited a family named Ruoff. Senter told O'Brien that Mr. Ruoff had been a high-ranking member of the Wehrmacht and was a member of the DuPont family of Wilmington, Delaware, in the United States.

Then the driver drove the two officers up the Autobahn to Heidelberg, where Senter spent several hours trying to locate a CIC agent by the name of Maxwell. They spent the night at the Seventh Army Special Service Center. The following morning, on November 25, they crossed the Rhine on a pontoon bridge the engineers had built and drove towards Metz. They came to a village — a few buildings and houses on each side of the road — named St. Avold. Senter suddenly exclaimed that he had been stationed there and had some friends there who would put them up for the night. They came to a small white frame house set back a little on the south side of the road and were invited into the Mengers' residence.

O'Brien never learned what Albert Menger did for a living, but the interior of the house included several oil paintings and a small grand piano. O'Brien noted that the quality of the paintings seemed out of proportion to the rest of the furnishings. Both the Mengers seemed like working-class people, not university-educated. Again with them, Senter and O'Brien went into their "officers on leave looking for primitive art" routine. Menger repeatedly urged that they try Paris, not Brussels, as the men had initially suggested. Senter conversed with the Mengers in German, much of which O'Brien did not understand, but apparently Senter asked Menger to "play along with the game." Menger indicated he had some paintings other than those on the walls. Senter asked to see one of them, whereupon Menger went to another room and returned with a large framed oil painting on wood. This was soon recognized as Cranach's *The Blessing of Christ,* one of the pictures being sought.

Both Senter and O'Brien kept poker faces and did not let on that they had any unusual interest in this particular work. They did inspect it, and O'Brien was certain that it was one of their targets. Senter later confirmed this, and they agreed that they would leave the picture where it was so that others down the black market chain might not be alerted by the Mengers that the other pictures were also being targeted. It was a calculated risk. If this painting was seized, they would have an even more difficult task in locating the other two.

At this point, O'Brien, in spite of his previous doubts, became convinced that Senter had a genuine interest in recovering the paintings. O'Brien now believed that Senter felt it was in his best interest to cooperate so as to alleviate whatever punishment a court-martial might hand him. It did not, however, completely remove O'Brien's feeling that, in a fit of depression over what "fate" had done to him, Senter might attempt to escape or even commit suicide. At least O'Brien felt that Senter was honestly trying to do the job they had been given while continuing to conceal the identity of any coconspirators as much as possible. The naive O'Brien did not have a clue that Senter and Menger were in cahoots and hoodwinking him big time.

When Senter told the family that they were going to the city of Luxembourg, Mrs. Menger asked him to deliver a package to her young son, who was attending the Ste-Marie Institute at Arlon, Belgium. She said the package was too large for the mail and asked Senter to deliver it to Aloyse Biever in Luxembourg.

The following day, November 26, 1945, the driver and two officers drove on to Metz, made a few inquiries, and then continued on to Luxembourg, where they delivered the package to Aloyse Biever. The two officers talked with Biever for more than an hour. Senter asked for the address of Louis Manteau in Brussels. As Biever was going through his files looking for the address, Senter noticed the certificate saying that the paintings were gifts to him, which was signed by Ursula Sachs and Jolanda Mayer-Caputo. He tore off the certificate and, as he was putting it into his pocket, told Biever that he would not have any use for it anymore. Apparently O'Brien was "ignorant" of this background and also of the fact that Senter had demanded another loan of 5,000 Belgian francs. Biever gave Senter the money and the two men left. From there they drove onward through Arlon to Brussels. After that Biever did not see Senter again.

O'Brien wrote the following in his report:

> Biever impressed me as a very shrewd individual, but we were unable to elicit any information concerning valuable art from Mr. Biever.
>
> It is interesting to note that the Mengers knew we were going to Brussels by way of Luxembourg City and would therefore have to pass through Arlon but instructed Senter to deliver the package, addressed to Arlon, in Luxembourg City, instead of delivering it to the proper address.[2]

Surely by now O'Brien must have known that the Menger family was using a willing Senter to smuggle items of value from France to Luxembourg. It appears from writings dating from the late stages of his life that O'Brien was this trusting.

By the evening of November 26 they were getting into the Ardennes forest, a mountainous, sparsely inhabited area that had been the scene of murderous fighting during and after the Battle of the Bulge. They paused briefly to see the town of Bastogne, where the 101st Airborne had made such a gallant stand against Hitler's last gasp attempt to win the war. There was still damage to some of the buildings, but that battle had taken place almost a year earlier and much of the destruction had been repaired or cleaned up.

The men turned north from there, traveling along a narrow road that wound through the mountains and came to a cleared piece of ground, perhaps four or five acres, on the east. Beyond this field was a large valley and beyond that was a mountain ridge parallel to the road. This ridge was several hundred feet higher than the field. In the field were six disabled American Sherman tanks, dug into the field perhaps four feet deep. All of them were facing the ridge on the opposite side of the valley. This was the scene of a tragedy. During the Battle of the Bulge, the commanding general of an American armored division had ordered his division to attack down this narrow road in an attempt to reach and relieve Bastogne. A battery of German artillery, firing 88's, a larger, more powerful weapon than the Shermans were equipped with, had zeroed in on the column creeping along this narrow track in the wilderness. In desperation, these two tank platoons had attempted to dig in on this

7. The Charade Continues

field and provide counter-battery fire to protect the column. Outgunned, with the Germans sited on the reverse slope of the ridge, they had no chance, and all six were destroyed. Tanks belonged in open terrain, where they could maneuver. On a narrow track like that road, they were almost helpless.

After stopping for a few minutes to view this terrible scene, O'Brien, Senter, and their driver moved on. It was getting dark, and the Ardennes seemed even more dark and foreboding than before. Senter pretended that he was not sure of their position, how far they were from Liege, or even whether this road would take them there. He had taken this route several times in the previous months while dealing in the art trade. O'Brien was concerned that a knocked-out bridge, which in this deserted area might not yet have been replaced, would force them to retrace their steps back to Bastogne through the forest in the dark, but Senter knew better.

It was late and they had not eaten since noon. As they were creeping along the road, they saw a glimmer of light off to their left and decided to stop and make sure they were still headed in the right direction. They pulled off the road, got out, and—walking 50 yards or so through the trees—came to a cabin, the source of the light. O'Brien knocked and a man opened the door. In French, O'Brien told him that they were Americans going to Liege and asked whether they were on the right road. Yes, they were. Then O'Brien asked the man whether they could heat some rations over his fire or stove, since they were hungry. The man nodded noncommittally and the three entered the one-room cabin. The man's wife and a small boy were also there, and it turned out that the man was a farmer, although in the dark the travelers had not seen anything that looked like a farm. In any event, they sat dawn with their mess kits at a little wooden table and the wife bustled about heating the food. There was enough food that the family could join, and they all sat and had dinner. There were absolutely no amenities. The family had a wood-fired stove, which provided warmth as well as place to cook, and some rudimentary bunks where they slept; that was it. There wasn't much conversation, either, although the family were responsive when something was said. During the meal, something suddenly bumped forcefully into one wall of the cabin. The visitors jumped up, startling the farmer and his family, and started over to the door from which the sound came. At that, the farmer jumped up, got ahead of them, and opened the door. O'Brien then looked out the door and into the face of a cow! The shed where the few animals were housed was part of the house, and when the door was opened, the odors of the barnyard floated in. The dinner hour over, the visitors piled back into the command car and continued on their way to Metz, where they were able to find quarters for the night.

Next morning, continuing the masquerade, Senter and O'Brien continued on to Brussels, arriving there about 10:00 A.M. The question at this point was: where does one start looking? In this large European city, in the confused aftermath of a six-year war, how does one locate a pair of stolen paintings? So it was decided to start with art stores. There were a variety of such stores on one of the boulevards of downtown Brussels. It was a beautiful sunny morning, crisp but not cold, and they found a several-block area on a boulevard that had a park with trees and grass down the middle. It was a lovely street, and the weather was almost spring-like. Having no other choice, they started at one end of the art store area and went from one shop to the next, entering, sauntering around looking at the various pieces displayed, talking with the proprietor, and trying to get a feel for the possibility that this was the destination of the two Cranachs. In these establishments they did not disclose the real nature of their visit, saying only that they were shopping for a painting. Several hours were spent at this, with no results.

O'Brien was beginning to think that unless he could obtain more definitive information from the Mengers or some other source, the paintings would never be found. Of course Senter was playing a game of make-believe but guiding O'Brien in the right direction so that he would find the missing paintings and leave Senter looking innocent. The game had to end soon, and it did at the next shop. The shop of Louis Menteau was a little more upscale than most of the others, but as explained by O'Brien, that did not account for what happened thereafter. O'Brien turned to Senter and said, "I don't know why, but I think this is the place. I'm going to try a different approach." They entered the shop and were greeted by Menteau himself. Without further ado, O'Brien pulled out a copy of his orders to recover the paintings and said to him in French, "I am Captain O'Brien of the American Army. We are here to recover two Lucas Cranach paintings that have been stolen. This is a copy of my official orders. Are they here in your shop?" Menteau just stared at him for about 10 seconds and then said, "Is this really official?" O'Brien said, "It is very official. If you or someone here can read English, this order will prove it."[3]

O'Brien was not certain whether Menteau was part of the ring or simply a noted dealer who was being used without his knowledge. O'Brien tended to favor the latter interpretation, for without hesitation, Menteau told O'Brien that he had one of the paintings there and that the other was at a restorer's shop, being worked on. He went into the back of his shop and returned carrying the portrait *Frederick the Magnanimous*, the portrait of an unidentified male about which they had been told. Menteau then proceeded to tell them that he had received the paintings from two men from Luxembourg, a Mr. Biever and a Mr. Menger, who told him that these pictures were being used in connection with a financial transaction involving Biever's firm. Menteau also told him that a third painting, *The Blessing of Christ*, was on its way and would be there in a few weeks. O'Brien gave him a receipt for the painting, and then O'Brien accompanied Senter and Menteau to an old brick building a few blocks away. Up on the third floor they found a loft in which a M. Philippot had a studio. Philippot was an expert restorer, and he had the portrait of *John the Constant* on an easel. The portrait had been completely restored — so much so that it scarcely resembled the original. The purpose of the extensive restoration was to make it less easily identified as stolen property. In other words, the painting could be presented as a new and hitherto undiscovered painting by Cranach. Both paintings were then seized by Senter and O'Brien.

At this point, the men had two problems. First, the driver became so ill that he could not drive any further. Whether it was due to his carousing on the previous night in Liege or whether he had some kind of bug, O'Brien did not know, but he was no longer available for duty. O'Brien took over the wheel, Senter sat with him in front, and the driver lay down on the back seat. The only means they had of protecting the paintings was a couple of old GI blankets, which were wrapped around the two pictures and placed on the floor of the back seat. Senter and O'Brien were hungry, as it was now noon. O'Brien drove around Brussels until they saw a small diner. The driver had no interest in food, so they left him to guard the paintings and took some C-rations into the diner and talked the Belgian cook into heating them. O'Brien gave the cook a pack of cigarettes, making him most happy to oblige. That done, they faced the second problem.

They were in Brussels, it was afternoon, and the third picture was in St. Avold. If Menteau or Philippot were so inclined, they might be able to inform Albert Menger that the two paintings had been seized. The officers had to get to St. Avold before the Mengers were notified, so off they went. O'Brien drove while the driver slept in the back seat; they pulled up in front of the Mengers' house in the late afternoon. By prearrangement, O'Brien kept the motor running in case they should have to make a hurried exit while Senter went into the house to recover the third painting. This had to have been Senter's idea. He returned with it in less than five minutes, after which they wrapped it in a blanket and took off. Only Amelie Menger was home, and though O'Brien did not know what Senter had told her, apparently she gave him no argument. In fact, upon taking the painting, Senter told Amelie: "I shall write you from Bremerhaven," implying that he was leaving Germany from that port city. She did not know that he had also taken the paintings from Brussels.

The roads in Europe at that time were in very poor repair. Most were passable, but one's average speed on them would be no more than 35 to 40 miles per hour. It was getting colder, and the open command car provided little protection against the wind. The men stopped once, briefly, and tried to heat some rations over a large tin can into which they put some sand, gravel, and gasoline to make a cooking fire. It worked to some extent, but only enough to take the chill off the food. Trying to heat water in a canteen cup to make instant coffee made the cup so hot that you could not put it to your lips, but the water remained lukewarm.

They reached the Rhine about 2:00 A.M. and crossed on the pontoon bridge. U.S. Army Military Police stopped them on the east bank, at Mannheim, and examined their papers; then they took off again into the night. The temperature continued to drop, and although O'Brien had a pair of GI gloves, his hands grew so cold that when he tried to use the Zippo lighter to light a cigarette, he could not turn the little wheel to make it spark and ignite. Fatigue began to take its toll too. They had been on the road for over four days under less than ideal conditions. O'Brien had been up since before 6:00 A.M. the previous morning, and it was now well past 2:00 A.M. Senter offered to drive, but O'Brien did not trust him enough to let him do so. With the pictures in their possession, there was still the possibility that Senter might try to take off with them and use them to finance his escape to Italy or Switzerland. Dawn came and things were a little easier, but they sat and drove with almost no conversation. About 8:30 A.M. they entered Munich and drove directly to the Munich Collection Center where they delivered the three paintings, still wrapped in the GI blankets.

O'Brien then dropped Senter off at the Evacuation Hospital where he was temporarily assigned, and went on to his own apartment. The driver had recovered enough by then and was able to return the car to the motor pool and get to his barracks. After a hot bath, O'Brien slept until late in the afternoon, and except for writing a report, that was the end of his part in the Senter saga.

O'Brien saw Senter one more time. Late in January 1946, O'Brien received orders to join the 287th Engineer Combat Battalion as adjutant to be returned to the United States. He went to Headquarters in Munich to sign out and obtain the necessary clearances before he left the city. He had just finished and was walking down one of the corridors when he ran into Senter coming the other way. They said hello and Senter told him that his courtmartial was to start that day. He asked O'Brien if he had submitted a report of the trip and O'Brien replied that he had. Then Senter asked if O'Brien had included the names of those who had been involved in the affair, and O'Brien again replied yes. Senter sort of shrugged and said, "Well, OK, that's all right. It doesn't matter," and they shook hands and parted.[4]

Lt. Donovan Senter failed, throughout the complete investigation, to reveal or admit the truth until compelled to do so because of Jolanda Mayer-

Caputo's written confession. Aware of these denials and knowing that Senter was guilty of several military violations, Lt. Walter W. Horn took only marginal interest, writing that he was engaged in other and more important missions. His obligation to track art looted by the Nazis had priority, obliging him to relocate the other Cranach paintings that had been stolen from the Göring collection at Berchtesgaden and also incriminating an American army officer. After all, the three paintings had been recovered. But Capt. Edwin C. Rae had other ideas and turned the case over to Maj. J. H. Peacock for general court-martial.

Peacock charged Senter with five specific violations. Primarily Senter was charged with wrongfully aiding and abetting Ursula Sachs, a German civilian, in violation of Military Law 52. This charge was in reference to Senter's acceptance of the Cranach paintings from Mrs. Sachs. The court valued the paintings at $4,000 each.[5]

Through Senter's defense lawyer, the trial was postponed and postponed. Meanwhile Senter had asked to work for the military government in the Transportation Branch. Because of his service as a faithful and efficient officer and with good recommendations, he was assigned the highly responsible position of denazification officer for Bavaria and promoted to captain. "Denazification" involved the efforts made by the Allies to remove active members of the former National Socialist Party from public or semipublic office and from positions of responsibility in important private undertakings. At first, denazification had significant consequences, as those who were not rehabilitated could not be appointed to important offices or granted specific licenses—for example, to publish newspapers. In his new position, Senter could make the decision as to who had been reformed from Nazism and would thus be available for the better jobs.[6]

As for denazification, a divisional staff officer, tongue in cheek, summed up the German attitude as follows: "All Germans, given the opportunity, presented loud disclaimers of any shred of affection for the Nazi Party. The Allied forces are obviously here under a misapprehension; as such a universally loathed institution could never have existed among these people."

Finally on May 20, 1946, Lt. Donovan C. Senter was tried in Munich, Germany. Edwin C. Rae, Ursula Sachs, and Jolanda Mayer-Caputo testified for the prosecution. Under cross-examination, Jolanda testified that Walter Horn had dictated the statement that she had signed in jail and had also told her that Senter had gone to Paris and she would not see him again. In their testimony, she and her mother stated that Senter had accepted the paintings.

In testifying for himself, Senter also admitted that he had accepted the valuable Cranach paintings from Ursula Sachs. Lying, Senter stated that he

Lt. Donovan Senter in his role as Bavarian denazification officer in Munich, 1947.

had no intention of selling them and valued them for their esthetic qualities. Senter further told the court,

> As a trained research sociologist who has taught at the University of New Mexico, Harvard University, and the University of Chicago, I have always been more interested in intellectual things than in my own personal aggrandizement. My interest in these pictures was due to their esthetic value and arises out of a long-time penchant for ancient painting on wood. My publications in archeology and iconography will lend proof to this statement.[7]

The court was not informed that the paintings were subsequently recovered with the help of Capt. William G. O'Brien, and they had no way of knowing that Senter had received a large amount of money for the paintings.

At the conclusion of the trial, Senter was found not guilty on all five counts. This verdict caused Judge Samuel M. Hogan to write the following:

Lt. Donovan Senter's identification card, issued on June 14, 1946, while he was stationed in Germany.

> If this is a sample of the court-martial available to [the] military government branch of our service, these officers should be banned from sitting on court-martial. Each member of the court should be reprimanded for violating his oath as a court member. In view of the evidence and their oath, these court members had no choice but to find Sender guilty. It is recommended that each member of the court be reprimanded for this miscarriage of justice.[8]

Judge Hogan knew that Senter, earning $200 a month in the army in 1945, was interested in his own personal aggrandizement, but the full extent of this greedy con artist's ambition was not realized until the investigation of the missing Crown of Hesse jewels stolen from Kronberg Castle. For Senter was a suspect here, too, through his contacts with Albert and Amelie Menger of St. Avold, France, and this investigation by the governments of France and Luxembourg would indeed reveal that Senter had received a large sum of money in connection with the three Cranach paintings.

During the preparations for Senter's court-martial, Paul Helberg had returned from Germany and entered Brooklyn College as a student on the G.I. Bill — an act of Congress that provided college education for returning World War II veterans. Helberg became friends with student advisor Peter Blos, a German psychoanalyst with a degree in education and a Ph.D. in biology, who was born on February 2, 1904, in Karlsruhe, Germany. Blos had studied education at the University of Heidelberg and then obtained a doctorate in biology in Vienna. To escape the rise of Nazism, Blos fled Vienna in 1934 for the United States and in time settled in New York, where, as a teacher, he also continued his analytic training. During their friendship at Brooklyn College, Helberg informed Blos that he had a Lucas Cranach painting in his possession. In the conversation, Helberg lied to Blos by saying he took the painting from the Führerhaus or Nazi Headquarters Building in Munich. Blos contacted the Metropolitan Museum of Art and informed them that Helberg was willing to surrender the picture to the proper authorities provided that the painting was not returned to Germany but was displayed in an America museum. Blos further stated that Helberg would surrender the painting in good faith.

Blos wrote: "I would appreciate it if you could advise me how to proceed in this matter because the student has entrusted me with this confidence and I promised to obtain for him authoritative advice."[9]

The U.S. Army was indifferent to Blos and Helberg's intentions and shortly thereafter the painting was seized by U.S. Customs. Helberg had stolen the Cranach painting from the Göring collection. The painting, *Philip Melanchton*, shows Melanchton in a black robe against a turquoise background; it is 20 by 14 centimeters in size and was stolen from the Göring collection on July 4, 1945. In 1941 Göring had finagled the small portrait from the giant Dutch electronic firm of Phillips. Was Senter telling the truth about his supposed involvement with the other Cranach paintings? The painting was returned to Germany in 1949.

Chapter 8

Unanswered Questions

The Lorraine American Cemetery and Memorial in France contains the highest number of graves of American military dead killed during World War II to be found in Europe. Most of the 10,489 men buried were killed while driving the Germans from the fortress city of Metz toward the Siegfried Line and the Rhine River. Initially, over 16,000 Americans were interred in the St. Avold region, largely from the U.S. Seventh Army's Infantry and Armored Divisions and its cavalry groups. St. Avold was a vital communications center for the vast network of enemy defenses guarding the western border of the Third Reich. The cemetery is three quarters of a mile north of St. Avold (Moselle), France. The commander of the cemetery in 1947 was Capt. Joseph Samuel Holsinger. Incredibly, he too was once a resident in the home of Albert and Amelie Menger in St. Avold.

On February 14, 1947, Holsinger escorted by jeep Mrs. Amelie Menger from her home in St. Avold, France, supposedly to visit her son at the Ste-Marie Institute at Arlon, Belgium — a trip of about 70 miles. Holsinger noticed that Mrs. Menger was carrying a large heavy suitcase. Upon arriving in Arlon, Mrs. Menger learned that her son's holidays had been postponed by eight days. Holsinger suggested she call the director of the school and request a short leave of absence for her son while she was in Arlon. Mrs. Menger declined and Capt. Holsinger considered the idea that she had not actually gone to see her son. This was confirmed when she asked him to drop her off on the return trip at the Cravet Hotel in the city of Luxembourg. As she was walking near the hotel, she "accidentally" met the small daughter and maidservant of Aloyse Biever. Mrs. Menger then went to see Maria Rieger, the 35-year-old wife of Aloyse Biever; the gentleman who had been involved with Senter and the Cranach paintings. She stayed eight days with the wife and child of Aloyse Biever without ever trying to visit her son.

On February 24, Holsinger drove to Luxembourg and picked Mrs. Menger up at the Cravet Hotel for the trip back to St. Avold. He noticed that the large suitcase was conspicuously missing but did not suspect that she had spent her time at the home of Aloyse Biever and his wife. Mrs. Menger was guardedly clutching a crammed handbag.

Suspecting that he had been bamboozled, Holsinger, on the following day, told Jean Victor, the public security officer of Luxembourg, about Mrs. Menger's trip. With a bit of investigation, Victor established that Mrs. Menger had indeed stayed at the home of Biever. He then obtained a search warrant and conducted a search of Biever's home, where he recovered a diamond bracelet and a golden necklace set with large diamonds valued at 15,000 Reichsmarks ($1,500 in 1945). Biever reported that he had purchased the jewelry from an unidentified German at the apartment of art dealer Erich Beltz in Cologne, Germany. Biever was arrested for defrauding the Luxembourg treasury.[1]

Following Biever's arrest and with the cooperation of the French police, the Mengers' home was searched on the afternoon on April 10, 1947. In Menger's office were copies of three letters from Lt. Elmer Teply. All three incriminated Lt. Donovan Senter.

The French police read a letter dated January 15, 1946, written by Mrs. Amelie Menger and addressed to Senter. The letter had been returned with the notation "not at this address." The letter read as follows:

> Dear Mr. Senter:
> I have just come back from Luxembourg, and I am very surprised about the news received by Mr. Biever. My husband and I cannot believe it.
> I had brought André back to school to Belgium. He is an outstanding pupil and learns very well. However what is the use of it altogether. Mr. Biever gave me no money with which to pay the school fees. I cannot pay with French francs either. It would be a pity if I had to take the boy from the school. Please, let me have a letter by return of mail, so that I will know what you are going to do, and tell me what I am to do.
> Monsieur Biever told me that you had picked up the paintings in Brussels. I think you should know perfectly well that we cannot afford to lose our money.[2]

The other two letters were sent from the United States and were from Lt. Elmer Teply, who was trying to help the Mengers locate Senter. The second letter from Teply, dated July 13, 1946, contained the following: "Anything new in the picture affair yet? Have you got your money back?"

From this minor act by Capt. Holsinger (of reporting Mrs. Menger's trip to the Luxembourg police), the connection between Senter, Menger, and Biever became evident to Emile Henriot of the Strasbourg police and Jean Victor of the Luxembourg police, both professional investigators. They established the following true story concerning Donovan Senter. On June 14, 1948, their findings were sent to the military government, Office of the Director General of Justice, Berlin. Their letter reads as follows:

8. Unanswered Questions

Subject: Lieutenant Donovan C. Senter

I have the honor to submit to you the enclosed records of pretrial investigation conducted by the lower court at Sarreguemines (District of Moselle, France), the copies of a report of the attorney attached to the court of appeals in Colmar, and the communication of the Minister for Foreign Affairs concerning the facts for looting with which Donovan C. Senter, Lieutenant in the U.S. Army is charged.

I would appreciate, if you would be kind enough to advise as how you decide to deal with this case.

The Chief of the Secretariat in Berlin[3]

The French enclosed records containing much of the material used in writing about this sordid affair. These are summarized below.

Because Senter was caught in the act by the Americans, he agreed to recover the valuables. Therefore, on November 23, 1945, he and Capt. William G. O'Brien began Senter's fantasized trip into the black market art world during which they "recovered" the paintings. Several weeks later, Biever went to Manteau's office in Brussels and found out about the seizure of the paintings. He then drove to the home of the Mengers, and there Mrs. Menger showed him a postcard from Senter notifying her that he had departed for the United States by boat. The postcard was just another of his continuing deception, as Senter was still in Munich.

Senter had obtained more than $5,000 from Menger and Biever. In 1945 this represented more than two years' pay for Senter. Both the 38-year-old Biever and 55-year-old Menger knew that they had only advanced a fraction of the value of the paintings to Senter. Both men had previously dealt with each other in other transactions and each expected to make at least a commission on the sale of the paintings. They had already jointly agreed on a percentage to be split between them. Their anticipatory greed is no excuse for Senter's theft of their funds.

Senter obtained a divorce from Florence Hawley on June 6, 1947. He had retained his high-profile job as a Bavarian denazification officer until his return to the United States on April 12, 1947. Thereafter he remained in Washington, D.C., for a few months. He was discharged from the army on July 30, 1947. Apparently he had quickly dropped his affair with Mrs. Sachs and her daughter, Jolanda Mayer-Caputo, for on October 22, 1947, 19-year-old Phyllis Baierle of Jirkow, Czechoslovakia, arrived in the United States and was married to Senter six days later. Phyllis' mother, Hildegard, eight years older than Senter, lived with the couple. After Senter left the army, he worked for the U.S. Department of Agriculture in Mexico City.[4]

On October 19, 1948, Senter reenlisted in the U.S. Army and attended school at Brooks Army Medical Center at Fort Sam Houston, Texas, where he trained as a clinical psychologist. In 1946, Fort Sam Houston was chosen as the new site for the U.S. Army Medical Field Service School. Senter remained at Brooks Army Medical Center as an instructor in clinical psychology until 1951. Then, for about a year, he served at the 6103 Army Hospital at Camp Cooke, California, as an assistant clinical psychologist treating soldiers returning from Korea. The hospital was near the ocean; the mornings were cold and foggy. The wards were one-story barracks connected by covered corridors that creaked beneath the patients' feet. Sand drifted over the linoleum floors in the wards and in the passageways. Senter, his wife, and his mother-in-law lived in nearby Santa Barbara. Camp Cooke is known today as Vandenberg Air Force Base. Later, Senter served briefly at Camp Kilmer, New Jersey, as clinical psychologist. In November 1952, he transferred to the 97th General Hospital in Frankfurt, Germany, as chief clinical psychologist. This large hospital was previously known as the Herman Göring Luftwaffe Hospital. In 1955, Maj. Donovan Senter relocated to Fort Bragg, North Carolina, where he served as social science Instructor in the Psychological Warfare School. He was relieved of active duty on October 31, 1957, with the rank of lieutenant colonel. His forwarding address was 1345 Columbia Road, Albuquerque, New Mexico, although there is no evidence that he returned to Albuquerque.[5]

After Senter left active duty, his wife Phyllis and her mother detached themselves from him. Phyllis then married a U.S. army officer of about her own age who, however, committed suicide shortly thereafter. Senter took several courses while attending the University of Mexico in Mexico City. He was also run over by a truck and spent considerable time recuperating in an Army Veterans Hospital.[6]

At some point Senter married yet again, this time to a woman named Doris. This was ironic, as his first wife and mother were both named Florence and both his last wife and her stepmother, Doris Capron, were named Doris. But his activities from October 1957 to the early 1970s are shrouded in mystery.

Donovan Senter showed up alone in early 1970 in Albuquerque. He was living in a small Volkswagen camper that he kept at different times in his two brothers' Albuquerque backyards so that he could use their bathroom facilities. He enjoyed playing in bridge tournaments throughout the Southwest. In 1981 Senter traveled to Reno, Nevada, to compete in a bridge match. During the night of January 6, 1981, while using a cooking stove to stay warm, the 71-year-old Senter died of asphyxiation while sleeping in his Volkswagen camper in the lot of a shopping center in Reno.

On May 29, 1950, Senter's first wife, Florence Hawley, married Bruce

Ellis, becoming Florence Hawley Ellis. But out of the ordinary and surely owing to ill feeling, 11-year-old Florence Anita (Don-Anita) Senter's name was legally changed to Andrea Hawley Ellis. Florence Hawley Ellis taught at the University of New Mexico for 37 years. After retiring from the University of New Mexico, she established herself at the Ghost Ranch of Abiquiu. A museum there bears her name, the Florence Hawley Ellis Museum of Anthropology. She died in 1991 and there is no doubt that she was one of the most influential women in anthropology of her time. She left a great legacy. The daughter, Andrea, died in an automobile accident on February 10, 2009.

Willy Sachs spent the last years of his life mainly on the Oberaudorf Rechenau estate, where, on November 19, 1958, at the age of 62, and suffering from depression, he committed suicide.

Donovan Senter took many secrets to his grave. Today he is buried in the Veterans Cemetery, Santa Fe, New Mexico.

Part III
Plundering Priceless Manuscripts

Chapter 9

The Capture of Bad Wildungen

On March 24, 1945, after a swift crossing of the Rhine River, the Western Allies encircled the Ruhr, the industrial center of western Germany. Trapped in this pocket were 325,000 German soldiers. Their commander, Field Marshal Walther Model, dissolved his Army Group B and committed suicide. On March 30, Good Friday, the fast-moving 7th and 9th Armored Divisions captured the resort town of Bad Wildungen.

In the spa town of Bad Wildungen were about 40 buildings containing approximately 7,000 wounded German soldiers. A month later, on May 2, 1945, when the Twelfth Army Group, commanded by Gen. Omar Bradley, established its headquarters in the Fürsten Hotel, Bradley reported that the hotel still had an odor of antiseptic clinging to the rooms that had been used as a German hospital ward.[1]

Upon entry into the well-known hospital center, American soldiers immediately erected barriers to control entry to the buildings, sealed off the administrative buildings, and occupied the stately Goecke Hotel. Its upper floors housed the town's administrative offices and the basement, provided with a steel door, was filled with museum treasures that were under the exclusive care of Frau Hubert Vonhoff, the hotel's owner. The main boulevard became a large tank compound. Soldiers and freed prisoners of war began combing through the homes in search of wine and souvenirs. The First Army had brought along Dutch and Polish civilians who had police authority, but understandably they were not willing to prevent the looting.[2] Within hours of the occupation of Bad Wildungen, the vaulted basement of the Goecke Hotel had been plundered. Frontline combat troops usually took bottles of wine and small items that could fit in the pocket of a field jacket. The larger valuables were taken by the more educated troops in the follow-up support groups. One headquarters and headquarters company had the lighthearted motto "You shoot 'em, we loot 'em."

The village of Bad Wildungen, First Army Headquarters and scene of large-scale looting from three large art repositories by U.S. troops (courtesy National Archives).

The most valuable and delicate paintings and objects of art from various German municipal galleries were stored in two concrete repositories in the town of Bad Wildungen and the basement of the Goecke Hotel. The two concrete bunkers, one a very long two-story building and the other three stories in height, were under the care of Felix Pusch, the provincial conservator. The longer building contained some 2,000 paintings; there were also cases of stained glass, famous musical instruments, and a great deal of superb sculpture, Greek and medieval. The finest works of art from the museums and churches of Frankfurt, Hanover, Wiesbaden, and Kassel resided in these bunkers.[3]

Although Pusch was not responsible for the repository at the Goecke Hotel, Frau Vonhoff asked Pusch to help rummage through the hotel's basement. On April 25, 1945, Pusch arrived at the hotel with a horse-drawn wagon and, after some difficulty with the military government, gained access to the basement, the floor of which was littered with empty picture frames, smashed crates, and broken artwork. Pusch loaded the wagon with debris and other things from the cellar and took the fragile cargo to his printing shop for safekeeping. Pusch also took a number of the more valuable paintings to his home, along with many ivory and gold objects. He later hid the gold objects within the walls of his home. In fact, he hid them so well that he soon "forgot" about them and their hiding places. In his home he also stored *Still Life* by

Renoir and paintings from the other two bunkers. A year later, Pusch's misplacements were discovered and it took the help of the Bad Wildungen fire brigade to remove the walls and recover the missing items.[4]

When James J. Rorimer, the first American Monuments, Fine Arts, and Archives (MFAA) officer, arrived in April 1945, Dr. Friedrich Bleibaum, the curator of Greater Hesse, was in charge of the operations regarding the repositories and had completed an inventory and photographs of the valuables. There were 388 paintings from Kassel, 110 from Hanover, 127 from Mainz, and others from Aachen. Stained glass, altars, and other ecclesiastical objects of importance from many German churches had been stored in Bad Wildungen. Rorimer wrote: "At Bad Wildungen I found the carefully concealed massive accession books of the Frankfurt museums."[5] Private property included 1,343 paintings, 63 pieces of furniture, and 23 sculptures. Quickly and not surprisingly, thieves broke through three bolted iron doors without leaving a scratch and stole 114 small paintings plus two valuable manuscripts, the *Liber Sapientiae* and the *Willehalm Codex*, which vanished from the cellar of the Goecke Hotel. The paintings included the half-length portrait titled *Youth in Red Cloak* by B. Fabritius, *the Fish Market at Leydeu* by Jan Steen, and works by Ruysdael, Bol, Tiepolo, Carot, Courbet, Cézanne, Marees, Thoma, and Matisse. Equally devastating were the missing manuscripts — for example, the first and last pages of the *Liber Sapientiae*, which contained the poem *Hildebrandslied*. These losses were probably the greatest single blow to art and literature resulting from World War II.

The *Hildebrandslied Codex* and

The wooden front cover of the priceless manuscripts known as the ***Willehalm Codex***, seized by a U.S. Army officer from the vaulted basement of the Goecke Hotel in April 1945. At that time the book was stamped and bound in calf leather. Today, owing to misuse during it absence, the leather cover is gone; all that remains is this board, to which the leather was bound (courtesy Universitätsbibliothek Kassel, Landesbibliothek und Murhardsche Bibliothek der Stadt Kassel).

Page one of the two-page tragic poem, the *Hildebrandslied,* the oldest example of writing in the German language. It begins: "I have heard tell, that two chosen warriors...." This valuable document was obtained by Lieutenant Bud Berman (courtesy Universitätsbibliothek Kassel, Landesbibliothek und Murhardsche Bibliothek der Stadt Kassel).

the *Willehalm Codex*, the two chief possessions of the Kassel Library, were taken from the war repository. They had been packed together in a small box and stored for safety in a bunker at Bad Wildungen in August 1943. The bunker was reported to have been carefully guarded until the last months of the war, when the custodians were displaced. The American Monuments, Fine Arts, and Archives (MFAA) officers were not immediately informed, when Allied troops entered the town, of the repository and its importance. In June 1945 the state conservator of Greater Hesse reported to the American military government that the bunker had been entered and the two famous manuscripts were missing. At the time it could not be ascertained whether the box with the manuscripts had been removed by German civilians, displaced persons, or American troops.

During the eighth century, paper or vellum was usually made from calfskin that had been scraped clean of hair and smoothed with fine-grained pumice rock. After it was cut into squares, the pages were inscribed using a sharpened goose quill moistened in ink. These codexes or handmade books were usually covered by a wooden board bound in leather.

This "modern" Latin text was titled the *Liber Sapientiae* or "Book of Wisdom." After the completion of the *Liber Sapientiae*, as supplies of vellum were rather limited, monks carefully filled the empty spaces with prayers and other small writings.

The brilliance of the *Liber Sapientiae* was the filling-in of the originally blank first and last pages with the poem of Hildebrand. Fifty years after the completion of the *Liber Sapientiae*, two monks took turns copying pages of *Das Hildebrandslied*, the tragic story of Hildebrand, onto the flyleaves of the *Liber Sapientiae*. This work is not only the oldest example of German poetry but also the oldest example of writing in the German language and is therefore priceless. The poem recounts the story of Hildebrand and his son, who after many years of separation meet and, without knowing each other, engage in combat. The poem breaks off with no indication of the outcome. There is an early Norse saga that refers to the *Hildebrandslied* and says that the son was killed, but in the later sagas the son is defeated and forced to recognize his father.

The *Liber Sapientiae* with *Das Hildebrandslied* remained on the shelves of the Fulda cloister library until the library was destroyed by Hessian soldiers in 1632 and the library's manuscripts were stolen or destroyed. Miraculously, the *Liber Sapientiae* eventually found it way into the Kassel Library.[6]

That book and the *Willehalm Codex* were the two most valued books in the Kassel Library. The *Willehalm Codex* of Wolfram von Eschenbach is a bound manuscript of the 14th century, containing 396 folios and 62 miniatures. Thirty-three of the miniatures are completed and the rest are partly finished. The script is a fine, precise, pointed Gothic minuscule of a severe style. The poem by Wolfram von Eschenbach relates the heroic deeds of the Christian knight Willehalm. In one of the miniatures illustrating Willehalm's adventures, the hero is kneeling before Charlemagne. The illumination of the manuscript shows strong English influence. The ornamental initial on the first page was executed with skill and versatility. Framed in a triple Gothic arch, Christ in Glory is bestowing His blessing; the Evangelists' symbols are at the corners. Below, the donor of the book, the Landgrave of Hesse, kneels in prayer; beside him is his coat of arms with the lion of Hesse.

These two books had survived centuries of battle, looting, and mistreatment. The Kassel Library gave them a safe haven until the beginning of World War II. To avoid their destruction by fire bombings, the books were placed in a gray wooden chest and hidden in a vault in the town of Bad Wildungen.[7]

Chapter 10

Lieutenant Bud Berman

Irwin Berman was born in Detroit, Michigan, on February 27, 1917. His father was Hyman Berman and his mother's maiden name was Lillian Danto. On November 28, 1936, at the age of 19, he applied for a Social Security card, which was required for his job in Detroit. In the early 1940s he was living in Forest Hills, a 2.4-square-mile neighborhood in the central part of New York City's borough of Queens. This neighborhood was home to a mix of middle to upper-class residents. Historically, Forest Hills had been home to a large Jewish population, with more than ten synagogues. Irwin Berman was single, had completed two years of college, and had been a buyer for a department store. On September 19, 1942, in Queens, Irwin Berman enlisted in the U.S. Army as Bud Berman.[1]

With his newly acquired name, Bud entered the U.S. Army. On July 1, 1943, after basic training, he along with 17 other enlisted men was assigned to the 6th Signal Center Liaison Team at Camp Crowder, Missouri. Originally established south of Neosho, Missouri, in 1941, the post was to serve as an armored training center. As it was being constructed, however, it was redesignated as a U.S. Army Signal Base. Private Berman's highly specialized unit, consisting of only 21 men, was commanded by Lts. Joseph Beauregard and Walter G'Schwend. The men selected for this unit had very high IQ scores and an aptitude for mathematics. The training emphasized radio operation, encryption/decryption, and a general mastery of the French language. After five months of training, the unit was ready for overseas duty. Subsequently Bud Berman was granted a furlough, letting him return to New York in early December.

On December 12, Berman's unit transferred to Camp Shanks, New York. The camp was located in Orangetown, New York, about 20 miles north of New York City; if served as a point of embarkation for troops going overseas during World War II. Dubbed "Last Stop USA," the camp was the largest army embarkation point. On the evening of September 25, 1942, over 300 Orangeburg residents met at the Orangeburg School to learn that their homes,

Bud Berman's Social Security Death Index and this application by Irwin Berman both contain the Social Security number 375 07 4148, thus confirming that Bud and Irwin Berman are the same person.

lots, and farms were being seized for the immediate construction of a military camp.

On December 29, 1943, after a stay of two weeks to make final field inspections, identify any problems, make any necessary repairs, and replace anything that could not be repaired, the 6th Signal Center Liaison Team embarked for Staten Island to board the HMS *Samaria*. This trusty, decrepit, and sooty troop transport hardly resembling the Cunard line cruise ship she had once been.

For Bud Berman the passage was relatively calm regarding the weather and totally undisturbed by any German naval activity. The ship docked at Liverpool, England, on January 6, 1944. The unit then traveled 100 miles south by rail to Stourport-on-Severn, Worcestershire. For the next five months the 6th Signal Center Liaison Team moved to several locations with "intensified classes in French given by the noncommissioned officers of the detachment."[2]

The invasion for Fortress Europe was imminent, and on April 14, the detachment was alerted for departure and attached to the 17th Signal Operations Battalion. On May 17, one month later, M.Sgt. Bud Berman, chief code clerk, and the members of his detachment boarded the USS *Achernar*, the headquarters ship for the general staff of the First Army, in Bristol Harbor. In the position of chief code clerk for First Army Headquarters for the invasion of Europe, Bud Berman was in the crème de la crème position of the U.S.

Signal Corps. Once aboard ship, radio communication was established, cryptographic means were made available, and various cabins of the ship were set up as message centers. On this highly classified mission, no one was allowed to leave the ship. The ship exited the northeast port of Bristol on May 28 and continued on its 300-mile trip, arriving at Plymouth Harbor two days later. This port was the assembly area for the D-Day invasion of Normandy.

During this entire time radio silence was enforced on the *Achernar*. Now in port, the general staff of the First Army was boarded, with Gen. Courtney H. Hodges in command. On the night of June 5, 1944, in the center of the invasion flotilla, the ship set sail for the coast of France, where it arrived early on D-Day and dropped anchor off Omaha Beach. At 2:50 A.M. in the early morning of June 6, 1944, communications were established between First Army Headquarters and the Army's corps and divisions. From that hour on, Berman was on the go, day and night, maintaining signal communications for the Allied D-Day invasion. He verified the authenticity of incoming messages, decrypted and encrypted messages, and determined the sender, time, and date from the call signs.[3]

Allied forces intended to convince Hitler that Normandy was actually a diversion for a greater attack in northern France. Preparations for Operation Overlord took 3½ years and involved the combined industrial, military, and intelligence powers of the British Empire and the United States. The plan involved a series of well-planned deceptions to ensure the success of the Allied invasion of Normandy. The shortest distance from England to France was from the Cliffs of Dover to Pas de Calais. Hitler assumed that the Allied forces would use this route to invade France. Considering this, the Allied forces created the fictitious First U.S. Army Group. This group consisted of "one million men," including dummy landing craft, dummy paratroopers, and light and sound schemes. Gen. George Patton had a commanding role in this fabricated army, which amounted to the greatest and most expensive ruse ever planned. But as Robert Burns's poem says, sometimes the best-laid plans of mice and men go astray.

The D-Day invasion took place of June 6, 1944. It began with overnight parachute and glider landings, massive air attacks, naval bombardments, and an early-morning amphibious landing; during the evening, the remaining elements of the parachute divisions landed. The operation was the largest single-day amphibious invasion of all time, with over 130,000 troops landed and an additional 195,700 Allied naval and merchant navy personnel involved. About 6,900 vessels were used, including 4,100 landing craft. The landings took place along a stretch of the Normandy coast divided into five sectors: Utah, Omaha, Gold, Juno, and Sword.[4]

On the evening of June 6, a copy of the VII Corps field order had been picked up by the German 914th Regiment from a boat that had drifted ashore at the mouth of the Vire River (Seine Bay). On the late afternoon of June 7, 1944, in the southern quarter of the village of Vierville, during a counterattack, the plan of V Corps was taken by the Germans off a youngish U.S. Army officer who had been killed in action.[5]

Therefore, within 36 hours of the invasion, the Germans had the complete plans of the American Army for the invasion of Normandy. For these invasion plans to have been removed from a ship had to be one of the major security violations of World War II. Therefore how important was the Allies' large-scale deception plan versus German military might?

This deception plan for the invasion was scheduled to continue for another six weeks. The broad plan covered deception operations designed to cause the German military to make strategic dispositions in Norway against Allied military threats, to deceive the enemy as to targets of General George Patton's large phantom army in England, and to induce the enemy to make faulty tactical dispositions by threats against Pas de Calais.

The fact that the Germans now had possession of the invasion plans had no effect on the German conduct of operations. This throws considerable light on the tactical and strategic problems facing the enemy command. From the plans, German Seventh Army learned that the major immediate objectives of the American forces were Cherbourg and St. Lo. However, the Germans could not have profited materially from this knowledge. Rommel was not free to shift the weight of his defense to the American flank to block either the assault on Cherbourg or the planned move southward toward Brittany. The major operational threat, from Rommel's point of view, remained the possibility of a British breakout at Caen and a sweep to Paris. In short, the Germans' complete knowledge of American intentions did not alter the logic of the battle. It was fought by an overwhelming force of the Allied armies in direct engagement of the German Army in a massive battle resulting in the ultimate destruction of the German Army. The U.S. Army was unaware of the capture of these plans until after the war, when captured German documents were examined.[6]

Thus, if enough men and weapons are poured into a confused battle situation, an enemy can be overwhelmed rather than defeated; and if masses of manpower and equipment are sent in, the probability is that sooner or later, by the grace of God, somebody will do something right.[7] And this may well have been the case for the subsequent breakout of Normandy.

During all of this invasion activity in Normandy, M.Sgt. Bud Berman kept working, regardless of shore-based artillery and heavy nightly bombing raids on the *Achernar*. After four days, the 6th Signal Center Liaison Team debarked the ship and went into bivouac near the First Army Headquarters

Command Post at Cricqueville. These four days of intensity were the highwater mark of the entire war for the 6th Signal Center Liaison Team and probably the highlight of M.Sgt. Bud Berman's military calling.

Once in the combat zone, the 21-man 6th Signal Center Liaison Team came under the direction of the First Army Signal Section and collaborated principally with the 17th Signal Operations Battalion. Their liaison work was primarily with the French and Belgian authorities.

After intense fighting, the First Army broke out of Normandy and continued eastward with the capture of Paris. Further advances brought the 6th Signal Center Liaison Team to Stree, Belgium, where Berman was promoted to second lieutenant on September 8, 1944.[8] The detachment had been living in tents, but because of the rainfall and approaching winter, they were quartered in the luxury Hotel Balmoral at Spa, Belgium. This resort, with its déclassé hotels and casinos, had served as the fashionable headquarters for General Paul von Hindenburg and had been the favorite watering place of Germany's Emperor Wilhelm during World War I. The First Army units occupied this same building complex overlooking a large lake. This was a relatively quiet period for the detachment, with only an occasional buzz bomb (V-1) dropping nearby. They remained in Spa until December 18, when Hitler's final counteroffensive, the Battle of the Bulge, forced the retreat of Gen. Courtney Hodge's First Army. The 6th Signal Center Liaison Team pulled back 25 miles to Tongres, as they were being strafed by enemy aircraft, and Lt. William C. Behn, the unit's liaison officer, was wounded by a buzz bomb. On January 18, after this 30-day battle, which had cost the Americans over 75,000 causalities and mauled the cream of Hitler's forces, the detachment returned to the Hotel Balmoral, where they remained until the middle of April.

The 6th Signal Center Liaison Team then crossed the Rhine River, pushing to Marburg, where they remained for 10 days. On April 14, 1945, Bud Berman and his detachment arrived in Bad Wildungen. They remained here for 10 days and established a communication center in the basement of the Goecke Hotel. *It was during this time that the Hildebrandslied Codex and the Willehalm Codex disappeared from the basement of the Goecke Hotel.* Bud and his unit then traveled to Weimar, and a few days later the unit received the exciting news that Germany had surrendered.[9]

The First Army was slated to transfer to the Pacific and continue the war against Japan. It appears that 2/Lt. Bud Berman was among the first to be selected for the South Pacific assignment, for on May 24, 1945, he was in Southampton, England, and boarded the USS *Monticello* for his return to New York City. The *Monticello* (AP-61) was built as *Conte Grande* in Trieste, Italy, as an Italian-flagged passenger ship capable of carrying 7,798 persons and was launched on June 28, 1927, for service in the North Atlantic tourist and passenger trade. In June 1940, the *Conte Grande* was in Brazil on one of her regular South American cruises. After Mussolini's attack on France, she was transferred to Brazilian registry and was purchased on April 16, 1942, by the United States.

The *Monticello,* with added armament, had space for 7,192 passengers, and from the passenger list, many appeared to be from the staff of the First Army. The passengers included four war correspondents and (army-classified) 2,430 liberated prisoners of war, escapees, and evaders. Aboard the ship were 510 medical patients, many described as suffering from psychoneuroses, burns of the hands and face, and other wounds. The ship also carried five dead soldiers under the classification of "Dead with Next-of-Kin List." The Army transport ship *Monticello* arrived in New York City on June 3, 1945.[10]

Chapter 11
The Rare Book Dealer

I have seen men hazard their fortunes, go on long journeys halfway around the world, forge friendships, even lie, cheat and steal, all for the gain of a book.
— *A.S.W. Rosenbach*

Dr. A.S.W. Rosenbach (1876–1952) of Philadelphia was one of the most prominent American booksellers in the first half of the 20th century. Flamboyantly bidding on treasures around the world, he helped to make the trade in rare books what it is today. Sometimes he would drive up prices to prove the value of books as investments for his clients, helping to build the collections of the Widener, J. P. Morgan, Rosenwald, Folger, and Huntington libraries and the Houghton Library of Harvard University, using the allure of Gutenberg Bibles and Shakespeare folios to build his own reputation. He was also a book lover who valued his volumes and manuscripts. Although many of the people to whom he sold books amassed collections that became central to America's great research libraries, he saw his own role as keeping great books moving, increasing their value, giving them the care and preservation they deserved, and putting them in the hands of those who would most appreciate them. One of Dr. Rosenbach's wealthiest clients was collector Carrie Estelle Doheny.

On June 11, 1945, Lt. Bud Berman of the American army walked into the Rosenbach Company on 57th Street in New York City and asked the owner to evaluate an old German book. A.S.W. Rosenbach and Philip Rosenbach, his brother, were the owners. John F. Fleming, the general manager, was unable to read the early German language in such an old script, so he asked Gretel Meyer to leave her desk and come into the reception room and read it. She saw the words *Liber Sapientiae—Codex*. Also on the first page was *Bibliotheca Kastelana*. This prompted Meyer to say to the American officer "You must have been in Kassel." He seemed surprised and asked her how she knew. She then pointed to the stamp of the Kassel Library. Meyer was familiar with German libraries, as she had been born in Germany in 1906; she held a law degree from a German university and a master's degree in library science from Columbia University. Then Berman left the book but received an acknowledgment on Rosenbach Company stationery dated June 11, 1945. It reads as follows: "Received from Lieut. Bud Berman 111-10 76th Road, Forest Hills, L.I., manuscript volume entitled *Liber Sapiencie*, circa 1350, small folio, bound in old pigskin rebacked, for the purpose of study." Meyer spent three days studying the manuscript. Later she opened the drawer of the Renaissance table in which the *Liber Sapientiae* sat in the vault, looking for a pencil, and saw that the page containing the ancient *Hildebrandslied* with the Kassel Library mark had been cut from the binding.[1]

Almost a month later, on July 6, 1945, Berman returned to the Rosenbach Company with a 14th-century vellum manuscript bound in blind tooled calf, which is the technique of using a heated tool to ornament the skin of a book's cover, so that it leaves a dark impression. This remarkable book was the *Willehalm Codex* manuscript. On that day, Berman dictated a letter written on The Rosenbach Company stationery authorizing Mr. Meyer Kahn, 350 Fifth Avenue, Room [suite] 3011, to act as his agent and have full access to the books that he had left with the Rosenbach Company. The authorization was signed, "Very truly yours, Lt. Bud Berman."[2] By then Berman's 30-day leave had expired and he returned either to his unit in Germany or on to a forwarding position for an assignment in the Pacific Theater to fight Japan. Ten days later, Meyer Kahn, supposedly working at 350 Fifth Avenue, which is the Empire State Building, came to the Rosenbach Company to discuss the Kassel manuscripts. Apparently dissatisfied, he took the books, as his letter of receipt of the *Willehalm Codex* was amended by a handwritten note at the bottom saying "received book mentioned above." It was dated July 16, 1945, and signed by Meyer Kahn. But on the back of the letter is written "and Latin Manuscript "Liber Sapiencie" 14th? century, 4 to 76 numbered pages bound in old sheepskin, blind tooled and enclosed in black cloth box." Kahn apparently caught a cab back to the 30th floor of the Empire State Building carrying the *Liber Sapientiae* and *Willehalm Codex* manuscripts. However, it appears that the first page of the ancient *Hildebrandslied* from the *Willehalm Codex* was now missing.[3]

Twelve days later, on a foggy Saturday morning, Col. William Smith was piloting a U.S. Army B-25 bomber and smashed into the north side of the Empire State Building. Most of the plane hit the 79th floor, creating a hole in the building 18 feet wide and 20 feet high. The plane's high-octane fuel exploded, hurtling flames down the side of the building and inside through hallways and stairwells all the way down to the 75th floor. The plane crash killed 11 office workers and the 3 crewmen while also injuring 26 others.

It would appear that Kahn and the valuable manuscripts on the 30th floor escaped any injury or damage. Based on information from Berman's letter and the fact that he had named Meyer Kahn his agent, at this time Kahn seems to have been shopping around for another buyer for the manuscripts. But in fact and according to army records, Kahn was a technician fourth grade (Tec/4) stationed 45 miles away at Fort Dix, New Jersey.[4] Kahn was indeed in New York and the address at the Empire State Building played a role in the charade, but why was this scheme needed? If needed, Bud could have resorted to his birth name, Irwin, and been untraceable.

Meyer Kahn then wrote Bud Berman a letter explaining that he had collected the two manuscripts from the Rosenbach Company. Berman was uncertain about Kahn's letter and then wrote to "Dear Mr. Rosenbach." The letter is undated, but must have been written a week or so after Japan issued its intentions to surrender on August 15, 1945, as Berman states in the letter "within the next 60 days — at which time I shall be a civilian." Berman would not have been a civilian if hostilities with Japan had still existed. The letter states that Berman trusted Mr. Rosenbach and knew that his company could obtain the highest value for the two German manuscripts. Berman also wrote that the sale would be unconditionally final, regardless of future actions taken by the U.S. government, "that books picked up in Germany were to be returned. I feel that such will not be the case — thousands of books — pictures etc., were sent home — none of us knew at the time and as a matter of fact still don't know the value of the things we sent back."[5] What did he send back? What else did Lt. Bud Berman loot from war-torn Europe?

On October 4, 1945, Berman was discharged from active duty. On that same day he received his mustering out pay and left Fort Bragg, North Carolina, on a trip to his home on Long Island. Now the civilian Berman returned to the Rosenbach Company with the two manuscripts. After a couple of days of negotiation, Berman received $7,000 for the *Liber Sapientiae* and *Willehalm* manuscripts. (The top of the invoice contains the date November 10, 1945, but written in the body of the receipt and invoice is 10/10/45; therefore November appears to be incorrect and the transaction took place on October 10, 1945.) A few days later, the secretary of the Rosenbach Company told Miss Meyer that the *Liber Sapientiae* sold for $2,000 and that, because of its attractive illuminations, they had sold the *Willehalm Codex* for $10,000.[6]

The Rosenbach Company then sent the *Liber Sapientiae* to Dr. Curt F. Bühler, Keeper of Printed Books, Pierpont Morgan Library, a complex of buildings in the heart of New York City. The Morgan Library began as the private library of financier J. Pierpont Morgan (1837–1913), one of the preeminent collectors and cultural benefactors in the United States. Rosenbach requested identification and authentication of the book. First things first; the astute Dr. Bühler microfilmed the complete document including the cover and back. Bühler and various scholars and technicians studied the manuscript, and on December 11, 1945, he wrote a letter to the Rosenbach Company, stating:

> A few weeks ago your office submitted to me for exanimation a medieval manuscript consisting of Neolesiastious [?], the Book of Wisdom and various other excerpts from the Old Testament and miscellaneous [illegible].
>
> During the course of studying the manuscript I discovered that it is an early product of the *scriptorium* of Fulda that has been preserved for more than two hundred years in the provincial library of Kassel, Germany, where it was Manuscript Theological 54. You will find it described and illustrated in:
>
> Die Landesbibliiothek Kassel, 1580–1930, p 30
>
> A lengthy bibliography concerning it is given by G Ehriesmann: Geschichte der deutschen Literatur, p 121
>
> Due to the great interest this manuscript has held for scholars throughout the world, I felt that you should be apprised of its provenance and importance.[7]

At the time of Dr. Bühler's examination he noticed that one page of the *Hildebrandslied* had been removed. One has to question why Dr. Bühler did not notify the proper authorities regarding this stolen manuscript. The Kassel Museum authorities were left with the impression that the two priceless Kassel manuscripts had been stolen by displaced persons and had been smuggled into East Germany.

Nothing more happened until 1950. At that time the Rosenbach firm published a catalogue that offered for sale the original copy of the Declaration of Independence signed by Benjamin Franklin and Silas Deane together with the letter of transmittal addressed by the two Americans to the Prussian minister on the occasion of their presentation of this Declaration copy to Frederick the Great. They had sent the document to the German king on February 14, 1777, hoping to win his support for the recognition of the United States. The copy of Franklin's Declaration of Independence, now missing from the Prussian State Archives in Berlin, was spotted in the catalogue by German authorities in Bonn, who subsequently submitted a claim for the looted document. The U.S. Department of State turned the case over to U.S. Customs. Upon further investigation, the Customs officials learned that the document belonged to Philip H. Rosenbach and was valued at $75,000.

On September 15, 1950, customs agents K. A. Marr and Eman S. Franks interviewed Philip H. Rosenbach, who claimed that the Declaration document had never been outside the United States and in further conversation said that several years before he had sold the document to a lady on condition that upon her death the document would be returned to him, based upon her will.

Rosenbach declined to give further details concerning the sale of Franklin's Declaration of Independence. In the same conversation, however, Rosenbach claimed that he had sold the document to "someone out west," but again failed to furnish details.[8]

Actually the Declaration of Independence signed by Benjamin Franklin and Silas Deane, the greatest document of American history that the Rosenbachs ever owned, was purchased by Philip Rosenbach in Berlin in 1912. In October of that year it was sold to Isabella Fishblatt for $5,000. Philip later regained the Declaration with hints that it was given to him by Fishblatt, who was his lover.[9]

A few days later Rosenbach called the agents and said that he had found the invoice. The agents visited the firm and Rosenbach produced an old invoice book that had an entry dated April 24, 1911, for the purchase of the Declaration of Independence. Later, the customs agents asked to review the invoices of items acquired by the Rosenbach firm. They were informed that all records five years and older were routinely destroyed by the firm. Therefore, in 1950, the firm retained only records from 1947. How convenient that they had an invoice from 1911, considering that the document was purchased in 1912, but nothing for 1945 and 1946.

While they were there, the customs agents questioned Philip Rosenbach and John F. Fleming about the purchase of the *Liber Sapientiae* and *Willehalm Codex*. During this investigation by the Bureau of Customs, *The New Colophon*, an art journal, published that the *Liber Sapientiae* had recently been acquired and was part of the Estelle Doheny Collection in Los Angeles. The agents again interviewed Philip Rosenbach and John F. Fleming, and only when they were shown a copy of *The New Colophon* were they able to identify the bound manuscript as part of a block of books sold to Mrs. Edward L. Doheny of Los Angeles for $85,000 in January 1949. Both readily stated that it had been purchased from an army officer, but neither could recall his name. Rosenbach then lied to the agents by saying that the book had been purchased through their Philadelphia office by his brother A.S.W. Rosenbach. This brother, who was 77 years old, had suffered a complete physical and mental breakdown and could not be interviewed. He died a week later, and his brother Philip died the following year. During the interview, it was established that the *Liber Sapientiae* had a value of less than $4,000, which was below the threshold for the value of a cultural artifact; therefore the customs agents closed the case regarding the manuscript.[10]

Chapter 12

The Papal Countess

Carrie Estelle Betzold was born in Philadelphia on August 2, 1875. She and her German immigrant parents moved to Los Angeles in 1890. Edward Laurence Doheny, her future husband, was born in Fond du Lac, Wisconsin, on August 10, 1856, to poor Irish immigrants. He left home at a young age to prospect for gold and silver and became the pioneer developer of oil in Southern California. Mr. Doheny discovered the Cerro Azul oil fields in Mexico.

Carrie Estelle Bertzold and Edward Laurence Doheny met early in 1900; they were married August 22, 1900. They located their home in the parish of St. Vincent de Paul and developed a strong affiliation to the Vincentia Fathers (Congregation of the Mission), supporting their ministries in education and missionary work. The affiliated order of Sisters, the Daughters of Charity, also received the Dohenys' special interest. The impact on the Dohenys of St. Vincent's teachings of loving the poor is evidenced by their great generosity to many Southern California organizations serving the unfortunate.

The Dohenys built St. Vincent's Church on the corners of West Adams and Figueroa in Los Angeles as a gift to the archdiocese. It was characteristic of the Dohenys that they were involved in all stages of the design, from selecting the architect to personally selecting many of the contents. The first mass was celebrated on April 25, 1925. Soon after, Pope Pius XI conferred upon them the title of Knight and Lady of the Equestrian Order of the Holy Sepulcher.

Mrs. Doheny began to explore the field of book collecting. She had always enjoyed reading, liked books, and had kept them about her in generous numbers, but she could spare little time for hobbies and had scarcely thought of books as collectors' items. To an unusual degree, she had shared in the business life of her husband, which, for many years, involved almost continuous travel by motor, by rail, and by sea in the *Casiana*, their yacht. During this period Mrs. Doheny's collecting instincts found an outlet in gathering a variety of objects reflecting exquisite craftsmanship, feminine charm, or playful ingenuity, such as jades, glass paperweights, laces, and fans. It is not surprising, therefore, that among her first purchases of unusual books were bindings set with jewels or with miniatures and books with concealed paintings on their fore edges. Her collection of such examples was probably the largest ever assembled by an individual. The Dohenys led a quiet life until Edward died on September 8, 1935. Carrie Estelle Doheny then began to dispose of some of their properties and other time-consuming holdings, but she did not decrease the scope of her charitable work.

Carrie Estelle Doheny always attended Rosenbach's summer exhibitions showing all the many books that had been brought from New York to California. At these gatherings she basked in the presence of movie director Frank Capra and other Hollywood celebrities and book collectors. Laughingly, she would comment that all she knew about rare books was where to sign on the dotted line. Hopefully Lucille Miller, her full-time librarian, kept her well advised.

In early 1939, Mrs. Doheny was elevated to the rank of papal countess by Pope Pius XII. (Rose Kennedy was also elevated to this royal status in 1951 by the same pope.)

For many years, Mrs. Doheny quietly but steadily bought important manuscripts and books, placing them in the Estelle Doheny Collection in the Edward Laurence Doheny Memorial Library at St. John's Seminary, a memorial to her husband. In this way she amassed a remarkable collection of early manuscripts, incunabula, bibles, Americana, first editions of English and American authors, and literary and historical manuscripts and documents as well as examples of fine printing, bindings, illustrated books, and fore-edge paintings.

The redoubtable A.S.W. Rosenbach sold Mrs. Doheny some of her most spectacular illuminated manuscripts. In 1949, his brother Philip, on his annual visit, presented her with the great Liesborn Gospels of the 10th century. This volume had carved bindings and Rosenbach mentioned a very high price. Mrs. Doheny objected, gently reminding him that he had just sent her a letter asking one-third of this figure. She sent Miss Miller to get the letter, and Rosenbach went pale, mumbling about a mistake, which, however, Mrs. Doheny was willing to forgive. She was enchanted by the Liesborn Gospels and also the manuscript the *Liber Sapientiae*; therefore she purchased both for $85,000. These were added to the library of some 6,500 volumes that she had assembled.[1]

According to an article in the literary journal *The New Colophon* in 1950, St. John's Seminary in Camarillo, California, was home to the *Liber Sapientiae*, but the case involving its origins had been closed by the U.S. government. Nothing further happened until January 1952, when Arts and Monuments

Advisor Ardelia R. Hall of the Department of State became involved. She was passionate in her attempts to recover looted cultural property. In her position since 1945, she had worked on 66 cases, recovering 1,300 items of art that had been brought illegally into the United States. The 56-year-old Hall had no investigative authority but was most forceful in enlisting the help of other government agencies. She immediately immersed herself in the task of recovering the Kassel manuscripts looted from Bad Wildungen.

On January 16, 1952, Hall received her first information regarding the *Liber Sapientiae* via a phone call from Karl Kup at the New York Public Library. He told her in full about the purchase of the manuscript by Mrs. Doheny.[2] Hall then wrote Cardinal McIntyre of Los Angeles asking for information about the manuscript but received no response. Then, on March 6, 1953, she wrote another letter to McIntyre, to which he responded on April 7, 1953, stating, "This description does not fit what we have in our library."[3]

On May 5, 1953, Ardelia Hall sent McIntyre a registered letter beginning "My Dear Cardinal McIntyre." This long letter gave a complete description of the *Liber Sapientiae* and stated that Mrs. Doheny should reimburse the library for the cost of the manuscript. Hall further wrote:

> should you require additional information as to the obligation of the Rosenbach company to make such reimbursement, the Department, under the established procedure, will be able to request assistance from the Department of Justice.... It is desirable to conclude this matter as soon as it is convenient to you. Objects of cultural importance lost during war, are returned to the claimant government under arrangements described on page 339 of the enclosed Department of State Bulletin.[4]

After a few more terse letters, on June 26, 1953, Cardinal McIntyre of the Archdiocese of Los Angeles delivered the *Liber Sapientiae* manuscript to the customs officials in Los Angeles. On July 1, 1953, to cover all bases, Hall received one last letter from McIntyre requesting a receipt for this document from the claimant government. "It was understood should this not be delivered to that government the manuscript should be returned to us." On August 13, 1952, the Collector of Customs delivered to Edward Blaisdell Fenstermacher, diplomatic courier of the United States, one bound manuscript alleged to be the *Liber Sapientiae*, containing one page of the *Hildebrandslied*, to be delivered to the Commissioner of Customs, Washington, D.C. A year later the *Liber Sapientiae* was returned to Germany.[5]

Ten years later, in January 1962, Ardelia Hall received what appeared to be a break in the case. Edgar Breitenbach, chief of prints at the Library of Congress, told her that Gretel Meyer, a Library of Congress employee, had held the *Liber Sapientiae* in her hand while working for the Rosenbach firm in 1945.

Of course with this information from Breitenbach, Ardelia Hall walked across the street to the Library of Congress and, on January 30, 1962, had a long talk with Gretel Meyer. She told Hall about the purchase of the manuscript; in fact, she had written down the name of the officer who sold it and had it at her home. Then, a few days later, Meyer changed her story and said that the book purchased by the Rosenbach Company was not the *Liber Sapientiae*. She further stated that she could not find the name of the American soldier. After the interview closed, Hall wrote:

> Because Miss Mayer is apparently frightened to be in any way involved in the case, it might be advisable to interview her again, in the presence of the Assistant Chief of the Division. I have seen her twice and each time I tried to reassure her and told her that members of the Library of Congress staff had always been willing to advise the Department of State, but she does not seem to believe me and seems to be in a panic. She apparently has neurotic or psychological handicaps.[6]

The page of the *Hildebrandslied* and the *Willehalm Codex* were still missing. After the death of the Rosenbach brothers, their estate and collections were established as a public foundation in Philadelphia. On October 26, 1953, Ardelia Hall wrote, "I am hoping that the very distinguished men who are among the trustees of the Rosenbach estate may be more cooperative than the firms when the Rosenbachs were living, but I am not too hopeful in finding the information which the firm refused to give."[7]

An American army officer who would sell the priceless *Liber Sapientiae* for $7,000 surely would not have known enough to remove the most valuable page of the book. The book did not contain the page when it was examined by Dr. Kurt F. Bühler of the Pierpont Morgan Library. Is the missing page somewhere in the estate material left by the Rosenbachs?

Unbelievably, *yes*. Regardless of the deception over the years, the missing *Hildebrandslied* page never left the Rosenbachs' collection. On the morning of February 3, 1972, Edwin Wolf II, library manager and biographer, under questioning by Lessing Rosenwald, the revered collector and friend of the Rosenbachs who had just stepped down as president of the Rosenbach Foundation, responded that the page had been in the library as long as he could remember. In one quick short statement, the location of the most sought-after missing document of World War II had been revealed. A month later, on March 3, while rummaging through a tall, ornately decorated cupboard in the attached townhouse of Dr. Rosenbach, the museum curator accidentally stumbled across the *Willehalm Codex*. Even more amazing was the fact that the *Hildebrandslied* had been kept between the pages of the missing *Willehalm Codex*.

After several board meetings and various ceremonial gatherings, on

September 22, 1972, both precious manuscripts were returned to representatives of the Kassel State Library. Today these most imposing manuscripts are on display behind shatterproof glass.

Unfortunately the Estelle Doheny collection was later dissolved. She was without doubt Los Angeles's greatest woman collector and its most zealous collector of Bibles. Sadly, her books were also dispersed at auction, even though, in 1940, she had established a library in memory of her husband, the Edward Laurence Doheny Memorial Library, at the Archdiocese of Los Angeles.

The archdiocese interpreted her intentions differently. By the terms of her will, Doheny's bequest became an unrestricted gift in 1983, some 25 years after her death. In 1987, the archdiocese announced that it would be "redeploying this asset" to endow the seminary and to modernize its library facilities. A lavish color brochure presented the calculated net worth of the Doheny collection at $20 million and explained that the cost of upkeep was so great and the number of visiting scholars so small that the archdiocese was paying "an effective subsidy of $1,700 per scholar." During the next two years a series of auction sales in London, New York, and Camarillo dispersed the Doheny Library and gained for the Archdiocese the princely sum of $34 million, far more than it had anticipated. The most highly valued item in the collection, a Gutenberg Bible, went to Japan for more than $5 million, a record-breaking price.

In the late 1940s or early 1950s, Berman established a successful clothing manufacturing company, Bud Berman Sportswear, headquartered in the Empire State Building in New York. By 1957 he had 12 manufacturing plants spread out across the United States. Berman later expanded still further, with factories in Hong Kong, Taiwan, and Japan. On June 2, 1958, he sold the company to Cluett, Peabody & Company, which formed the Arrow Company division to manufacture, merchandise, and advertise Arrow products throughout the world.

In 1967, in Palm Springs, California, Bud Berman wrote, narrated, and recorded a Vietnam protest on a long-playing 33⅓ rpm record entitled *For Too Long I Have Remained Silent: Let's Talk About Viet Nam*. This recording was, according to the notes on the record jacket, sent gratis to 2,500 "prominent Americans." A bulleted double column list on the verso of the album lists the 32 categories of "prominent Americans," among them U.S. senators and congressmen, college presidents, union leaders, doctors, and so on. In an early statement, Berman employs the phrase "we veterans of World Wars I and II" as a claim to the authority to make his case. The narrative spoken by

Mr. Berman is a plea to people of influence in the United States to end the war in Vietnam as an act of civic and moral obligation.[8]

In 1977, Berman joined the Kellwood Company, a St. Louis manufacturer of clothing, home fashions, and recreational equipment. According to the Records of Trading of Securities by Corporative Insiders, Berman made 37 transactions involving Kellwood stock between June 11, 1986, and April 10, 1991. Records about the Proposed Sale of Unregistered Securities by Individuals reported three transactions for Bud Berman, two in 1990. The largest amount is $253,053. These are public records and merely reflect his stock trading activities.

Berman died on March 7, 1991, in Osprey, Florida, at 74 years of age. Except for his Vietnam protest, he maintained a low profile. In fact, his obituary in the *New York Times* made no reference to parents, date or place of birth. It was as enigmatic as Bud Berman's times of yore.

Chapter 13
Other Bad Wildungen Robberies

In 1945 there were two large repositories in Bad Wildungen; they had no windows and the steel doors were securely locked. The buildings were under the custodianship of Felix Pusch; therefore the U.S. Monuments, Fine Art, and Archives (MFAA) officers had no concern regarding their safety, and they remained at Bad Wildungen through the winter of 1945. In February 1946, they were moved to the Wiesbaden Collection Center.

One of the greatest problems at the end of World War II was the collection and return of cultural objects to their countries of origin. To provide a means of organizing and processing these cultural objects, the U.S. Army established several collections points in the U.S. Zone of Occupation. The two main and longest-surviving collection points were at Munich and Wiesbaden. The Munich Collection Center contained over a million objects and the Wiesbaden Collection Center eventually housed about 700,000 objects.[1]

In July 1945, the Wiesbaden Collection Center was established in a large former Luftwaffe building. The center was under the command of Capt. Walter Farmer; during his tenure it contained great treasures from the Berlin museums. After Farmer's departure to the United States, the Wiesbaden Collection Center was placed under the command of Capt. Edith Standen. Her father was English and her mother a Bostonian; Edith herself was born in Canada, but by 1945 she had become a naturalized American citizen. Educated in England, she was later in charge of the Joseph Widener Collection, the most noteworthy art collection of its period. When it was given to the National Gallery in 1942, Standen found herself out of a job and joined the Women's Army Corps. One of the first matters Standen oversaw was the shipment of artworks from Amorbach and Bad Wildungen.[2]

Like the repository in the basement of the Goecke Hotel in Bad Wildungen, in the first week of April 1945, the Amorbach Castle Depot repository had also been looted, in this case by the Seventh Army's 2756 Engineer Combat Battalion. Also at this time, Lt. Sinclair Robertson "helped" Dr. Albert Rapp, curator of the Städel Museum, remove 34 of the most valuable paintings from Amorbach. Robertson appropriated six of these paintings in payment for his help.[3] (The complete story is told in my book *The Spoils of World War II*.)

On February 8, 1946, a total of 402 paintings of the Städel Museum were trucked into the Wiesbaden Collection Center from Amorbach Castle and assigned inventory numbers 2051 to 2452. Next were the works from Bad Wildungen, which arrived on February 27 and 28. The second shipment included some of the finest paintings ever assembled — works by Dürer, Vermeer, and Botticelli. Between the first shipment and May 8, a total of 13 shipments of valuables were transferred from Bad Wildungen to the Wiesbaden Collection Center.

Now, as the last paintings arrived, something strange happened. It was discovered that 140 of the paintings that had been stored in Bad Wildungen and Amorbach were missing. This included the six taken by Robertson. The missing works were 93 from the Städelsches Kunstinstitute, 33 from the Städtische Galerie, and 14 privately owned paintings. On June 28, Edith Standen had reviewed the missing paintings and noted that the Jordaens *Portrait of a Doctor* was included among them and that it had been purchased in Paris in 1941 for 100,000 francs. This meant that upon recovery, the Jordaens painting would be returned to France as the country of origin, as it had been purchased during the Nazi era.

On July 27, 1946, the missing art from the Bad Wildungen bunker became the number one priority of investigator Bernard B. Taper, a U.S. art intelligence officer and a young, enthusiastic, knowing, and energetic person. Because of his further investigation into this case, however, Taper, sadly enough, became persona non grata and was transferred to Berlin.[4]

As for the 140 missing paintings, Bernard Taper began an investigation and on July 27, 1946 wrote:

> The following steps were taken by the Art Intelligence Officer in this case:
> (1) Meeting with Captain Standen, Wiesbaden Collection Point in order to study lists and photographs of missing art works 21 July.
> (2) Meeting with Mr. Holzinger, director of Städel Museum, and interrogation of him as to circumstances of disappearance 22 July.
> The next step in this case will be conference with German district attorney at Kassel, who has been conducting an investigation.[5]

On August 25, 1946, Taper wrote:

> An illustrated booklet, with photographs of the main items which are missing, has been printed and is being distributed to museums, art dealers, and interested government agencies. The discovery of but one of these missing

paintings will provide the all-important clue which may lead to the solution of what to the present appears an almost insoluble case. The undersigned hopes to undertake intensive investigation of this case in the near future.

And indeed a booklet titled *Diebstahl von Genmälden* (Stolen Paintings) was published and distributed. The first page contained the following:

> The paintings in this list belong to the Städelsches Kunstinstitute, Frankfurt am Main, to the Städtische Galeries, Frankfurt am Main, and to private owners; have been stolen out of deposits of these museums. Both museums ask for your kind assistance in this affair.
>
> The artists' names in this list are given in alphabetic order; measures are indicated in cm, first height, then breadth. As it is very likely the paintings on canvas have been cut from their wedged frames, the measurements may have been reduced.[6]

The case went cold and sometime in 1948 all but 25 of 140 missing paintings published in the booklet *Diebstahl von Genmälden* were found in the basement of the Städelsches Kunstinstitute. Did someone secretly place them there under stress? Was it a high-ranking American army general or a museum director?

Four of the 25 paintings were eventually recovered in Germany. Those four included two of the six paintings taken by Lt. Sinclair Robertson, one of which was Rubens' *A Satyr and Three Nymphs Frightened by a Thunderstorm*. On February 16 and 23, 1962, Christie's in London placed 10 of the 21 missing paintings on auction. On August 7, 1963, and again in 1984, a private owner sold one of the missing Städel paintings to a New York art dealer. Therefore 12 of the 21 missing paintings have surfaced.[7]

In 1948 Howard B. Travis, giving his address as the YMCA, Los Angeles, walked into the Los Angeles County Museum and asked the director whether a small ivory diptych he had had any value. Travis told the director that his brother had obtained this object during the war. The carved ivory represented scenes from the passion. The left panel showed Jesus entering Jerusalem, the washing of his feet, and Judas' kiss. The right panel showed the Last Supper, Christ on the Mount of Olives, and the Crucifixion. The director, William R. Valentiner, who had been born in 1880 in Karlsruhe, Germany, recognized the 14th-century French ivory diptych as an important museum piece. Fortunately, he held onto the piece and turned it over to U.S. Customs. He made several inquires and learned that the diptych belonged to the Kassel State Museum, inventory number VI 154. It had been looted from the repository in the basement of the Goecke Hotel in Bad Wildungen. This $5,000 object was then returned to the Kassel Museum by the proper army authorities.[8]

Two years later, another painting taken from Bad Wildungen surfaced in Los Angeles. Capt. Jerry P. Frary had purchased Rubens' *St. Catherine*, formerly in the Municipal Art Gallery of Dusseldorf, in 1945 near Bad Wildungen. *St. Catherine* was one of 16 Dusseldorf Museum paintings that had been stolen from Bad Wildungen. Frary, then living in Encino, California, and a police sergeant with the Los Angeles Police Department, had Michael G. Frary, his brother, take the painting to the Los Angeles County Museum for evaluation. James B. Byrnes, the curator, immediately recognized it as a work by Rubens and took the painting to William Valentiner, his boss, for confirmation. Valentiner recalled that a soldier who wished to dispose of it through sale had brought the painting to him about a year earlier. Byrnes photographed the painting, made a notation that it was on a wood panel 21 inches high by 17 inches wide, and labeled on the back, "*St. Catherine*, collection number 734." Byrnes then returned the Rubens to Michael Frary.[9]

Byrnes sent U.S. Customs a letter and photograph of the painting. The Department of State then contacted Jerry Frary, who retained Harry S. Apster, a lawyer, to handle the matter for him. Upon being contacted by U.S. authorities, Apster seemed to be totally unfamiliar with the case and did not demonstrate great cooperation, but instead stated that he and his client were taking the case up directly with the Department of State. A year later, Frary surrendered the painting to U.S. authorities.[10]

At that time Frary disclosed that he had acquired a second painting from the same person while serving as an army officer in Europe. The painting, by B. C. Koekoek, was tentatively identified as painting number seven reported missing from the Dusseldorf Museum. Frary delivered the Koekoek to U.S. Customs. After they received the painting, it was discovered that it did not match the description of the missing Dusseldorf painting.

The Department of State began to look for a home for the recovered Koekoek. As they wrote to various museums in Germany, they received the same response from all: "No picture by B. C. Koekoek is missing."

In 1952, customs officials seized from Valentine Lavin of Canton, Ohio, two more paintings that had been stolen from the Bad Wildungen repository.[11]

On November 15, 1961, two paintings unidentified as to ownership were turned over to the German Embassy in Washington, D.C. One of the paintings was *Portrait of a Man in Armor*, by Nicolaes Maes; the other was the Koekoek seized from Jerry Frary.[12]

Part IV
The Schwarzburg Castle

Chapter 14

The Robbery

During World War II, 89 divisions were activated by the U.S. Army. By comparison, Germany, with half the population of the United States, organized 313 divisions. A U.S. Army division is the smallest composite unit capable of operating independently and at the time was composed of 14,037 soldiers. The nucleus of a division in World War II were three regiments, totaling 9,207 soldiers. The rest of the men were primarily assigned to artillery and tank battalions with 497 medics and, interestingly enough, 114 men assigned to the division band. Behind the story of a division lie countless untold achievements in supply and service branches. Working in obscurity, the men of the Quartermaster Company, Signal Company, Medical Battalion, Ordnance Company, and Division Headquarters normally receive only a footnote in the history of a division.

One of these divisions, the 102nd Infantry Division, was formed in September 1942. After two years of organization and training, they arrived in Cherbourg, France, on September 22, 1944. By May 1, 1945, after 173 days of combat in Europe it was over for the 102nd as far as actual fighting was concerned. During the combat phase, the division saw 1,077 of its young men killed in action.[1]

Hordes of German soldiers and civilians, fleeing from the advancing Soviet Army, crossed the Elbe River by every conceivable means to surrender to U.S. forces. German military personnel crossed individually and by units, but always under protection of a white flag. Because of the terms of the Geneva Convention, there was no choice but to accept their surrender. Over 100,000 German soldiers surrendered to the 102nd Infantry Division during this period. Many civilians also did so. Some were returned to the eastern bank of the Elbe, but others managed to get through the lines to western Germany's interior. The huge influx of German prisoners clogged the evacuation channels to the point of bringing the evacuation of prisoners to a complete standstill. The feeding and housing problem was enormous. But with the use of army rations, captured Wehrmacht stores, and civilian food, the prisoners were fed.

Temporary enclosures were constructed. Medical aid was provided and sanitary measures were installed, but shelter was at a minimum. Thus VE Day, May 8, 1945, found the 102nd Infantry Division deployed on the west bank of the Elbe River faced with the problem of guarding, feeding, and ministering to 100,000 prisoners of war.[2]

Immediately following V-E Day, the division set about the task of organizing and perfecting the military government and administering the enormous population of the division's area. Some German prisoners of war were evacuated to camps in rear areas. Others were placed in enclosures wherever housing and other facilities were available in the area. Allied liberated prisoners of war and displaced persons were collected in camps and segregated according to nationality, Negotiations were begun with the Soviets with a view to sending their nationals across the Elbe to them and accepting from them French, Belgian, and other Western Europeans who were then evacuated to the West. This system worked very well, and before the end or the month, many thousands had been cleared from the area.

Allied military government detachments were placed at strategic locations. Local officials were screened and left in office or replaced according to their background and associations with the Nazi Party. Local utilities and essential facilities were repaired and put into operation. Surveys were made of local food stocks and necessary steps taken to guard and distribute food on hand.[3]

Beginning May 26, 1945, the 102nd Infantry Division started moving to the province of Thuringia, approximately 175 miles south, to relieve the 89th Infantry Division. The division headquarters was located in Gotha. There were no new problems but just more of the same. The move was completed and responsibility for the sector was assumed on the morning of May 30. There were more than 60,000 displaced persons in the division's area of assignment and most of them were restless. In Thuringia, every effort was made to collect, segregate, and evacuate German war material, ammunition, and equipment. Ammunition dumps, some enormous and some small, were found in woods, fields, and innocent-appearing farm buildings; in one case a machine gun was found in a tennis court. Some dumps were complete with up-to-date signal, engineering, and ordnance equipment. Others were practically exhausted. But all presented a problem from a transportation point of view. A dragnet was spread by the CIC for war criminals and other wanted German persons. Hundreds of people were screened and many SS troops, party members, and officials were arrested and imprisoned. One 48-year-old Nazi Party member went into the woods and hung himself. He had made statements insisting that he would not be taken by the Americans. There was no reason to arrest him and, as the army investigator wrote, "He overestimated his importance."[4]

14. The Robbery

Personnel of the division were becoming restless, as they had visions of going home or to the Pacific to finish the war with Japan. These troops did not have an interest in occupation duty in Germany, especially with a non-fraternization policy. This most unsuccessful policy prohibited any kind of contact with Germans, including conversation, shaking hands, and even giving children candy. The American soldier did not feel at ease with this policy, which was strictly enforced by the commander of the 102nd. The standing joke with the troops was "Copulation without conversation is not fraternization." Fortunately this unpopular policy was dropped by the end of July.

Several hundred soldiers of the 102nd requested Red Cross emergency leave to return to the United States for personal problems, family problems, and health reasons. With the combat stage over, the army approved many of these requests and many soldiers returned. After this leave, a soldier would be reassigned to a military unit in the states. Another function of the American Red Cross was the supplementary supply of cigarettes. After the move to Thuringia, the field director of the Red Cross sent his driver on a 500-mile round trip to the Ninth Army Headquarters warehouse to obtain 18,000 packs of cigarettes. The director reported: "Half a case [250 packs] was turned over to Chaplain Boswell of the 327 Medical Battalion for the express use of patients at the clearing company who missed out on the P-X issues."[5]

Within the large land area occupied by the 102nd Infantry Division was the village of Schwarzburg, 30 miles south of Weimar, occupied by Company F, 406th Infantry Regiment, 102nd Infantry Division. In the pandemonium of postwar Germany, Company F, commanded by Capt. Paul N. Estes and three platoon leaders — Lts. Walters Jr., Wooten, and White — was responsible for maintaining law and order for Schwarzburg and 20 other villages. Walters was responsible for roadblocks and checking the towns for weapons and other forbidden items. The officers lived together in a hotel in Schwarzburg, but Walters stated: "I did not get to know Estes well, as he seldom confided in his officers."[6]

On a hill overlooking the town was the Schwarzburg Castle; Lt. Wooten was responsible for its safekeeping. One guard was posted at the entrance of the castle to prevent anyone from entering or leaving without proper authority. As far as the guards knew, they were protecting a supply of submarine parts, as the upper story contained prisms, parts of periscopes, and similar items. Most members of F Company did not know that the castle also contained a trove of art treasures.

2/Lt. Cecil A. Wooten, a newly commissioned officer recently assigned to the 102nd, inspected the castle and, in the basement, noticed many tables covered with objects made of porcelain. Many were decorated with the crests of old Prussian families — families that Wooten thought were probably wealthy. He did not know that all this porcelain and other art treasures had been stored there by the Thuringia State Museum, located in Weimar. Until 1943, the paintings had remained on exhibit in a museum known as the Staatliche Kunstsammlungen zu Weimar. In 1943, to protect these artworks from anticipated bombardment, 121 of the museum's paintings were stored in the cellar of the Schwarzburg Castle.[7]

Hundreds of paintings and objects of art from other collections were also stored in the castle, which, with its broken windows and shattered doors, had a number of possible entrances. But members of Company F guarded only the main entrance. Three Germans lived within the grounds: Herr Fassbender, an architect, and his wife as well as a groundskeeper. Fassbender was an ardent Nazi; he had designed the Hotel Elephantine in Weimar. He was at Schwarzburg to maintain and reconstruct the castle as a future residence for Adolf Hitler and a site for Nazi Party functions. The Fassbenders lived in a well-constructed building and, according to Lt. Walters, the architect and his wife were often seen in the company of Capt. Estes.[8]

On June 12, 1945, Dr. Walther Scheidig, director of the Thuringia State Museum, visited the castle. A guard obtained the keys from Capt. Estes and opened the cellar door for Scheidig's inspection. The visitor opened a few wooden crates and concluded that the basement depository was safe and everything was in order.

Dr. Scheidig returned on June 27, 1945, once again to check the basement. To his surprise, some of the cases had been opened and the contents strewn about the floor. The American guard brought to the attention of Scheidig that the most valuable of the paintings, Albrecht Dürer's *Hans Tucher and Felicitas*, two panels on wood, were missing. The paintings were small, about 11 by 9.5 inches, and could easily be hidden. The guard assured Scheidig that he had nothing to do with the disappearance and did not know the whereabouts of the paintings, but *this* soldier apparently knew something about art. Scheidig reported the loss to Capt. Estes, who responded that he was not responsible for guarding the art but only for protecting the submarine parts stored in the castle. Estes advised Scheidig to remove the art — an impossible task considering the complete destruction of the country and transportation system. In fact, Germany's museums did suffer their greatest losses in the confusion that prevailed once hostilities had ceased.[9]

During a conversation with Lt. Col. Isaac A. Gatlin, 2nd Battalion Commander, 406 Regiment, Capt. Estes mentioned the painting *Venus with Cupid*. Gatlin was headquartered in Bad Blattenburg, about 10 miles from Schwarzburg. They then went to the castle together to view the painting and noticed that it, Cranach's *Venus with Cupid*, was missing. This is a very attractive representation of Venus in the nude showing little sympathy for Cupid

14. The Robbery

This valuable painting by Lucas Cranach the Elder, titled *Venus with Cupid*, was described by officers of the 102nd Infantry Division as "a painting of a child with a fly on his nose." It is actually a bee. This is one of 13 paintings stolen by U.S. soldiers from Schwarzburg Castle. This painting found its way into a Yale art gallery in the early 1970s and was sold to a Swiss collector, after which the trail goes cold (courtesy Kunstsammlungen zu Weimar).

(her son), who is complaining about the bee sting he got while trying to steal some honey. Estes, in a cursory investigation of the missing painting, described it as "a painting of a child with a fly on its nose, which appeared very real ... allegedly valued at one million dollars."[10]

Following the visit, on July 2, 1945, the 102nd moved into Bavaria and the Soviets occupied Thuringia. Capt. Estes promptly forgot about the incident of the Cranach painting, but the boy with the fly on his nose would not fade away.

On July 19, 1945, Scheidig revisited Schwarzburg Castle, now under guard of an official, one Herr Ehle, and the local police. As they entered the castle, it was obvious the locks had been broken open and paintings plundered. Several had been removed from their frames. The frames, left behind, were now scattered on the dusty floor. A case of ivory-inlaid pistol from the state armory had been broken open and some of these antique weapons were gone. The average American soldier may have been uninformed with regard to art, but when it came to collecting guns, they were obsessive. Some of these valuable pistols surely left the castle in soldiers' pockets. Herr Ehle told Scheidig that this pillaging was done by the American soldiers the night they left Schwarzburg. It was obvious from the grimy prints of American-made rubber soles and the numerous cigarette butts lying about that the intruders had been American soldiers. For answers, Scheidig looked to architect Fassbender and his wife. But as Herr Ehle reported, they had left with the Americans. The stolen Dürer and Caspar David Friedrich's *Landscape with Rainbow* were priceless.[11]

Dr. Scheidig was stymied; the Soviet troops were sending to Russia all cultural property of international renown that they could find in their occupation zone. On July 25, 1945, Scheidig wrote a short report to the director of the Weimar Museum, reporting the looting of the repository by the 15th American Infantry Division, commanded by Capt. Paul Estes. Scheidig made one mistake; there *was* no 15th American Infantry Division. But on the report next to the words 15th American Infantry Division he drew this shoulder sleeve insignia:⊙.[12] This was unquestionably the 102nd Infantry Division, the Ozark, named after the Ozark Mountains.

Scheidig wrote several comprehensive reports describing in detail the incident at Schwarzburg. These were mailed to German officials in Weimar and Berlin. This was rather risky at the time; any attempt by an official from the Eastern Zone of Germany to communicate with any Allied power was punishable by the Soviet authorities. Scheidig's efforts included contacting various German museums and administrative organizations, the Allied Control Council, the Soviet Military Administration, the U.S. Department of State, and the Fogg and Germanic Museums at Harvard, all at extreme risk to himself and all to no avail.

The most valuable painting stolen by American soldiers from the Schwarzburg Castle was Caspar David Friedrich's *Landscape with Rainbow on the Island of Rügen*. This oil painting on canvas was cut from its frame. It is still missing (courtesy Klassik Stiftung Weimar).

Then, according to Thomas Foehl, deputy director of the Weimar Art Museum, in later 1945, some 200 paintings were pillaged from Schwarzburg Castle by Soviet troops; these have never been seen again.

Nine years later, on October 21, 1953, Dr. Walther Scheidig wrote to Ardelia Hall, MFAA officer of the U.S. Department of State, requesting her help in the recovery of the valuables stolen from Schwarzburg Castle. He wrote that the castle had been guarded by troops of the 15th American Infantry Division and included a sketch of the 102nd Division patch. He further reported that Churchill J. Brazelton, who had attended Princeton University and was from Waco, Texas, could assist in the recovery of the missing valuables.[13]

At the insistence of the Department of State, on July 19, 1954, the army initiated an investigation into the 1945 theft by questioning Paul Estes at his home in Miami, Florida. Estes acknowledged "That painting of a child with a fly on its nose" was missing. He denied any knowledge of the theft of the remaining paintings. He concluded his short interview by stating that all officers and enlisted men were permitted to visit the castle and go where they pleased; that the war had just ended and everyone was relaxed and not worrying about what happened to their former enemies, the Germans. Estes readily agreed to take a lie detector test, which proved inclusive.[14]

Lt. Col. Isaac Gatlin had remained in the army and was questioned at Fort Gordon, Georgia. Gatlin "did not recall Weimar Castle or the incident of the missing painting of a boy with a fly on his nose." He stated that when his division left Thuringia, they moved out by unit, did not meet at a rendezvous point, and had no direct contact with the Soviets. He said, "I do not know of any individual who had any particular knowledge or liking for art."[15]

Several former officers of the 102nd were interviewed, and they too had no knowledge of the art theft and stuck by the story of being aware only of the missing painting of a child with a fly on its nose. The army investigators also checked with the local art dealers in the towns of the officers being investigated, and this too proved negative. On January 20, 1955, the investigation concluded with: "From the foregoing ... it is concluded that this investigation has failed to identify the person(s) responsible for the theft of the paintings from the Schwarzburg Castle, Schwarzburg, Germany, in July 1945."

In 1955 Ardelia Hall wrote Scheidig that the investigation of 10 months had failed to provide one clue that would help in finding the missing paintings. All the officers could remember was a painting with a child and fly but nothing about the Albrecht Dürer. It does seem that Gatlin's statement — that the men in the 102nd Infantry Division had no knowledge or interest in art — was true, and the paintings selected by the thief were the most valuable ones at the castle. What was the involvement of architect Fassbender and his wife? An ordinary soldier would not be able to tell which of the paintings were of great value, but a German architect would have known. Was Dr. Walther Scheidig being deceitful? Did he take the paintings? Were the officers of the 102nd maintaining a code of silence? The U.S. government took the stance that the art had been stolen by one of the Germans or confiscated by the Soviets.

Chapter 15
A Break in the Case

In May 1966, more than 20 years after the fact, 62-year-old attorney and art collector Edward I. Elicofon was contacted by his friend Gerard Stern, an art dealer, who told Elicofon that he had recently seen two of Elicofon's paintings listed in a German book describing stolen art treasures of World War II. Stern, apparently, had a fabulous memory for the 1965 catalogue, which focused on art missing from German museums. It contained thousands of descriptions, and Elicofon's collection, consisting primarily of oriental art, included roughly 2,000 paintings, porcelains, and other art objects kept in his home in the Flatbush section of Brooklyn. To have made the connection was amazing. The two men took the paintings to New York's Metropolitan Museum of Art, where they were described by one official as the discovery of the century. The paintings included Albrecht Dürer's portraits in the form of a diptych *Hans Tucher and Felicitas*, stolen in July 1945 from the Schwarzburg Castle. Dr. Walther Scheidig of the Staatliche Kunstsammlungen zu Weimar had been vindicated. The discovery was publicized in a front-page article in the *New York Times* on Memorial Day, May 30, 1966.[1]

Elicofon told the *Times* that one day in 1946 a young man about 25 to 30 years old came by his home saying that he had been sent by a friend of Elicofon. Under his arm he carried a package containing eight paintings, which he said he had bought in Europe. Elicofon picked out the two portraits, dickered with the young man over the price, and agreed on $500, which he paid in cash. The young man gave him a receipt, which, after 20 years, Elicofon could not find. "I never saw or heard from him again," Elicofon said. He framed and displayed the paintings in his home along with his many other art objects. The *Times* article stated that the legal issues were so complicated that if Elicofon desired he could hold the paintings for years before the case was settled. How right this prediction was.

Later, in court papers, Elicofon would swear that he had purchased the unsigned Dürer paintings in the spring of 1946 for $450 from a young American ex-serviceman who appeared at his Brooklyn home and claimed to have purchased the paintings in Germany. This is not the only inconsistency in the *Times* story. The eight looted paintings consisted of four oil paintings on wood and the remainder on canvas. The four paintings on wood together consisted of more than 6 by 1½ feet of wood and the four remaining canvases were about the same size, more than a young man could carry under his arm. Moreover, the individual who had selected the paintings and kept them in his possession for a year knew the value of the paintings. They would not have been sold at such a ridiculously low price.

Ardelia Hall had retired two years earlier, in 1964, but on the day this story made the *New York Times* she at her home on Cambridge Plaza in Washington, D.C. She wrote Dr. Scheidig a letter and mailed him a copy of the *New York Times* article. In the letter, she said that she was going to Montague, Massachusetts, and gave Scheidig her address and phone number in Montague. Although it was Memorial Day, she had contacted the Department of the Army and had no doubt that they would reopen the investigation.

Hall received two letters from Scheidig addressed to her home in Hunting Hill Field, Montague; she responded in July 1966:

> I am glad to learn that you have retained an attorney in New York. Not only the dealers, as you mentioned, but museums are interested in buying the Dürers. Their lawyers have come to me inquiring about the ownership. I have referred then to the State Dept. and will write more about that when I get my typewriter. There is so much money involved in the purchase even of these stolen paintings, that I am writing now to suggest that your attorney file an attachment of your ownership so that the paintings will be taken into custody of the court.[2]

Hall and Scheidig could have used some advice from Sun Tzu, an influential ancient Chinese military strategist: "Know the enemy and know yourself." At this point Hall and Scheidig had no idea of who would be their real enemy.

On January 27, 1969, the Federal Republic of Germany brought suit in the district court for the Eastern District of New York against Edward Elicofon to recover the two paintings by Albrecht Dürer, alleged to have been stolen in 1945 from Schwarzburg Castle in Germany during the American occupation. The Federal Republic of Germany asserted that the paintings, executed in the year 1499, were the property of the German people, having been in the possession of a state museum at the time of theft, and that the Federal Republic of Germany's government was the only one that could properly represent the German people in an American court.[3]

Elicofon's claim in the case was fairly straightforward; his ownership arose out of his uninterrupted possession of the Dürer paintings from the time of his good faith purchase of them in 1946 from an American serviceman in Brooklyn to his discovery in 1966 of the identity of the paintings. Elicofon advanced the theory that the paintings may have been removed from the castle by Fassbender, a German architect who lived on the grounds and was allegedly a de facto custodian of the stored artwork. Elicofon maintained that under German law, Fassbender could have conveyed good title even though he himself did not have title, and that the good faith purchaser or transferee could in turn have transferred good title to Elicofon.

Then, on March 25, 1969, in a bolt from the blue, the grand duchess of Saxony-Weimar claimed possession of Dürer's diptych *Hans Tucher and Felicitas*. She claimed legal ownership of the portraits on the basis of a divorce settlement with Grand Duke Wilhelm Ernst. To the surprise of everyone, the grand duchess was granted permission to intervene based on a claim that the Dürer masterpieces had been part of the collection of the grand duke of Saxony-Weimar since 1824 and that title to the paintings rested in her through an assignment from the grand duke. Thereafter Elicofon, the grand duchess, and the State Art Museum of Weimar all demanded the paintings.[4]

The grand duchess of Saxony-Weimar claimed that the two Dürer paintings had been in the possession of successive grand dukes of Saxony-Weimar since at least Goethe's time in 1824. They were part of what was known as the Grand Ducal Art Collection. By 1913 the paintings, along with other art objects, were displayed in the Grand Ducal Museum in Weimar. The grand duchess maintained that they were the grand duke's personal property and continued to be the personal property of his successors. The State Museum of Weimar contended, to the contrary, that the paintings were public property on the basis of 19th-century dynastic law, a 1921 settlement between the Grand Duke Wilhelm Ernst and the newly established Territory of Weimar.

The grand duchess responded that in 1848 the Grand Ducal Art Collection was declared to be a family trust in which title was vested in the grand ducal family until the male line became extinct, thereby removing the collection from the domain of property held as sovereign. However, according to the State Museum of Weimar's German law expert, the title to the Dürer paintings passed to the Territory of Weimar automatically in 1918.

The German province of Thuringia, which was created by Federal German Law on April 20, 1920, was first included as the municipal association of Sachsen-Weimar-Eisenach, the territory over which the grand dukes formerly presided. The municipal association was dissolved effective April 1, 1923, and the assets of the Weimar District became the property of the Land of Thuringia. The Grand Duke, beginning on January 21, 1921, would each year receive from the Territory of Weimar an annuity of 300,000 marks, out of which all claims of the grand ducal family to civil lists, maintenance, and other gratuities would be paid. The annuity would continue to be paid to existing male descendants of the grand duke after his death, and upon extinction of the male line a reduced annuity of 100,000 marks would be paid to his female descendants. As further settlement for the concessions made by the grand duke, particularly in ceding highly valuable collections and objects of art, the grand duke was to be paid a special compensation of 3 million marks.[5]

By this time, about 1924, the collection was no longer called the Grand Ducal Art Collection but rather the State Art Collection of Weimar (Staatliche Kunstsammlungen zu Weimar). The annuities under the 1921 agreement were paid to the grand duke's heirs until 1945, when payments ceased, as the war had been lost by Germany and the Allies would not make these payments. In 1948 the right to the annuities was extinguished by expropriation through an act passed by the Province of Thuringia, then under Soviet control.[6]

What the grand duchess failed to tell the courts was that in October 1946, she and the duke had smuggled out of the Russian Occupation Zone gold, silver, and jewels valued at $5 million. The property was found by German border police and turned over to the U.S. Army First Constabulary Brigade in the town of Eschwege. The property was inventoried, tagged, and loaded onto a 2½-ton truck and taken to Frankfurt, Germany. There it was turned over to American authorities at the Foreign Exchange Depository. In the late 1960s, the property had been turned over to the officials of the West German government.[7]

The Elicofon, grand duchess, and State Art Museum of Weimar case continued. After 15 long-drawn-out years of legal appeals, the United States District Court, Eastern District of New York, named the State Art Museum of Weimar the true owner of the two Dürer paintings and directed that they be returned to Germany. Elicofon's additional appeals of the court's decision were denied and the Dürer portraits were restored to the Weimar Museum in 1982. By the time of the return of the paintings, Ardelia Hall had died, Dr. Walther Scheidig had also died, and, after 38 years, the U.S. Army had lost all interest in World War II matters.

In 1979, two years prior to the settlement of the case, for some arcane reason Edward I. Elicofon, the defendant, asked the United States District Court, Eastern District of New York, to interview and obtain sworn affidavits from the same 102nd Division officers who were investigated by the army in 1954 regarding their activities while occupying Schwarzburg Castle. This cross-examination was more formal than the first, when army investigators asked the former soldiers comfortable questions. The penalty for untruthfulness with a federal court is a bit more severe than with the army.

Former Capt. Paul N. Estes, company commander of F Company at Schwarzburg, told the federal interrogator more than he had told the army investigator of 1954. He recalled seeing an antique pistol with a handle in the shape of a ball. This may well have been one of the ivory-inlaid pistols from

15. A Break in the Case

the state armory. He also remembered playing bridge with the German architect Fassbender. But the four men investigated again stuck by the story as told by Estes:

> I have been informed by defendant's counsel that a Dr. Walther Scheidig, who I am told was the Director of the Weimar Museum during the period of the American occupation of Schwarzburg, has testified that he visited Schwarzburg at least twice during June 1945 to inspect paintings supposedly stored in the Castle; that, on each occasion, he requested from me the keys to a storeroom located in the Castle and supposedly containing numerous paintings and other art objects; that, on his second inspection, he discovered that the two paintings reproduced on Exhibit A were missing; that he reported this to me in the presence of one of my lieutenants; and that I advised him to remove the remaining works of art.
>
> Although almost 35 years have passed since I left Schwarzburg, and my memory of some of the names and places have faded, I am certain that the story told by Dr. Scheidig simply never happened, at least insofar as I am supposed to have played a part. I am confident that I would have remembered events as dramatic as those recounted by Dr. Scheidig if they had in fact occurred. I never met a Dr. Scheidig or any other man representing himself to be the Director of the Weimar Museum and never had any part in the events the Dr. Scheidig describes. In particular I never received any report that the two paintings reproduced in Exhibit A were missing, and I have never seen either of them.[8]

Chapter 16
Churchill "Chuck" Jones Brazelton

As part of this investigation the U.S. Eastern District Court of New York subpoenaed and took the affidavit of Churchill J. Brazelton, who had been mentioned in Dr. Scheidig's 1945 annotations. In the spring of 1945, he was a lieutenant on the staff of the U.S. First Army. Brazelton told the investigating authorities that he met Dr. Scheidig in 1945, that they had a mutual interest in antiques and objects of art, and that Scheidig helped him obtain a pair of antique pistols.

Brazelton testified, "Dr. Scheidig and other German civilians I met in Weimar were quite apprehensive about the then rumored approach of the Soviet Army. I recall Dr. Scheidig telling me that, if it became known that the Russians were to occupy Weimar, there would be a number of people in Weimar and the vicinity who would be interested in selling art objects."[1]

On December 3, 1980, less than a year after giving his affidavit, at the age of 60, Churchill "Chuck" Jones Brazelton died. Who was he? Brazelton was born on September 25, 1920; his well-connected parents were Thomas Berry and Pauline Battle Brazelton of Waco, Texas. He attended Episcopal High School in Alexandria, Virginia, and graduated from Princeton in 1943. He was drafted into the army and assigned to Fort Sill, Oklahoma, where he was able to secure a spot in Officers' Candidate School. He was at Fort Sill for the year of 1943 and was then assigned to Fort Washington, Maryland, to be trained in journalistic censorship. On February 27, 1944, he sailed from New York to Northern Ireland. Three months later, he was assigned to Supreme Headquarters Allied Forces Europe in London. He remained there until October 7, 1944, when he was transferred to Paris. There a young Lt. Brazelton found himself "living a king's life at the government's expense, and getting paid for it!" In Paris he charmed his way into the elite social circles of the Parisian aristocracy. For four months, which he called "the finest of my life," he was a regular guest at their clubs, chateaus, and cocktail parties.[2]

On January 31, 1945, Brazelton was promoted to first lieutenant and transferred from Paris to First Army Headquarters at Spa, Belgium. In this luxurious setting Brazelton worked as a press liaison and censor and spent most of his days with war correspondents from the major U.S. radio networks and wire services. These included NBC, CBS, and the Blue Network, which was the on-air name of an American radio production and distribution service. The correspondents' task was to report the truth and keep up morale, but the two were not always compatible. It was Brazelton's job to try to facilitate this.

At this point Brazelton decided to make his first trip into Germany with the press corps. The purpose of his trip was to travel with a couple of war correspondents to get a firsthand picture of just what was going on on the front lines. On the last day in February they started out at 10 A.M. from Spa. They quickly drove through the now captured but still formidable defenses of the Siegfried line; their first stop after 31 miles was the German city of Aachen.

The city had first been attacked on September 29, 1944, when the First Army began an offensive with the ultimate objective of taking Duren and Cologne. Between the First Army and this target lay the city of Aachen, which had great symbolic status in the Nazi ideology. The birthplace of Charlemagne, it evoked memories of the glories of the Holy Roman Empire and had captured Hitler's imagination. "The city," the Führer ordered, "must be held at all costs." And it almost was, owing to the Nazi counterattack of the Battle of the Bulge in December. Now, five months later, the First Army had taken Aachen and was continuing toward Cologne.

Even through the ruins, it was obvious to Brazelton that at one time this had been a very fine city. Now, however, there was nothing but rubble. Aachen was completely deserted except for a handful of pitiful looking civilians wandering aimlessly about in the ruins.

From Aachen Brazelton and his party traveled on the Autobahn and drove 18 miles, crossing a pontoon bridge over the Roer River to the village of Duren. On the way they saw not one building standing. In Duren, everything was completely destroyed except the statue of Bismarck in the central square. It was formerly facing east into Germany, but the concussion from bombs and shelling had turned it completely around, so that it faced west. From Duren they drove past large guns hurling shells at Cologne, eight miles away. There was German wreckage everywhere, countless German bodies, and dead animals that had been lying around for two or three days, as the war was moving too fast to allow time for burials. The trip concluded with the group's arrival at the headquarters of the 3rd Armored Division close to the Erft Canal.

Headquarters was a large, badly damaged castle. Brazelton toured the castle and noticed many pictures of high-ranking Nazi officers, one of which he took as a souvenir. In addition to the picture, Brazelton picked up two small cut crystals, several covered vases, and a Meissen figurine.[3] Then Brazelton and the members of the press corps had a steak dinner with the officers of the 3rd Armored Division. Afterwards a major asked if they would like to see a prisoner-of-war cage.

What a sight it was. It was just a big barnyard with chickens, cows, horses, and geese running wild and all intermingled with hundreds of Nazis, lots of civilians, captured members of the Volksturm (People's Army), and many American interrogators, military police, and officers. Right behind the barn the big guns were booming, and shaking the ground every few seconds. The press corps asked many questions and found the answers most interesting. The local leader of the Volksturm, who was about 60 years old and quite fat, was asked why he joined the Volkstrum. He answered that he did it for business reasons, so that the local citizens would purchase his merchandise. Then he was asked why his unit did not fight when the U.S. Army approached, and he said they figured that if the German Wehrmacht could not stop the army, they certainly could not. They had therefore surrendered their village without firing a shot.

One German sergeant volunteered his story and said his mother was living in London and his father in New York — that World War I had interfered and they had never married. He further stated that Germany was a mess internally, that transportation was almost nil, there was no food, and that German soldiers were beginning to desert. Two captured medical aid men, when told that they could return to their own lines (according to the Geneva Convention), refused to return. Many of the prisoners seemed to be scared to death and jumped every time the guns fired, while others were happy to be prisoners and seemed anxious to give information in order to help the advancing Americans.

Leaving the camp, the major took Brazelton and his group up to the front line, which was right at the Erft Canal. Here the 3rd Armored Division was attempting to throw a bridge across the canal near Bergheim, where ancient gates stood astride the road to Cologne. The road they should have taken had just been shelled by the Germans. So they took an alternative route and after about two miles arrived at a destroyed house with an American tank sitting in its shadow. Someone in the house yelled for them to leave the jeeps quickly and get into the house's cellar. They followed these instructions and found the members of the tank crew inside. The crew had been stopped by machine-gun fire from about 50 yards away. Brazelton and the reporters waited for the fire to die down and then, as the drivers turned around the jeeps, crawled along the ground and returned to the jeeps, which took off as fast as they could. Brazelton wrote: "I wasn't a bit nervous — still couldn't believe the Germans so close — but one of the correspondents, a young lady about 30, was scared to death."[4] Then they arrived at the village of Bergheim, which had been taken while they were enjoying their lunch.

That was Brazelton's total exposure to combat. Although many other war correspondents would work in close proximity to the front-line troops, he did not. Despite the fact that this was his one and only visit to the front lines, Brazelton was later awarded five campaign stars. His party then returned to the safety of Spa, Belgium, in time for dinner, as indeed it had been a difficult day. He wrote: "It was indeed the most interesting experience I have ever had."

Three days later, on March 3, 1945, the souvenir vases, crystal, and Meissen from Brazelton's visit to Germany were placed in a big wooden box to be mailed to his mother, Mrs. T. Berry Brazelton, Palm Court, Waco, Texas. He wrote his mother that he had salvaged these items from the wreckage of a chateau and that the crystal vases would look nice on her dressing table. He added that the little Meissen figurine was slightly broken, but fine in every detail.

That same day Brazelton wrote to "Dearest Mother":

> One [letter] said the box of perfume and so forth had arrived.... It is always a relief to hear that things arrive safely. Hope the luck keeps up. Were the lipsticks and powder colors you could use? I doubt they were the ones you usually get but I had to guess. The cream in the blue jar is to use before applying the makeup. Tell me exactly which of these things you like and if they are the right colors, if not what would you like so when I go back to Paris, I can get you some more.... I think you will enjoy using it when you go out in the afternoon or evening. It is all black except for the monogram, which is in royal blue. All the ladies use them in Paris. I hope you will enjoy it.... Someone brought the last part of your Mother's Day present from Brussels today and I shall mail it tomorrow. It came out more beautiful than I expected and I am very happy about it.... Open it when all three boxes arrive. Two boxes I mailed last week and they are rather small flat boxes.... I hope you will like them. I certainly send them with lots of love. Had a wonderful mineral bath and rubdown today which made me feel fine.

In addition Brazelton wrote that he was sending home a fine bottle of cognac, a gift of friends from Paris; a little enamel snuff or trinket box that a lady had given him; a little book, *Long, Long Ago*, by Alexander Woolcott; and a can of paté de foie gras and lobster that he thought his mother might enjoy.[5]

This enjoyment was to be had during the deadliest war ever with an estimated death toll of 62 to 78 million, which included 250,000 American soldiers. Indeed, as Churchill Brazelton concluded one of his letters, "So you see I am not living a bad life."

On March 18, 1945, the press corps moved into Germany, following the advance of Allied forces. Brazelton's press camp formed the nucleus of an assembly of some 200 correspondents from Europe and America; his job was liaison and censorship. Among the war correspondents he worked with was Bill Downs of CBS. Downs had been hired by Edward R. Murrow and was known as Murrow's boy; this gained him entry into the inner circle of reporters. Murrow was head of CBS in Europe and his honesty was renowned. Another, Gordon Frazer, was the first correspondent to make a radio broadcast while crossing the Rhine River, and John McVane, of NBC, made many broadcasts while with the fighting forces in Germany. When these delayed broadcasts were taped, Brazelton was in the room with the reporters to ensure that there were no security violations. One of the stars was *New York Times* reporter Gladwin Hill. Born in Boston in 1914, Hill graduated from the Phillips Academy in Andover, Massachusetts. After graduating from Harvard, he was hired by the Associated Press, where he won coveted assignments as a columnist and a writer of features, roaming from coast to coast in search of material. In 1942 he was sent by the AP to London as a war correspondent. For two years he covered the Allied air campaign against Germany alongside his arch competitor Walter Cronkite, who was then with the United Press. Tall, handsome, a natty dresser and possessed of a deep, resonant voice, Hill stood out even in the august company of the journalists gathered in Germany. But it was his aggressive reporting that attracted the most notice. He became the first reporter to fly aboard an American bomber on a raid into Germany, and he witnessed the Allied invasion of France in 1944 from another bomber. Brazelton noted to his mother that there were several very attractive women among the correspondents, which helped considerably toward making things cheery.

The day Brazelton's press unit moved into Germany he had only army rations, but as he wrote, his mother's package of sardines, mackerel, turkey spread, fruitcake, and so on had arrived, so he had a fine lunch. On this day Brazelton wrote to his mother:

> The army always treats the correspondents like kings and working with them we are able to benefit quite often in ways that would not come to the ordinary army man. Usually they demand comfortable quarters and get them when the rest of the army headquarters is sleeping in tents. This is the worst place they have ever had so I imagine they will complain and perhaps soon we will move to another nice chateau.
>
> The last one was very nice but had been wrecked by the hordes of Americans who had stayed there from time to time. However this is Germany and the

way these men hate the Germans no one gives a darn what happens to anything they own. After the horror and destruction they have thrown to the rest of the world they deserve and will get no sympathy. Nothing we can ever do will repay them for all they have done. If by chance you really do feel sorry for the Germans as knowing your sympathetic feelings, I imagine you do, forget them. These people hate us and would have ... willingly done to our country what they have done to Europe. As anyone who has fought the Germans or has ever had any dealing with them knows, the only good Jerry is a dead one.[6]

Brazelton was echoing the sentiment of all Americans at that time, as the rallying cry was "The only good German is a dead German."

Brazelton's press unit's biggest problem in their new quarters was the lack of hot water. Apparently the army knew of the correspondents' demand for comfortable quarters, as a few days later they were housed in the fine 19th-century Ringhotel Rheinhotel Dreesen, situated along one of the most beautiful parts of the Rhine River in Bad Godesberg on the outskirts of Bonn. From this hotel Brazelton sent a little pottery vase from Hitler's bedroom as a souvenir and wrote to his mother that he had several [unreadable word] of odds and ends to send and would send them as soon as he could find boxes to pack them in, as getting wooden boxes was most difficult. Apparently Brazelton's souvenir collection was accumulating as a few days later he sent a large crate by commercial freight and told his mother that it would take several months to arrive. He advised her that he had paid the freight to New York and that when she was contacted to pay from New York to Waco, he would repay her. What could have been in this large crate?

In a letter dated April 13, 1945, Brazelton described a recent mailing of a package with a set of small good fruit glasses of different colors bearing the Prussian coat of arms that he had found in a Nazi headquarters, a brass eagle off the top of a flagpole at Nazi headquarters in Duren, several pieces of fine 17th- and 18th-century glass, nine bottles of good Rhine wine, a book, and other things. "Oh yes, I sent rather nice oil painting — a small oval portrait of a lady. You asked for two small figures for the little shelves so I found two in a wrecked home and confiscated them."[7]

Two days later, on April 15, the First Army Press Unit transferred across the Rhine River into the lovely resort town of Bad Wildungen, completely untouched by the war. It was here that Gen. Omar Bradley established headquarters for his Twelfth Army Group, the largest single military force ever assembled by the United States. Brazelton and his press corps moved into one of the finer hotels with hot and cold running water. He remained in Bad Wildungen alone, as the war reporters moved out to be closer to the action on the front lines. But of course they had to file their stories with Brazelton before they could be forwarded to their home papers for publication in the United States.

It was here at Bad Wildungen that Brazelton, in a letter dated May 3, described some items his mother had been sent:

> The jugs are typically German.... The pair were made at Frechen on the outskirts of Cologne in 1570. The blue one with the pewter top is early 18th century. The pair may make attractive lamps. As for the glass, it is very early Roman glassware and has a great deal of value, I imagine.... The little wooden blocks were the stands for the three pieces.... They were in perfect condition when I found them. I am proud of these five pieces so take good care of them for me. Do not wash them or handle them very much as the crust on the outside will come off. The crust comes from being buried for about 2000 years.

Brazelton's mother also asked about a fur rug; Brazelton responded that he had taken one from the library of a fine Nazi home in Cologne and he imagined it to be wolf or bear or something like that. He also stated that a Mr. Parma had sent him a letter asking that he send him a wooden box of antiques for his living-room coffee table.[8]

With the war winding down and the correspondents at the front lines, Brazelton was just sitting around with very little to do; but May 5, 1945, would be the highlight of his World War II experience and a day that he would never forget.

That morning Gen. Omar Bradley and his staff left from nearby Fritzlar, the American airfield, and flew to Leipzig in two C-47s. Earlier that morning Brazelton and his staff started in a long convoy to meet with the general about 10 miles from the Elbe River, a distance of about 200 miles. They had been invited by Soviet Marshal Ivan Stepanovich Konev, commanding general of the Ukrainian Army Group, to a celebration banquet. It was a great thrill for Brazelton to ride in the convoy with armored cars leading and following them. They joined Bradley's party about 10 miles from Torgau, where both sides of the road were lined with hundreds of American soldier honor guards as far as eye could see. About a mile from the Elbe River the Soviet honor guards were lined up, all in colorful dress uniforms. As the convoy passed, the guards came to attention with a snap that could be heard over the roar of the motors. Behind the honor guards were thousands and thousands of Soviet soldiers in grimy uniforms lining the road and all smiling, waving, and saluting.

At the Elbe River an armed escort was waiting, consisting of motorcycles and cars, all covered with branches and garlands of fresh flowers, which also covered the temporary bridge thrown across the river. Next to this bridge was another under construction. Brazelton noticed that the Soviets were cutting down trees and taking the logs and cut timber to the river to construct a more substantial bridge. Except for a crudely fashioned steam engine on a pile driver, their methods of construction were the same as they had been for hundreds of years. Using this technique, they did not have the problem of transporting tons of steel, and the construction process did not seem to bother the Russians.

On the far side of the Elbe River Soviet banners had been draped along with brightly lettered welcome signs and three large lithographs of Roosevelt, Churchill, and Stalin. As they were leaving the bridge, a Russian riding a bicycle along the side of the road cut right in front of Brazelton's jeep. Traveling rather fast, there was no way to avoid hitting him. On impact, the Russian flew up and hit the windshield, smashing it hard, bending the whole thing back, and injuring the correspondent in the front seat beside the driver. The Russian, a young fellow, was still living when Brazelton walked back to check on him, but he could not have lived more than a few minutes, as he was a horrible sight to see.

The accident damaged the jeep badly enough that it could not keep up with the convoy and had to drop back. They got lost on the wrong road for about an hour, trying to return to the proper road. Brazelton finally found a Soviet officer in a jeep who spoke French and said for the Americans to follow him. As they rounded a corner, a Soviet truck sideswiped the officer, wrecking his jeep. The driver of Brazelton's jeep had to take to the ditch to avoid smashing into the truck. Still lost with no one to ask for instructions and in a very cold blinding rain, they drove around aimlessly, freezing with the missing windshield. Two Soviet soldiers then stepped in front of the jeep and, as the jeep slid to a stop, its bumper touched one of the soldiers. By that time they were all "fit to be tied" and the driver was shaking so badly that he could hardly hold the wheel.

While they were lost they observed that the real Soviet Army consisted of every imaginable vehicle that could move, including horse-drawn farm wagons, which were the primary mode of transportation. Brazelton, like most Americans, did not realize that the highly mechanized German Army was actually 80 percent horse-drawn. Thus the Soviet Army was comparable to the German Army in the utilization of horses. The expensive German automobiles captured by the Soviets had their original paint jobs, unlike the cars captured by U.S. forces, which were painted olive drab. There were also many women soldiers among the Soviet troops.

At last Brazelton and his group found their way back to the main road, which was easily identified with many flags and guards. At all the crossroads were women military police, who looked very attractive and were extremely efficient. A motorcycle escort finally picked up Brazelton's party and led them to Marshall Konev's headquarters, which were in a beautiful German castle. A red carpet ran from the drive to the door of the castle, which had flags, garlands of flowers, and large portraits of Stalin, Churchill, and Roosevelt hanging from its walls. The Soviet officers were all in their brilliantly colored dress uniforms, covered with medals and wearing highly polished boots. The Americans in their field clothes looked distressingly plain in comparison.

The luncheon was undoubtedly the most lavish ever, as it consisted of 12 courses, each containing as many as 10 different dishes. All of the food had been brought from Russia. There was black bread, cucumbers, fresh caviar, sardines, salmon, steaks, roast beef, chicken cooked four different ways, lamb, pork, and various cold meats. All of this was cooked to perfection and washed down with the finest wines and champagnes plus the inevitable Russian vodka. Everything was served in beautiful china, crystal, and silver, undoubtedly all looted from the better homes in Germany.

Brazelton was not impressed with the Russians' table manners, as they reached across the table and speared with their forks any food they wanted. Women soldiers were waiting on the tables, and there was one for every five men, so as soon as a dish emptied, a full one immediately took its place. There were numerous toasts, during which the only point of etiquette was that each glass had to be emptied in one gulp. After a few of these, the language barrier disappeared and Brazelton also began to fork his food from a distance. Everyone smiled and slapped one another on the back. They all exchanged insignias and Brazelton's uniform began to look like that of a Russian officer.

After lunch Marshall Konev had arranged for a wonderful show in the ballroom of the castle. It began with the singing of the "Star-Spangled Banner," sung by a male chorus who spoke no English and had memorized every word. Brazelton had never heard it sung more perfectly. It was followed by numerous male and female dancers and singers. The performers for the two-hour show had been especially picked by Konev to perform for Gen. Bradley.[9]

Afterwards Konev and Bradley walked out into the garden and a Russian orderly led out a stallion whose army blanket bore a red star. Konev handed Bradley the bridle and a handsomely carved Russian pistol. Anticipating the exchange, Bradley gave Konev a new American jeep with an attached holster holding a highly polished new carbine rifle. Bradley then presented Konev with the 12th Army Group banner, which had been carried since D-Day.[10]

After more cheering, saluting, and shaking of hands, the party was over and the Americans reluctantly left their host. It appears that Bradley's Russian horse was turned over to Col. Fred L. Hamilton, chief of the U.S. Army Remount Branch, and shipped to the United States on the troop transport *Stephen Austin*, arriving at Newport News in October 1945. The horse was then shipped by rail to Front Royal, Virginia, the army's veterinarian center and breeding station.

Brazelton returned to Bad Wildungen and a few days later was transferred

On May 11, 1945, Supreme Allied Commander General Dwight D. Eisenhower poses with the U.S. Twelfth Army Group officers at Bad Wildungen, Germany. Left to right (front row) Lieutenant General William H. Simpson, U.S. Ninth Army; General George Patton, Third Army; General Carl A. Spaatz, U.S. Tactical Air Force, General Eisenhower, General Omar Bradley, Twelfth Army Group; General Courtney H. Hodges, First Army; General Leonard T. Gerow, Fifteenth Army; (back row) Brigadier General Ralph P. Sterling, Ninth Tactical Air Command; Lieutenant General Hoyt S. Vandenberg, Ninth Air Force; Lieutenant General W. B. Smith, General Eisenhower's Chief of Staff; Major General Ralph P. Weyland, Nineteenth Tactical Air Command; Brigadier General Richard E. Nugent, Twenty-ninth Tactical Air Command (courtesy National Archives).

125 miles west to Weimar, Germany. By now the war was over and Brazelton and the First Army were in the designated Soviet Occupation Zone of Germany. Here he quickly mailed home two packages and noted that books in the second box contained a series of very beautiful pictures of Spain, concluding that he was pleased his mother had liked the luncheon set so much. Then in his only undated letter, written between June 8 and 20, 1945, he wrote that he had gotten, for $6, a wonderful set of dueling pistols made in 1720. "Will tell you about the best later." Strangely enough the bottom half of the next letter, typewritten, was carefully removed with a pair of scissors. Who had cut that letter in two and what did the missing half contain? Could this have been about "the best"? What was "the best"? Did it concern the missing 13 paintings?

Churchill Brazelton was present when General Bradley received this horse from Marshal Ivan Stepanovich Konev, commanding general of the Soviets' Ukrainian Army Group. At Bad Wildungen, General Eisenhower looks over the horse given to General Omar Bradley. The generals appear bewildered (courtesy National Archives).

While Brazelton was in Weimar, Dr. Walter Scheidig enabled him to purchase something Brazelton had always secretly dreamed of but never thought he would own: a Gobelin tapestry. This tapestry, in absolutely perfect condition, was 11 feet 3 inches (3.43 meters) wide and 14 feet 7 inches (4.45 meters) long. It was originally one of a set of six, each representing two months of the year. This one represented September and October. The fineness of a tapestry depended to a great extent on its borders, and this one had the finest of borders. As described by Brazelton, it was the finest tapestry of its period that he had ever seen "in or out of a museum."

The border was very wide and depicted fruits, flowers, bows, and sheafs of arrows as well as animals and many others objects. The center contained a woodland scene with people harvesting crops, picking cherries, and tending to animals. Another area showed a village with hunters chasing an animal and many other activities. On the bottom were woven the initials BVB and M.D. Vos, which indicated that the tapestry had been made by Master Craftsman Marcus de Vos in Brussels, who worked from 1655 to 1690.[11]

Now Brazelton was of the very few people to own a tapestry by de Vos.

His ownership put him in the ranks of the king of Sweden and other royal families of Europe. To carry his new possession (with an estimated value of $3,000 in 1945), he had a man in Weimar make a wooden box fitted with a padlock. The box was large — the size of an army footlocker.

During this time Dr. Scheidig gave Brazelton a woodcut of a tiger attacking a zebra. The woodcarving had been done by one of Germany's finest engravers of animals. Scheidig also gave Brazelton two enameled boxes, one of which was French, from about 1770 and the other a Dutch brass and copper snuffbox of the period 1720 to 1730. The pistols that Brazelton mentioned in his affidavit as having been obtained from Dr. Scheidig are described as two dueling pistols circa 1700 that he "was crazy about." They had walnut inserts with brass, and he intended, someday, to hang them in a crossed fashion.[12] He wrote about these items again in a seven-page letter on July 20, 1945, to his mother.

Then he picked up an 18th-century Italian woodcarving of two cupids' heads, painted and gilded. He had found it in a battered castle in western Germany. It was a fine piece of work and he mailed it home and to see what his mother would think about this acquisition. To justify his theft, he wrote: "It was probably stolen in Italy and sent home by some Nazi officer." In his following letter, he wrote: "Dr. Scheidig, the Director of the Museum and the man who arranged for the purchase of my tapestry gave me a very nice woodcut of a tiger attacking a zebra."

The plan was for Weimar to be turned over to the Soviets, and Brazelton, along with correspondents from 15 different countries, was anxiously awaiting transfer to Berlin. On July 4, 1945, Brazelton was transferred to Berlin and participated in the Allies' triumphal entry into the Soviet-controlled city. One month later, through a persuasive crusade on his part, the press liaison job ended and Brazelton returned to Paris, where he worked for the army's Visitors' Bureau, entertaining generals, congressmen, and other VIPs. He remained in Paris until April 29, 1946, when he returned to the United States and was discharged from the army at Fort Dix, New Jersey. He carried his treasured Gobelin tapestry with him on his return.

In the postwar era, Brazelton returned to Paris and worked for three years with Morgan Bank and then with the American Embassy for two years as an economic analyst. He returned to the United States and opened an antique shop in New Orleans. A few years later, he moved to New York City, where he lived on 54th Street and opened an antique and art business on Madison Avenue. A lifelong bachelor, Brazelton devoted most of his time and energy to building up one of the most outstanding collections of 17th- and 18th-century French furniture in the United States.[13]

Who took the 13 paintings from the Schwarzburg Castle? Paul N. Estes' lieutenants were by now successful businessmen: Clinton R. Walters, the president of Alamo Steel; John S. Gwynn, partner in the law firm of Oven & Gwynn; and Cecil A. Wooten, vice president of Chicago Bridge and Iron. They all stuck by Estes' story of having never met Dr. Scheidig. The former army officers had no reason to perjure themselves. Dr. Scheidig, on the other hand, had immediately started to try to recover the missing paintings and wrote down the details in 1945. Had Scheidig been duped? Did he meet someone masquerading as Capt. Paul N. Estes? Was Scheidig in cahoots with someone to make money on the paintings and was his investigation just a red herring? Did Brazelton and Scheidig set out to bamboozle the Weimar Museum?

Brazelton was in Weimar when the paintings were stolen. He arrived in New York in the spring of 1946, when Edward I. Elicofon purchased two of the missing paintings. Brazelton knew the value of the paintings and we know that he was not averse to stealing art items of great value.

Chapter 17

The Nun and the Poster

In June 1998, Sister Rose Mary Phol, a former art teacher at the now-defunct St. John's Mater Christi Roman Catholic School in Astoria, Queens, New York City, took a painting to Frank J. Vaccaro, a furniture restorer in Rockville Centre, Long Island. The painting had been given to her by Msgr. Thomas Campbell, a native New Yorker who grew up during the Depression and was ordained in 1943. The monsignor claimed the painting came into his possession in 1972; he guessed that a parishioner might have given it to him. Sister Phol found the painting dark and kind of depressing but the gold frame around it was beautiful, so she promptly pasted a magazine print of the Blessed Mother over it and hung it in her bedroom. It was there for more than 26 years.

When the Long Island furniture restorer picked up the 8½- by 11-inch wooden frame in his shop and started to remove the magazine print that had been glued to it, he made an unusual discovery: he saw a pair of eyes looking back at him, covered in black paint. Peeling off the page, he found a nose and suddenly realized that he was looking at the painting *Bust of Christ*, painted in the 16th century by the Venetian artist Jacopo de' Barbari. The $5 million painting was one of fewer than two dozen of Barbari's known works and was considered a critical link between the Italian and Northern Renaissance schools. The fate of this missing masterpiece had been a mystery ever since its disappearance in the summer of 1945 from Schwarzburg Castle.

Recognizing that the picture might be valuable, he returned only the gold frame, telling Sister Phol that he had discarded the poster. He then traced the painting's provenance to Weimar and contacted the museum, identifying himself as a journalist or researcher interested in works by Barbari. A museum official told him about the looting of the museum's collection after the war.

On August 2, 1999, Vaccaro called again, telling the museum's director that he had possession of the Barbari painting and offering to return it for $100,000. In describing how he had found the painting, which he had had for about a year, Vaccaro did not say how he had obtained it. Dr. Ralph

Bothe, the director, said that this price was too high for a finder's fee and offered $50,000. The museum had caller ID and made a note of Vaccaro's phone number.

The following day, in the first of several conversations that were secretly recorded, Vaccaro described how he had discovered the painting, peeling away the print and cleaning off the black paint. "All of a sudden, I saw two eyes and then a nose, and then I realized it was a painting of Jesus," a transcript quotes him as saying. Vaccaro continued to insist on payment.

In one conversation on August 31, Vaccaro acknowledged that the painting belonged to the museum. "It doesn't belong to me," he said. But he also made clear that he believed himself to be "entitled to something after saving this painting." He added at one point, "I've stared at this painting night after night because it's so beautiful."

Dr. Bothe hired Thomas Klein, a Washington, D.C., lawyer, who contacted the U.S. Customs Service, which was more than willing to take an active role in retrieving the missing painting. Klein furnished the customs agents with Vaccaro's phone number and they taped a number of conversations between Vaccaro and the Weimar Museum officials.

Customs agent Bonnie Goldblatt, posing as a representative of the Weimar Museum, told Vaccaro that she wanted to pay the finder's fee and collect the painting for the Weimar Museum. She then traveled to the restoration shop on Long Island and asked for the painting. Vaccaro climbed onto a filing cabinet and pushed up a tile on the ceiling of his shop; then he took down the painting. As Vaccaro was waiting for payment from Agent Goldblatt, she presented him with her customs badge and stated the museum's position, which was that the painting was stolen property, that it belonged to the museum, and that they would not pay for its return. Thus on November 8, 1999, the painting was seized and then the furniture restorer from Long Island was arrested. He was charged with one count of possessing and trying to sell a stolen artwork.

That same Monday night Vaccaro was released on $10,000 bond by a federal magistrate judge in Manhattan. Michael Handwerker, his lawyer, said: "It was not, and is not, his intention to harm anyone. He acted in good faith and we're going to try to dispose of the matter." Apparently the lawyer's statement was acceptable, as Vaccaro was sentenced only to community service. Later the charges were completely dropped.

A year later, on December 6, 2000, the painting was displayed in the U.S. Customs House in New York while German authorities signed the customs documents and the painting was turned over to them. Rose Mary Phol, when she met with the German officials to return the frame (which she carried in a shopping bag), laughingly said "So much for my art expertise." Smudges of glue that Phol had used to secure the magazine print were visible on the black background of the haunting portrait. "Being a bureaucrat, I need a receipt," said Customs Commissioner Raymond W. Kelly, turning over the magazine-sized oil-on-wood painting to Dr. Thomas Foehl, vice director of the Kunstsammlungen Museum in Weimar.

The painting was flown back to the Kunstsammlungen zu Weimar that afternoon in a special wooden briefcase-box carried by Thomas Foehl, surrounded by armed guards. "This is like Christmas was to me as a young boy," Foehl said.[1]

Among the 13 works taken from the Schwarzburg Castle were the two 15th-century oil-on-wood panels titled *Hans Tucher and Felicitas* by Albrecht Dürer. Those two were recovered from Edward I. Elicofon. In July 1995, another missing painting, Johann Heinrich Tischbein's *Portrait of Lady Elizabeth Hervey*, was offered at auction by Sotheby's. It had been traced back to 1964 in the shop of an art dealer in New York's Upper East Side. The painting was sold several times and later presented to Sotheby's and auctioned off to an unnamed couple from St. Louis. Christopher Apostle, a specialist in Sotheby's Old Masters department, noticed the missing painting during research routinely done before a sale. Comparing its uniform pattern of cracks in old paint to that of the Weimar Museum's missing Tischbein, he ascertained that they were one and the same. Apostle alerted his colleagues and the Weimar Art Museum. The painting was returned to Germany in February 1997. Thus with the recovery of Jacopo de' Barbari's *Bust of Christ*, four paintings had been recovered. The Lucas Cranach, *Venus with Cupid, Pursued by Bees*, found its way into Yale University's art collection in the early 1970s and was eventually sold to a private Swiss collector. Then the trail goes cold.

Still, nine paintings also believed to have been stolen by American troops remain missing (see Appendix C). After extensive research and reviewing what others have found, the author is still no nearer to finding the person or persons who stole the paintings from the Schwarzburg Castle. A missing piece of this puzzle has a New York City connection.

Sister Rose Mary Phol died on September 5, 2006.

Part V
Vignettes of Looting

Chapter 18
The Gravediggers Pillage Reutti, Germany

On April 5, 1945, the 4460 Quartermaster Service Company arrived in France. Their principal function was the collection and burial of the battlefield dead. The first Americans had arrived in France on June 6, 1944, and from there had fiercely fought their way across France and into the heart of Germany. By the time the 4460 arrived, the fighting and dying for the most part was finished. From France they continued on their journey to Bensheim, Germany.

On April 26, the unit moved south 150 miles to the small village of Reutti, about 3 miles from Neu Ulm, Germany. The unit consisting of four officers and approximately 212 enlisted men who were attached to the 46th Quartermaster Graves Registration Company. The 46th's function was to supervise the burial of the dead. They also recorded and marked the gravesites and disposed of the personal effects of the deceased. Because of its topographical features and close proximity to the battlefield, the 46th Quartermaster Graves Registration Company had chosen Reutti as the site for an American cemetery. At that time the local battlefields were relatively free from extreme danger and the men of the 4460th traveled to various regimental collection points and picked up the soldiers who had been pronounced dead and so tagged by the medical corps. Every effort was made to identify the dead. If the identification tags were attached to the body, it was a comparatively simple procedure. Otherwise it was necessary to search the body for personal letters, take fingerprints, or compare dental work. Six bodies at a time were removed from the collection points by 2½-ton trucks with trailers and taken to Reutti, where they were buried immediately in order to prevent disease and also to maintain morale among the American troops. The actual gravedigging was done by German prisoners of war.[1]

Three years prior to capture of Ruetti by the Americans, Bernhard V. Limburger had purchased a house there in order to protect his family from the constant Allied bombings and also to safeguard the art collections acquired by his father and grandfather many decades earlier. These collections of furniture, oil paintings, oriental rugs, china, cut glass, silver and other objects of art, coins, and so on were most valuable. Other members of his family, numerous friends and even public institutions like the Museum of Ulm, sent their most valued art and other treasures to Limburger's home for safekeeping. In April 1945, it contained more things of value than most museums.[2]

On April 27, 1945, the 4460th arrived in Reutti, and at 2:30 in the afternoon Lt. Francis C. Elko told Mrs. Bernhard V. Limburger that her house was to be taken for military purposes. He told her that she had two hours to clear out and find a place where they could stay and take their personal belongings. Of course most of the time allotted to her and the two other families living in the house was taken up with finding new quarters and looking after the babies; as a result, very few things could be removed. The women were, however, told that they might return the next day to bring out some more things.

The following morning, when they arrived on the scene, the women were appalled to see a bonfire ablaze in the yard, fed by things of great value, such as priceless books of the 15th to 18th centuries. They immediately protested to the commanding officer who was headquartered at the castle in Reutti. He kindly promised to put a stop to such and other damage to the Limburger property. Nevertheless, this bonfire was seen to burn for another full week, being fed not only by a beautiful 18th-century cupboard and other objects of art but also clothing and items that were irreplaceable in Germany under wartime conditions. At the same time antiques and other furniture that, in the opinion of the Lt. Elko, were superfluous were thrown into a pile in a nearby barn.

On Sunday, April 29, Mrs. Limburger, Mayor Schaible, and several local farmers were allowed to remove many valuable art objects from the Limburger home. They stored them in a nearby locked building. This was a fruitless effort, as the building was immediately broken into and the contents sacked or destroyed. Following this incident, on May 5, the local policeman Mr. Frank and Mrs. Limburger, using a wagon and two horses, managed to move to safety many valuables that belonged to the Municipal Museum of Ulm.[3]

During the next week or so, every trunk, packing case, and piece of furniture in the Limburger home was ransacked. Although every single key for these things had been demanded by and given to Lt. Elko personally, who was at this time alone in charge, not one key was used but every piece was opened by the force of a hammer, chisel, saw, or knife, thereby doing irreparable damage to old mahogany, walnut, and other furniture that had been cared for and treasured for centuries. When permission was finally granted to remove the furniture and trunks from the house, the most valuable things had already been removed by the Americas.

A few days later, Dr. Limburger, having returned from a trip, immediately sought an interview with Capt. Francis E. Ewing, the commanding officer of the 4460th. Ewing dismissed Limburger's protests, saying that he had no reason to complain as he still had a roof over his head, which was more than could be said of most Germans, and that the Nazis had done the same things in occupied territories. Limburger answered that it seemed illogical to condemn a deed when done by the Germans and to approve it when done by the U.S. Army. Capt. Ewing then gave his word that, apart from the damage done before his arrival, he would see to it that nothing was taken from the house when Lt. Elko's platoon left.

After this conversation, Limburger was more than astonished when, a few days later, he saw a soldier in the yard putting extremely costly old china into a packing case while another was just closing the lid on an oriental rug. He immediately went to Lt. Elko and asked him to put a stop to the packing of his things. Elko refused, saying that that was unnecessary, as nobody would be allowed to send anything away. The next day Capt. Ewing complained that Limburger had hurt his feelings by even suggesting that American soldiers would take away anything not belonging to them. He emphasized that he had given his word as an American officer that nothing would be taken away.

On June 1, 1945, Limburger and his wife were allowed to inspect his house, which had been vacated by the 4460th but was still being used to house other American soldiers. As they went from room to room, Limburger and his wife compiled the following inventory of missing items:

1. Everything made of silver that they had not been allowed to remove from the house.
2. All antique and most modern china, cut glass, and Venetian glass.
3. Two stamp collections belonging to an aunt, worth over $30,000.
4. All table and bed linen.
5. All watches and nearly all clocks — among the latter museum pieces of great value.
6. Nearly all of the blankets, quilts, cushions, and curtains.
7. A whole case full of family miniatures, some of them of ancestors dating as far back as 1617.
8. Pictures, old Renaissance velvets, precious silks, a collection of antique and other coins, and countless objects of art.
9. Practically everything of any value in the way of clothes, underwear, stockings and shoes.

10. Every drop of wine and liquor — a few hundred bottles in the cellar were missing, but the whole estate was strewn with empty bottles.[4]

Also missing were 400 drawings and watercolors plus sculpture and furniture from the Ulm Museum. In one room was a packing case with a painting of great value that had been used as packing material for an antique mirror. The wooden packing case had been cut from the famous 16th-century wooden cabinets from the Ulm Museum.

The container had a label affixed to it marked "Passed by Censor." P.F.C. W. H. Murry had left this now valueless case stenciled with his military address as well as the name of the addressee:

> Mrs. Jenny E. Murry
> 953 Gloss Street
> Franklin, Tennessee[5]

Dr. Limburger wrote: "Considering the high code of honor I have always believed to exist in the American Army, it seems inconceivable that such acts are approved of in responsible quarters. Should I be right in this assumption and the matter be taken up, the chances of recovering at least some of the things now missing would be greater the sooner action was taken."[6]

Reutti was just one of 12 American cemeteries then located in Germany. On June 2, 1945, the 4460th left Reutti on the backs of 2½-ton trucks. As they were leaving, Limburger noticed that the troops were sitting on rugs and wrapped in blankets taken from homes in Reutti. They were being transferred to the Philippine Islands to continue the war against Japan. Their short stay in Europe was due to U.S. military strategy. The last units shipped to Europe were designated as the first to be removed and sent to the South Pacific. Several combat infantry division were shipped out with the 4460th, their mission being to "kill Japs." The objective of the 4460th would be to bury the American war dead from among the one million casualities expected as a result of the planned invasion of the Japanese homelands.

Hardened by daily contact with death and looking forward to a future apocalypse, these officers could not care less about the protection of valuable art objects. As noted in the history of one graves registration company, "those were the days when the thought most frequently spoken was 'How's looting?'"[7]

On July 17, 1945, the 4460th departed Calais aboard the U.S. Army Transport *Brazil* and arrived in Lingayen, Philippine Islands, on August 26, 1945. While in the Philippine and questioned about his role in Reutti, Capt. Francis E. Ewing denied any wrongdoing and stated that under the stress of wartime conditions he did his best to protect the rights and property of the German people. Ewing wrote:

To me, who is fairly acquainted with Mr. Limburger, he is just another suave, shrinking, pious, non-party, pro–American who caused some 10,000,000 American men and women to waste four or five years of their lives at war, some of whom are buried in one of his fields today, and he complained to me that we were using up his fields today, and he complained to me that we were using up all the ground that he had to raise crops on just to bury people.[8]

Ewing's reasoning was the same as that of most Americans in 1945. At that time and on this same theme, the American soldiers buried in Germany were being disinterred and reburied in Allied countries. Today, no American soldiers are buried in Germany.

On August 21, 1945, Monuments, Fine Arts, and Archives (MFAA) Officer James J. Rorimer investigated the outrageous acts of thievery in Reutti. He reported that 134 drawings belonging to the Ulm Museum were clearly damaged by being walked on by American rubber-heeled boots. And Rorimer noticed several more packing crates that had been prepared for shipment. He remembered one of the cases, packed by P.F.C. John Amaker, because the address was his hometown. It was addressed to

Mrs. Arrie Amaker
231 W. 140th St.
New York 30 New York[9]

In his book *Survival*, Rorimer wrote: "There is one such case, which should be made a matter of public knowledge. In 1945, a thick dossier was forwarded to highest American headquarters. It had the approval of our commanding general, or at least of his chief of staff, and the recommendation [was] that this case be returned to the United States for further investigation."[10]

In keeping with the times, Rorimer wrote the incident up in an anonymous way without revealing the individual names or that the 4460th was involved.

Chapter 19
The U.N. Red Cross Robbery

In March 1941, the mayor of Munich rented the dungeon room of the Hohenaschau Castle for the purpose of storing the large art collection of the Städtische Galerie and Lenbachhaus Galerie. The first shipment of art from the gallery was sent there on April 8, 1941, and the remainder followed in May of the same year. The castle was the private property of Baron Cramer-Klett. He was a fantastically wealthy individual with vast industrial enterprises and agricultural lands. After he had purchased the Hohenaschau Castle and its associated property in the valley of the River Prien, Cramer-Klett financed the construction of a railway line that opened up the Prien valley to the main line from Munich to Salzburg.

As the war continued, the castle was sold to the German government and used as a naval rest center. On September 4, 1944, the rest center was dissolved and the castle used as a medical hospital for the German Navy. During this time the valuables of the Städtische Galerie had remained in the basement and the key to the large lock was in the custody of Hans Lebel, the director of the naval hospital, and later Stephanie, his wife, who remained at the castle and in charge when her husband was inducted into the Germany Army.[1]

After the American occupation, in August, the naval hospital was taken over by a U.S. medical unit stationed nearby in Fischbach near Rosenheim. The American medical unit's surgeon came to the castle each day to make sure that it was secure and managed in a proper medical manner. The security of the castle was assigned to Battery C of the 58th Armored Field Artillery. The keys to the castle and to the dungeon remained with Mrs. Lebel.

On August 31, 1945, James Shields, representing the United Nations Relief and Rehabilitation Administration (UNRRA), came to Hohenaschau Castle to see if it could be used to house the many war refugees in the immediate area. Shields, a British citizen, was accompanied by Zarko Pavlovich, a former captain of the Yugoslavian Army. On September 1 and upon the request of Pavlovich, Mrs. Lebel gave the keys to him in the presents of Fridolin Göser. Pavlovich promptly put the keys in his trouser pocket.

There is some confusion concerning the keys, but on September 11, 1945, when Shields and Pavlovich left the castle, the keys were in the possession of Sgt. Leno V. Bonat of Battery C, 58th Armored Field Artillery. On September 24, Battery C moved from the Hohenaschau Castle to Bad Aibling. The keys were then turned over to P.F.C. Delbert Ripley of the military government in Rosenheim. From October 3 to November 27, 1945, the castle was occupied by Company A, 1st Battalion, 39th Infantry Division. The commanding officer was a Lt. Stratton.[2]

On October 1, Lt. Jonathan Morey, MFAA officer of Bavaria, asked the acting director of the Lensbach Galerie to inventory the paintings stored in the basement of the Hohenaschau Castle. At the conclusion of this inventory it was established that the most valuable 116 paintings were missing. The last time these valuables had been inventoried was in December 1944 by a Mrs. Lüttgens, the restorer of the Lenbach Galerie.[3]

On or about October 28, 1945, two German employees working in the basement of the castle noticed that the door to the dungeon had been completely torn off its hinges. They immediately informed Sgt. Norman Edwards, who placed a guard in front of the door. The door and lock were replaced and the German locksmith made a new set of keys. The job of breaking down this massive door must have created a loud noise that would have been heard throughout the castle. It could not have escaped the attention of the guards or the soldiers sleeping in the castle. Because of the boisterous forced entry, the commanding officer of Company A, 1st Battalion, 39th Infantry Division, assumed that his men were looking for liquor and thought no more of the incident.

A bit later it was discovered that during the time of the forced entry a painting by Lenbach, *The Head of a Girl*, and three Gobelin tapestries were stolen. Unlike the prior theft of 116 paintings, this painting had been cut from the frame. Gobelins were favorite loot for the Americans, as they could easily be folded and placed into a mailbag. So could the missing cutout painting.

On October 20, 1946, the overworked Lt. Walter Horn began to investigate the missing paintings. On December 3, he questioned Pavlovich concerning his possession of the key to the dungeon. Pavlovich initially told Horn that he never had the key; but after being confronted by a sworn statement by Mrs. Lebel, he said, "I visited the room with the paintings with Mr. Shields. Mr. Shields turned to key over to Sgt. Bonat on September 11."[4] On this same day Shields declared that he had never had any keys in his possession, nor did he ever enter any room in the castle that contained any paintings.

The following day Horn had Pavlovich jailed and put in solitary confinement. After four days in a cold cell without food, the deteriorating Pavlovich — in bad health due to sciatica, nerves, and rheumatism — was again interrogated by Horn. He swore by a picture of Christ that he was innocent and declared that the inconsistencies of his statements with Mrs. Lebel and Mr. Shields were the results of a faulty memory. After a severe grilling and much doubt that he was telling the truth, Horn allowed Pavlovich to limp back to his job at the displaced persons camp because of his failing health.

It is most doubtful that the paintings disappeared before September 1, 1945, because the keys to the dungeon had been in the possession of Mrs. Lebel from October 28, 1944, until September 1, 1945, and both she and her husband were unanimously described as honest, reliable people. Also a Mr. Richard Blaul had stored a painting in the dungeon in 1943 and had checked on the paintings around the middle of July 1945. He had been in the room on several occasions and was familiar with the locations of the paintings. On his last visit during July, Blaul did not observe any changes in the arrangement of the Lensbach paintings; he was convinced that the paintings must have been stolen between mid–July and the inventory of October 1.

Because the paintings selected were the more valuable of the lot, Horn was convinced that it was a professional organized job and not the type of pillaging normally done by the occupying troops, as most of the items selected were too large to go into a mailbag. Not only that, but to move the entire lot would have required the use of a truck. Horn suspected that during his interrogation Pavlovich might also have been covering for James Shields. On September 4, 1946, the investigation by Lt. Walter Horn was closed for lack of evidence. Today 45 of the paintings are still missing, as are the three Gobelins. Horn's primary suspects were Zarko Pavlovich and James Shields, although Sgt. Leno V. Bonat was never ruled out.[5]

Chapter 20

The Rabbi's Egyptian Ring

After a British air raid on Berlin in 1940, Hitler ordered that three massive flak towers be constructed to defend the capital from air attack. The towers, known as Flakturms, were situated in Friedrichshain; in the Tiergarten (zoo) adjacent to the city's zoological gardens; and at Humboldthain. These massive towers, 15 feet thick and made of concrete reinforced with steel, were designed for antiaircraft defense and as civilian shelters, with room for 10,000 civilians and even a hospital ward inside. During the fall of Berlin, these above-ground towers formed their own communities, with up to 30,000 or more Berliners taking refuge in each tower in the midst of the fighting. The largest was the Tiergarten Flakturm. Collections from Berlin's major museums and galleries were stored at Tiergarten and Friedrichshain. The largest item in the Tiergarten Flakturm was the Pergamon Altar, a massive marble edifice from the ancient Greek city of Pergamon. The priceless Trojan gold, the treasure of King Priam excavated in 1873 from the site of the city of Troy by Heinrich Schliemann, was also stored at Tiergarten. Stored with the Trojan gold was the large Egyptian collection, and stored in box with "Saal VIII" written on its side were 50 wide gold rings from ancient Egypt.

The Soviets, planning to recoup their looted treasures from the Nazis, had organized trophy brigades and were now removing treasures with a vengeance. The Americans and British had also organized the Monuments, Fine Arts and Archives (MFAA) unit to recover loot and return it to its country of origin, including trainloads sent to Russia. But the Soviets looted and shipped all the valuables to Russia. Within a few days of the capture of Berlin, the three Flakturms were emptied by the Soviets.

On October 19, 1945, in Moscow, an archivist opened a box with "Saal VIII" written on its side. It contained gold and silver jewelry from ancient Egypt. There were 49 wide gold rings. The fiftieth was missing from its nest.[1]

For seven months in 1945, Rabbi Joseph S. Shubow served as chaplain in Berlin. His duties included performing services for the many displaced persons (DPs) and well as U.S. military personnel. In Shubow's own words:

> The Lord is my witness that I did the best I could. The DPs were the most harried, distressed, impoverished, and broken people that I or anybody could have seen and in providing them with food, clothing, shelter, and protection I found that they could never express their gratitude sufficiently. I can still see their faces and hear their expressions of thanksgiving and gratefulness. A number of them insisted on showing me their personal gratitude by bringing me a Bible or a book of one kind or another or some family heirloom or trinket. God is my witness that in every instance I refused manifestations of appreciation, for I, as a rabbi and chaplain, conducted myself on the supposition that my extraordinary privilege of such service was greater than any concrete reward could ever be. But these good people insisted that I take a gift here and there and I have in my possession these sacred manifestations of the gratitude of human beings broken and shattered by the cruelty of the Nazi regime.[2]

Among the various token of gratitude the rabbi received was a ring that looked rather peculiar, but he paid no particular attention to it as he had never been interested in jewelry.

In the latter part of May 1946, the rabbi had the extraordinary privilege of returning to the United States as chaplain for the first boatload of refugees who came from Europe to America. Aboard the *Marine Flasher*, Shubow conducted daily services, taught classes in English, and conversed with the refugees about the glory of the United States, the land which they were to adopt as their own.

In 1951, on a road trip to Washington, D.C., for a reunion with the XVI Corps, Ninth Army Rabbi Shubow stopped by the New York Metropolitan Museum and asked for an appraisal of the Egyptian ring. Indeed it was confirmed as an original Egyptian ring and, surprisingly, the Met official recommended that the ring be appraised at the Museum of Fine Art in his hometown of Boston.[3]

After his return, the rabbi traveled to the Museum of Fine Art to chat about his Egyptian ring. The rabbi presented the ring to Mr. Dows Dunham and his assistant Bernard V. Bothmer, a German-born American Egyptologist, whose career began in the Egyptian Museum of Berlin. The rabbi's objective was to sell the ring to the museum. The museum officials recognized the slightly bent ring, which had a trace of the museum inventory number 22871 in India ink on the back, although partially obliterated. They informed the rabbi that they could not purchase the ring since it had probably been stolen from the Berlin collection. Rabbi Shubow told Dunham and Bothmer that in 1945 he had been in the U.S. Army in Berlin and had worked in a displaced persons camp in the Zoological Gardens. One of the camp's residents, a German, had given him the ring in return for his help with food and clothing. The German said he had found it in the Flakturm.[4]

The rabbi was informed that the ring was indeed original and a far better specimen than any in their collection of Egyptian artifacts. The ring was from the Giuseppe Ferlini Treasure, taken from the Nile city of Mero. Ferlini, an Italian explorer, had unearthed this cache of gold rings in 1830 from the pyramid of Queen Amanishakhto. Then the museum officials requested that Shubow leave the ring at the museum with Mr. Dunham for further examination. A few days later Dunham met with Shubow and told him that the ring must be returned. Shubow was reluctant and, as described by Dunham, "seemed very bitter against the Germans, quite understandable since he was a rabbi." Finally the rabbi stated that he would write to the inspector general of the U.S. Army for a ruling regarding the museum piece. Dunham agreed with the rabbi and wrote him a letter to be forwarded to the inspector general regarding this subject.[5]

Dunham immediately wrote Ardelia Hall of the Department of State informing her of the ring. She, in turn, contacted the collector of customs in Boston. As Shubow put it: "Probably this German who worked at the Berlin Museum during the days of Hitler saw this ring, he must have informed the State Department that such a ring was in my possession."[6]

The rabbi was furious with the Boston Museum for disclosing the ring to the U.S. Department of State. He went to the museum and demanded and received the ring. The rabbi then obtained the services of Friedman, a lawyer, and turned the ring over to him. During inquiries by the Department of State, Shubow insisted that he had no idea who had given him the ring, but he could identify some of the people who had given him Bibles and books that contained their families' inscriptions.

The collector of customs in Boston contacted Shubow and asked for the ring. The rabbi informed him that the ring was in the custody of his lawyer. If Shubow was heartfelt about these "gifts," why did he need a lawyer? Why would he play hardball on the return of the ring? On November 19, 1951, Collector of Customs J. H. Burke played his ace card by informing Shubow's lawyer that if he did not immediately turn over the ring, he would spread a report in the newspaper and the publicity would "do him [Shubow] considerable damage." Friedman tried to stonewall by stating that he could not contact Shubow. Burke would not back down and the lawyer subsequently turned the ring over to customs upon a receipt for the ring, with a statement from Friedman that "He relies upon the State Department to see that justice is done to all parties."[7]

The following day, Friedman wrote letters to Dean Acheson, secretary of state; John W. Snyder, secretary of the treasury; and to representatives John W. McCormack and Joseph W. Martin and senators Leverett Saltenstall and Henry Cabot Lodge. The letters all protested action of the collector of customs. Friedman wrote:

I want to call your attention to something that savors to highhandedness....
I, therefore am making application to you now, to know what are the facts
and on what ground you have directed the ring to be taken from Rabbi
Shubow, and request that his right is regarded to the same as property noted
and [request] an opportunity to inquire into his right or lack of rights in connection with said ring.[8]

The ring was seized in violation of the Tariff Act of 1930, specifically attempting sale of an antique previously entered for personal use without prior declaration of intent to sell. Rabbi Shubow, during his seven months in Berlin as a chaplain, by accepting "gratuities" for his services, benefited from the same people who had suffered hunger, starvation, and death from the Nazi tyranny. Department of State records indicate that the ring was recovered by the Bureau of Customs, Washington D.C. There are no indications that any of the other "gifts" to the rabbi were ever returned to the original owners.

Chapter 21
Frederick the Great's Handwritten Manuscript

John Murphy left the United States for Europe in June 1945. He was a chief warrant officer and on this tour of duty as a political adviser to the military governor of Germany. He was stationed in Paris and Frankfurt briefly and, after approximately five weeks, arrived in Berlin as convoy commander of classified files and documents.

Murphy lived near the Zeldendorf subway station and transacted a number of purchases and barters in that area. Throughout the ruins of Berlin in 1945, motley and hungry German peddlers traded valuables to the Americans for such things as cigarettes, candy bars, and food. Murphy came by a particular document in this manner. He spoke no German and claimed that a peddler had come to his flat one night with a bound manuscript, explaining in broken English that it was very valuable. The manuscript was handwritten with very small letters in French, signed by Frederick the Great. It was also noted that it had been written in Sans Souci, the former summer palace of Frederick the Great, king of Prussia, in Potsdam, near Berlin. The palace was designed as a private residence where the king could relax, away from the pomp and ceremony of the Berlin court. As king, he guided the growth of the provincial kingdom he inherited toward its place at the head of the German principalities. He earned a great reputation as a military commander and skillfully employed the limited Prussian resources to make his kingdom the most powerful German state; by the time he died, he had doubled Germany's land area. Frederick the Great was admired by Adolf Hitler, who had a portrait of him in his headquarters. Hitler envisioned himself as a regenerated Frederick the Great.[1]

Murphy gave the peddler a footlocker full of canned food and 25 packs of vegetable seeds for the 50-page manuscript, which was titled *Testament Politique du Roi Frederic II, D.A. 1752*. On the flyleaf were the words "König House Archives," which identified the manuscript as having been in the royal archives. Murphy wrote:

Some of my high school history had stuck. I realized that if this be the genuine article, it was indeed valuable.... My family in Baltimore had sent me a number of food packages which had recently arrived, and my footlocker had also arrived. One of these contained 25 packages of vegetable seeds (I'm a dirt farmer from the Eastern Shore of Maryland) as well as some tinned food. I decided to splurge. For almost a footlocker of foodstuffs and the seeds, I acquired my questionable treasure.[2]

The price sounds small, but at that time in Berlin a carton of cigarettes could sell for $100. A few tins of food could be swapped for a fine camera worth several hundred dollars. Mickey Mouse watches were going for $500, the market being Soviet soldiers returning to their homeland. At such a time Murphy's full footlocker could easily have brought him more than $500 worth of souvenirs. He did indeed "splurge" in this purchase.

Shortly afterwards, Murphy was reassigned to Frankfurt; he was granted 15 days' leave and visited Nice and Cannes. On his return to Frankfurt, he discovered that because of credits for his overseas service in Australia and India, he was eligible for 30 days of rest and recuperation in the United States. Because his orders called for his return to Europe, he carried only two large travel bags, known then as B-4 bags. One of these contained the manuscript. He traveled by train to Paris and by truck to Le Havre, where he and 1,200 other returning soldiers sailed to New York, arriving at about 3 P.M. in the midst of a snowstorm on December 2, 1945.

The day prior to Murphy's arrival, mimeographed customs certificates were handed out to all passengers. The certificate was to the effect that no one would be allowed to bring firearms, ammunition, government property, or stolen goods into the country. There was nothing to indicate the exclusion of purchase items of any type. The signed certificates were then collected in bulk and handed in. Murphy saw no one from customs. He then traveled to Camp Kilmer in New Jersey and arrived home in Baltimore on December 10, 1945, to spend Christmas with his family.[3]

After Christmas Murray traveled to Washington to visit some military friends and Gen. Charles H. Caldwell, his old boss, who asked if he wished to be assigned to Argentina. Murphy replied that he had to return to Europe. Caldwell, assistant chief of air staff for operations, then sent a telegram to Gen. James Bevans, chief of staff for personnel of the U.S. Forces in Europe and Murphy was quickly transferred to Gen. Caldwell's staff. He was then sent as a military attaché to Argentina, stationed in Buenos Aires. Because he was not returning to Europe, Murphy had to acquire a full military and civilian wardrobe. His belongings in Europe were eventually packed by the army and sent to his parents' home in Baltimore.

Upon his arrival in Argentina, Murphy was assigned to the intelligence division of the embassy staff in Argentina, where he remained for three years. After his return to the United States in 1950, Murphy married and purchased a home near Maxwell Air Force Base in Montgomery, Alabama. In his new home, Murphy had space for his acquisitions from Berlin. When these things arrived, he displayed numerous etchings, prints, Meissen china, and books, but he relegated his unauthenticated manuscript to his attic.

Then in 1951, Murphy read an article in *Life* magazine about a New Jersey housewife who had brought to a New York appraiser six confidential letters written by Mary Todd Lincoln, Abraham Lincoln's wife. Sigmond Rothschild had appraised the letters as worth more than $100,000. The same article disclosed that a watercolor painting by Hitler had been appraised at $1,500. An American soldier had brought the painting back from Germany. After reading the article, Murphy went to his attic and brought out his stored document. Through the mail, he made several offers to sell an original manuscript of King Frederick II.[4]

As a result, Murphy found out that the manuscript was worth at least $6,000. This was more than he had paid for his new house. The appraiser, Rothschild, wrote back that there was a question of ownership and thus obtained Murphy's permission to contact the U.S. Department of State. Murphy had contacted several antique dealers in New York City and the discovery created quite a stir, with several dealers contacting the German Embassy as well as various U.S. government agencies. One of the offers of the manuscript was sent to Mr. Walter Schatzki, a renowned book dealer in New York. Schatzki notified the U.S. Department of State of the offer and asked for their assistance in the matter. The publicity created by the discovery caused Murphy to write the following letter to Dr. Ernest Posner, a professor at the American University in Washington, on August 19, 1951. Posner was formerly the archivist of the Prussian Secret State Archives in Berlin and one of the authors of its official inventory published in 1938. For some reason the complete letter does not contain a single capital letter.

> i have been advised that you have acted as an informer to the state department.... i classed it [the manuscript] in the same category as the numerous art treasures passed off on other service personnel during the war years by the ungrateful populace of europe.... are we prepared to say definitely that it wasn't stolen by an unscrupulous underling of the german archive establishment? ... i have nothing to hide except that i do not wish to part with it for nothing without full justification.[5]

Murphy filed a petition on August 18, 1951, with the Supervisor of Customs, Washington D.C., for remission of forfeiture and penalties as delineated by the Tariff Act of 1930. Murphy wrote that he was unaware that antiques dated before 1800 had to be declared before being offered for public sale.[6]

On May 16, 1952, the manuscript of Frederick the Great belonging to the Königliche Haus Archives of the German State was returned to Federal Republic of Germany by the U.S. Department of State. This return marked the beginning of a bizarre tale.

Chapter 22
Berlin Central Archives

In 1943, to avoid destruction due to Allied bombing, the records of the Prussian Secret State Archives and about 28,000 parcels of documents of the Brandenburg Prussian Archives were moved to a salt mine at Stassfurt, near Magdeburg. During the closing days of World War II, the area of Stassfurt was consecutively occupied by Americans, British, and finally Russians. In January 1946, the Berlin Main Archives received a communication from Stassfurt that the archives stored there had remained almost completely intact and that the keys for access to the salt mine were in the hands of the Russian military commander of Stassfurt.

In October 1946, transfer of the archives from the mine into open storage buildings aboveground was started by compulsory labor units. During this transfer, theft of valuable documents occurred on a large scale, although most of the documents were sent by the Soviet Trophy Brigades to archives in the Soviet Union. The forced laborers employed to sort and catalogue the documents stole the most valuable ones, which they brought into Berlin's lucrative black market.

In Berlin, more and more of these valuable documents and letters were traced as having come from the repository at Stassfurt. The Berlin Criminal Police and Allied Military Police therefore felt compelled to warn bookshops and antique dealers regarding these thefts. As the Russians continued to remove this vast collection of documents in 1947 and 1948, thefts of these items continued at an alarming rate. Berlin was flooded with them.

Other valuable objects from the Prussian State Museum had been stored in the antiaircraft tower near the Berlin Zoo and had been packed into 11 large boxes for further removal. They were taken over by the Soviets in or around July 1945, together with other objects from Berlin museums. These rare archival museum documents were a "gold mine" for any opportunist in Berlin in 1946–1947 and many Americans took advantage of this situation.[1]

After the Frederick the Great manuscript was returned to Germany, Dr. Hans Bellee on November 5, 1952 wrote a letter to the German Foreign Office in Bonn. It began: "Dear Dr. von Tieschowitz,[2] The fortunate return of the stolen Testament of Frederick the Great to Germany through the efforts of your agency, prompts me to inform you of another theft."

In July 1947, Major Lester K. Born, then a U.S. Army archives officer in Berlin, appeared at the Berlin Central Archives and submitted a number of items for the appraisal of the archive's Dr. Bellee and his staff. Descriptions of the items removed from Born's briefcase follow:

> 1. Volume of average thickness, small folio, green leather binding (probably from the second half of the 19th century) with initials and monograms of King Frederick II pressed in gold, and embellishments on the covers and back of the binding, paper (18th century, hand-made) with gilt edges, containing, according to the inscription on the inside (frontispiece) title page [the following is in French]
>
> "Original letters and autographs of Frederick II of Prussia to Voltaire and his Counselor of Finance Faesch 1739–1766 his preface to the Henriade and his testament in verse" (document of the late 18th century).
>
> There follows a 28-page Table analytique (Index and Register in the French language, publication of the late 18th century); the 24 original letters then follow mounted individually sidewise on a separate page each without any further additions; only in the case of individual letters of Frederick the Great were strips of paper inserted with penciled notations (in the handwriting of a scholar of the 19th or 20th century) "written by the Crown Prince," "late," "not get printed," etc. 11 letters of Frederick II, in his own handwriting, (1741–1756) are addressed to Voltaire, five others to Faesch, on 4 pages there are drafts of poems by the King, in his own handwriting (with numerous corrections, additions, insertions, and one for the preface to the "Henriade"; finally there are four state letters [Kabinettschreiben] signed or countersigned (next to the Royal signature) by Podevil or Borcke, and a testamentary fragment (codicil by Frederick II, in his own hand, of 782.
>
> On an empty page, in front of the title page, upper left, notation (in pencil in the normal handwriting of the 18th century)? "AcC. Nr. 174 (1882)," lower right (likewise carelessly in pencil in the writing of a scholar of very recent times) "R. 94 (Friedr. II) IIII, L.a.2." Otherwise there is neither on the back nor on the covers nor elsewhere a signature or notation or a stamp which gives information regarding the origin and former repository of the volume.
>
> 2. Ten letters in her own handwriting by Queen Louise of Prussia to her sons "Fritz" (Fr. Wilh. IV) and Wilhelm (I) of 1802/04 and 1806/07 all papers loose, and evidently, to judge from writing book margins and perforations, taken from a volume or a collection, partly torn and soiled, in part with the original envelopes in which they were received and outside addresses without any signature or notation.
>
> 3. Two original letters from Hardenberg to Metternich and two from the former to Friedrich Wilhelm II (1807–18); paper loose, well-preserved, without any mark or notation.

4. Several original — partly incomplete — letters from Metternich to
   a. W. v. Humboldt (from 1810 on)
   b. Hardenberg (1809–20)
   c. Friedrich Wilhelm III (1821–39), all paper yellowed, partly torn, soiled.

5. One Court epistle (Rescript) of King August the Strong of Saxony, signed by the Monarch and countersigned by Count Brühl (regarding a tax levy, without address [1699]); paper well-preserved, with large Royal Seal (stamped wafer seal); without Chancellery or Archives notation and without signature.

6. Eight letters in her own handwriting, from Queen Victoria of Great Britain to Friedr. Wilhelm III and IV, and Wilhelm I (1838–81), English and German, all paper (correspondence paper with Crown and letterhead "Buckingham Palace" or "Windsor Castle") in a good state of preservation, in part with original envelopes; without signature or any other distinguishing mark.

7. One letter each, signed in his own hand (German) from King George II of Hannover-England and his wife, Queen Carolina, to the "Markgrave of Brandenburg (Alexander) in Bayreuth" (1757/58); paper, large Royal Seal stamped in red sealing wax, well preserved; without any mark or notation.

8. One letter in her own handwriting from Barbarina to an Excellency, on the reverse side marginal note in the King's (Friedr. II's) hands "kan noch 200 rtlr. erhalten F. 24.XI."; no year indicated, dated October 9; paper well preserved, on the reverse side, upper left, hardly legible in blurred writing (indelible pencil of recent times): "R 47 J."

Dr. Bellee noticed that items 2 through 8 were in large envelopes on which short, cursory references were written in pencil in modern handwriting regarding addressee; these could have been written by Maj. Born.

With the notes they took, Bellee's staff instituted careful investigations regarding these archives and found that the volume of documents had come from the Prussian Secret State Archives and consequently from the Stassfurt salt mine. Bellee concluded that "the archives material may, in the devious ways of those times, have come into the hands of the American archives officer."

Bellee informed Maj. Born of the result of his investigations regarding the origin and fate of these documents but heard no more on this subject, and the documents have thus far not been returned. He wrote: "Perhaps we shall succeed in some way in tracing and saving for Germany these valuable archives items also, which were in American hands in 1947."[3]

In the early 1950s Lester K. Born was employed by the Library of Congress as an expert in the field of microfilm technology. He was employed as a foreign service staff officer from February 27, 1956 to September 5, 1957. After serving some 11 months as a cultural affairs officer in Manila, Philippines, he was reassigned, without change in grade or salary, to Washington, D.C., as an instructor in the French language. Thereafter, on August 5, 1957, he received a letter from the director of personnel notifying him that it would be necessary "to terminate (his) probationary appointment" within 30 days because of "the severe cut in the agency's appropriation for fiscal year 1958" and the agency's inability to relocate him. Born's employment was terminated on September 5, 1957. He died in 1969.

In 1958, more than 350 letters from Frederick the Great, Ferdinand II, Emperor Josephus, Frederick Wilhelm, and many others were placed on the market by Richard H. Scalzo of the law firm of Scalzo and Scalzo of Niagara Falls, New York. They were offered to several New York dealers who recognized the documents as stolen and refused to purchase them. The law firm then wrote the German Embassy in Washington, D.C., furnishing an inventory and microfilm of a portion of the letters and asking $20,000 for the contents. The U.S. Department of State was given a copy of the letter to the German Embassy and began an immediate investigation. They began by examining Mr. Scalzo's military background and found that he was in the medical corps as an enlisted man from March 24, 1944, until his discharge on May 17, 1946, at Fort Dix, New Jersey. His service had included assignments with the 64th Field Hospital in Europe. His last assignment in Germany was in the town of Nachtsheim, near Stassfurt, and he left Europe in August 1945, several months before the robberies of the Prussian Secret State Archives in Stassfurt.[4]

Additional information was obtained from Scalzo, who told the officials of the State Department that he was representing a client and was exercising his client-attorney privilege by not disclosing this person's name. Scalzo further stated that his client had purchased the documents from a dealer in 1934. The State Department then filed a civil suit and had the documents confiscated. Meanwhile the inventory was being examined by Dr. Ernest Posner of the American University in Washington, who pointed out that one item on the inventory, "L'histoire de mon temps" by Frederick the Great, alone was worth $25,000. Posner also identified the documents as having been stored in the Stassfurt salt mine.[5]

On June 1, 1960, as the case heated up, the unidentified owner acquired the services of John T. Elfvin, a lawyer known as a rebel. Because of Elfvin's tenacity, the federal grand jury cleared the unknown man of criminal charges and demanded that his historic German documents be returned. But when the papers were to be presented to Elfvin, Customs Agent Paul A. Lawrence was on hand and seized them on grounds that they had been brought into this country illegally by the owner.[6]

The Department of State had learned that the owner of the documents was Fritz Otto Weinert. He had been born in Germany; lived in Milwaukee, Wisconsin, from 1929 to 1932, and then returned to Germany to work in Stassfurt from 1933 to 1947. In Stassfurt, Weinert, holder of a doctorate in technical sciences, had worked as a chemist for I. G. Farben, the major such company in Germany. He had listed his religion as "Gottglaübiger," a Nazi term for those who had left the church for political reasons; it implied a belief in God, without any religious affiliation. As a member of the Nazi Party, he would have had a difficult time reentering the United States; therefore he immigrated to Australia in 1948. He then returned to the United States in 1952 and settled in Niagara Falls, New York. The Department of State even managed to obtain an Australian passport picture of Weinert.[7]

The Department of State in its pursuit of documents of Frederick the Great obtained this Australian passport photograph of Fritz Otto Weinert. He had brought these priceless documents into the United States in 1958 (courtesy National Archives).

The time-consuming legal battle continued. In 1964 Ardelia Hall's position at the Department of State in reclamations was dissolved, and this ended the government's pursuit of property stolen from the former Axis powers. A clue as the final disposition of the 350 letters lies in the 1976 obituary of Richard H. Scalzo. It states, "In 1964 Mr. Scalzo was successful in arranging the purchase of several valuable German documents, including letters of Voltaire, Goethe, the Empress Josephine Bonaparte, and Baron Rothschild."[8] Apparently these documents were sold back to the Prussian Secret State Archives in Berlin. This explains why the archives refused to correspond with the author on this subject, responding only that they were distressed at the thought of purchasing back documents stolen from their collection.

Chapter 23
The Golden Book of Saarbrücken

In 1920 the province of Saarland was occupied by Britain and France under the 15-year provisions of the Treaty of Versailles following World War I. The capital of Saarland is Saarbrücken. After the original 15-year term was over, a plebiscite was held in the territory and on January 13, 1935, 90 percent of those voting opted in favor of rejoining Germany. In commemoration of the return of the Saarland to the Reich, on March 1, 1935, the city of Saarbrücken was visited by Chancellor Adolf Hitler; Franz von Papen, then deputy chancellor and the second most important man in Germany; Robert Ley, an alcoholic and leader of the German Labor Front; and Joseph Goebbels, propaganda chief. On this day these dignitaries were given the honor of signing the Golden Book of Saarbrücken. Three of the four signers and their families would be dead by their own hands within 10 years. In a Berlin bunker in April 1945, Hitler would first poison Blondi, his dog; then he and his wife Eva Braun as well as Goebbels and his wife Magda would kill themselves. The six Goebbels children were also given lethal injections. Earlier, in 1941, Ley's wife locked herself in a bedroom, wrapped her nude body in a pricey ermine coat, and shot herself in the head. After the end of hostilities, on October, 24, 1945, while imprisoned in Nuremberg, Ley hung himself with a towel. His 18-year-old mistress was killed in the course of an adventurous love affair. Only von Papen, the high-minded aristocrat, remained unscathed. He was arrested by the Allies, tried at Nuremberg, and acquitted on all counts.

The last signature in the Golden Book is that of Alfred Wünnenberg (no date, but possibly 1944). He was a four-star SS general and chief of all SS uniformed regular police (Obergruppenführer der Ordnungspolizei). He was born in nearby Saarburg and had the distinction, in August 1936, of commanding the first German military guard police in Saarbrücken. This happened after German troops occupied the demilitarized zone of Saarland on March 7. This was the first German act of aggression in World War II.[1]

The Golden Book of Saarbrücken was taken by Sergeant Walter Clark to his home in Omaha, Nebraska. He demanded an unrealistically high price for its return (courtesy City of Saarbrücken).

On March 21, 1945, Sergeant Walter E. Clark took the Golden Book of Saarbrücken (*Goldenes Buch der Stadt Saarbrücken*) from it storage area in the city hall. It reflected the history of changing conditions of the city and is of great historic value. It is also a register signed by visiting dignitaries and celebrities from early in the century until it came into Clark's possession. The names ranged from the first, that of Kaiser Wilhelm II in 1909, to the last, that of Obergruppenführer Wünnenberg. Clark insisted that the book was given to him as a gift by the bürgermeister while he was serving in Saarbrücken as an interpreter on the staff of the American military government. Clark obtained it a few days before American forces turned the city over to the French.

Clark mailed the book home to Omaha, Nebraska, and thought little more about it until 1948, when Saarbrücken city officials contacted him and asked that he return the book. The officials of Saarbrücken insisted that Clark took possession without being authorized or entitled to it in any way. They further insisted that he took the volume arbitrarily and against the will of Saarbrücken city authorities. The latter knew very well that the signatures of Kaiser Wilhelm and ranking Nazi officials made this a most valuable book in the United States. Clark, now an English teacher at Central High School in Omaha, ignored the requests and considered the book a war souvenir.[2]

The Saarbrücken city officials remained persistent and, over a six-year period, filed 14 requests through the French and German embassies for the return of the book. Clark by now had formed such an attachment to his souvenir that he was reluctant to part with it. After more correspondence, Clark agreed to return it if (1) the city compensated him with another souvenir of comparable worth; (2) the city paid for two first-class tickets for himself and his wife from Omaha to Saarbrücken so that he could personally return the book; and (3) the city paid for a six-week vacation in Europe for Clark and his wife and, further, gave them a per diem allowance to make up for their missed pay during the period of the trip. The stunned city fathers found this an expensive way to recover property that they considered rightfully theirs in the first place and turned the matter over to the Federal Republic of Germany, asking for its help in recovering the book. The officials stated that they were, however, willing to present Mr. Clark with another gift in place of the Golden Book, which would equally serve as a souvenir of the time he had spent in their town.[3]

On September 12, 1956, Mr. Clark made his case public with an article in the *Des Moines Register*:

> Mr. Clark described the book and stressed that it was a gift. He stated: This summer a letter came to him from Saarbrücken's top officials terming the book priceless to the city and containing an offer of adequate compensation if it were to be sent back or returned personally. Clark said he was willing to make the return on a personal basis. He further stated the Saarbrücken remained silent, thus, he said he was a bit startled when officials of the city recently turned down his offer to return the book in exchange for a six-week, all-expense tour of Europe.

But Clark said, the U.S. State and Defense Departments ruled that it was a legitimate war souvenir.[4]

Up until now France had been representing the city officials of Saarbrücken, for after World War II the Saarland once again came under French occupation and administration as France attempted to gain economic control of these German industrial areas, which contained large coal and mineral deposits. On October 26, 1956, the Saarland treaty declared that the Saarland should be allowed to join the Federal Republic of Germany, which it did after a vote on January 1, 1957.

Now the Golden Book case was taken over by representatives of the German government. On April 9, 1957, the Washington Embassy of the Federal Republic of Germany wrote the U.S. Department of State a four-page letter about the Golden Book taken by Clark. On May 8, 1957, Robert C. Creel, the officer in charge of German political affairs, wrote Walter E. Clark the following letter:

> The city of Saarbrücken has, as you know, been attempting since 1948 to recover for its municipal archives the city register or Golden Book which is now in your possession....
>
> In view of the assurance which has been received by the department that under no circumstances was any person in the Saarland competent lawfully to transfer possession of the book to you at the time you received it, and of the department's assumption that you would not knowingly take any action that might result in damage to the foreign relations of the United States, you are requested to make the Golden Book available to the department for transmittal to the government of the Federal Republic and ultimate return to the Saarland.[5]

A rare picture on a Saturday morning on September 3, 1960, was an empty parking lot in front of Saarbrücken's city hall. This puzzle was solved at 10:00 A.M. when two American military cars arrived with General Peter Schmick and a wooden box. It contained the Golden Book of Saarbrücken. With glasses of champagne, the military and city officials celebrated the return of the Golden Book after its absence of 15 years. The old book was retired to the city archives and a new Golden Book took its place to record the continuing history of Saarbrücken.[6]

Chapter 24

The Priceless Mainz Psalter

The Mainz Psalter was commissioned the archbishop of the German city of Mainz in 1457. It was one of the earliest psalters to be printed on the Gutenberg press. These biblical Books of Psalms were the most common type of illuminated manuscripts, often containing calendars, representations of saints, and portions of the Old and New Testaments.

The 1457 Mainz Psalter is regarded by those interested in such matters with almost idolatrous respect, for it is the first book with a date, the first book with a colophon, the first with a printer's mark, the first with two- and even three-color printing, and the first to contain music (although this was inserted by hand). Although 10 copies are known to exist, no copy or any fragment of a copy is in the United States. It would be difficult to estimate its value except to say that if the Library of Congress correctly appraised the St. Paul copy of the Gutenberg Bible in 1945 at $300,000, this book is worth a great deal more because it is so much more rare. (There may be some 40 Gutenberg Bibles and as many as 11 in the United States.)

By 1948 the Mainz Psalter was in the United States, but it had originated from the Landesbibliothek in Dresden. During the war, the German government sent the rare books from the Dresden Landesbibliothek to Czechoslovakia for safekeeping. When the Germans were driven out of Czechoslovakia, these books were left in Czech territory and were seized by the Soviets, just as they seized the Sistine Madonna from the Dresden Gallery, which is now in Moscow. Apparently some Soviet soldier "liberated" the Psalter while it was en route to Moscow and sold it to Vladimir Zikes, a bookseller in Prague. According to postwar Czech law, it was legal for Zikes to own German government or private property found or obtained in Czechoslovakia. It was not legal for him to export it from Czechoslovakia without a license from a bureau established for that purpose.

Zikes was a man of considerable experience, and he was undoubtedly aware that it would be possible for him to extract several pages from the book, particularly the first leaf with the great colored initial "B" and the last leaf with the colophon and printer's device, and to sell these leaves without any necessity of establishing provenance for at least $10,000 apiece. Knowing that it was only a matter of time until the Russians took over his country and realizing the value of this book but also the difficulties of selling it without a clear title which would be recognized internationally, Zikes wrote to New York bookseller Herbert Reichner, asking him if he would be interested in selling a copy of the Psalter. Reichner answered that of course he would, thinking that it might be merely a facsimile but being curious to know what it was all about. Nothing at the time was said to Reichner about the fact that this book came from Dresden and that it bore no bookplate or other mark of its provenance. The book arrived in New York by plane from Holland in October 1947. It had been sent with a consular invoice that contained several misstatements of fact: (1) that it was sold and not on consignment, (2) that it was valued at $320, and (3) that it was dated 1557 instead of 1457.

When the book arrived in New York, Reichner was astounded to find that it was actually the Dresden copy in its original pigskin binding. His first inclination was to return it to the Czech dealer, but before doing so he decided to seek the advice of William A. Jackson, librarian of the Houghton Library at Harvard University. A month after the arrival of the book, Jackson called on Reichner and was shown the book. Jackson advised Reichner to keep the book in his vault and say nothing about it — that he would approach the U.S. Department of State to find out whether they might approve of keeping the book in America. On February 10, 1948, Jackson traveled to Washington, D.C., and called upon Mr. William R. Tyler, an old friend, who stated that he was in charge of such matters in the State Department.

Jackson later claimed that he obtained from Tyler a promise that no attempt would be made to trace the present location of the book without notifying him, Jackson, in advance. The reason for this was that if the State Department should decide to seize the book, the identity of the Czech bookseller might be revealed; he could then be in very critical danger if the Soviets learned of the transaction. Furthermore, Jackson stated that Reichner had begged him not to reveal his name if it could possibly be prevented, because as a former citizen of Vienna he had had experience with bureaucratic officials. Although he was now an American citizen, he feared that such bureaucrats were of the same type in America as they were in Europe. Upon receiving this promise, Jackson proposed that a trusteeship be set up consisting of the Librarian of Congress, the Librarian of the Morgan Library, and the Librarian of Harvard, any two of whom would be empowered to decide when it was proper for the book to be returned to Dresden. He further suggested that the state department give its approval to the placement of the book in the custody of the Harvard Library under the control of these trustees and that no term should be set upon the time the book should remain at Harvard but that this should be left to the judgment of the majority of the trustees. At that time Jackson said that if the state department would approve of such a trusteeship, Harvard would endeavor to give the Czech bookseller $10,000 for his service to civilization in preserving the book intact. After some delay, he was informed that this proposal was viewed favorably by the department. He then went to Washington on April 23, 1948, to arrange the details.

At that time Jackson had a second interview with Ardelia Hall, who according to Jackson

> has some peculiar ideas; one is that there apparently does not exist an honest bookseller or art dealer. Another is that it seems impossible for her to recognize that this psalter is a printed book, of which there are other copies in existence, and not a unique manuscript. This, which would seem to be a small matter, involves in her mind questions of international copyright and a good many other things which effectually, it seems to me, prevent her from seeing such a proposal as this one in its proper light.

On April 23, when Jackson left Washington, he wrote that he had every confidence from the assurances of Tyler and Hall that the matter would soon be resolved. He did not hear from them in the next two weeks and telephoned sometime early in May, only to be told by Tyler that the book was being seized by the U.S. Treasury Department on the instructions of the U.S. State Department. This action was, of course, undertaken without regard to the promise that Tyler had given him that he should be informed before such an action was instigated. In the course of a week or so the F.B.I. traced the consular invoice and Reichner received a visit from officers of the Treasury Department, who took him and the book to their New York office, where the book was seized and a receipt given.[1]

The U.S. Department of State had a completely different view on this matter and wrote, in a top secret memo condemning the methods of America's oldest university, "In sharp contrast with the cooperation the Department of State has generally received from American museums and libraries, it may be asserted that the 1475 Mainz Psalter has been recovered by the Department in spite of the lack of cooperation from the Librarian of the Houghton Library of Harvard University."

The State Department went on to say that Jackson had outlined a scheme to obtain a book of psalms worth $250,000 that had been looted from the repository of the Dresden Library during the war. He had refused to divulge any information as to the whereabouts of the book, saying that it would invalidate the confidence placed in him by a refugee book dealer. Jackson had proposed that he be allowed to purchase the book secretly for $10,000, gambling that he would thus be able to retain the book indefinitely for the Harvard

University Library. He further contended that if the State Department did not agree with his proposal, "the book might be lost, mutilated, or returned immediately to Europe."[2]

The seized Mainz Psalter was placed in the custody of Collector of Customs in New York and from there, on March 13, 1950, was sent to the U.S. Wiesbaden Collection Point in Germany.

William A. Jackson was a tall man with an electric dynamism and a commanding presence. He was the first librarian of the prestigious Houghton Library at Harvard University. Arthur Amory Houghton Jr., an imperious figure, was the owner of Steuben Glass, and the founder of the Houghton Library. He and Jackson regarded each other with wary respect. Jackson was a raider for this library and died suddenly in 1964 at only 59 years of age.

Chapter 25
Raphael's
Portrait of a Young Man

It's the most valuable single thing that's still missing.
—*Bernard B. Taper*

The prelude to World War II came to an end on September 1, 1939, when Germany invaded Poland. During the siege of Warsaw in September 1939, the King's Palace, as a national historic monument, was not used by the Polish defenders as a stronghold or as a depot for military equipment or ammunition. But this fact did not prevent the Germans from shelling the palace, as incendiary bombs were showered on it. The roofs of two towers and a palace wing burned down. The fine Bacarelli ceiling, dating from 1780, was destroyed. And then the museum staff began trying to save the most precious objects by taking them from the palace to cellars of the museum. In this way, they transported the royal throne, a series of paintings representing Warsaw, pictures by foreign and Polish artists, and various sculptures, upholsteries, and jewels. With the exception of the relatively mild damage done during the siege, the palace came out of it in a fairly satisfactory state.

Poland, which had been jointly conquered by Germany and the Soviet Union, was divided first of all between the Soviet Union and the German Reich. Of the 380,000 square kilometers, approximately 200,000 square kilometers went to the Soviet Union and the remainder to the German Reich. That part of Poland which was taken over into Soviet Russian territory was immediately treated as an integral part of the Soviet Union.

After the invasion, the municipal administration of Warsaw in the first days of October had begun to build the temporary roof over the palace wing. In October Hans Frank, the Nazi governor of Poland, arrived in Warsaw. He stopped at the Warsaw Palace and declared that it should be pulled down; furthermore, he opposed any restoration of the building, which had been only slightly damaged during military operations. With his own hand, Frank tore the silver eagles off the royal canopy and put them in his pockets. By this act, he gave the signal for the general plunder of the palace installations, which lasted for several weeks.

The objects stolen from the palace were sent to four large storehouses in Warsaw. From there, they were distributed to various German contractors to transform the offices of the prime minister into "the German House"; to remodel the Belweder Palace for Ludwig Fischer, governor of occupied Warsaw; Gestapo Headquarters; and to enhance other Nazi government buildings in Poland. The collections from the Palace were also transferred to Krakow, where they were temporarily stored, in view of their ultimate transfer to Germany.[1]

The museum of Princess Czartoryski at Cracow contained over 10,000 works of art and were considered among the greatest of private collections, having been begun by Princess Isabel Czartoryski in the 18th century. The Czartoryski Museum dates back to 1801 and is the oldest museum in Poland. It boasts the country's most valuable collections of art, ancient handicrafts, and memorabilia connected with historical figures. Its best-known exhibit was Leonardo da Vinci's famous *Girl with an Ermine*, a superb portrait of the teenage mistress of one of Milan's rulers of the late 15th century. The Princess Czartoryski Museum occupied three old buildings at the northern edge of Krakow's Old Town historical center. The most valuable items from the collection were sent to the Sieniawa Castle in Goluchow during the early days of fighting. There the items were secretly walled up in the castle, but after the invasion a brick mason disclosed the hiding place to the Germans.[2]

In October 1939, Kajetan Muehlmann, a special commissioner of art on Göring's staff, brought three paintings to Göring from Poland. They were priceless: Rembrandt's *Landscape*, Raphael's

Raphael's *Portrait of a Young Man* is the single most valuable item still missing from World War II (courtesy Robert Kudelski, Warsaw, Poland).

Portrait of a Young Man, and Leonardo's *Girl with an Ermine*. In addition, Muehlmann sent about a dozen paintings to Berlin, where they were placed in safe deposit boxes in the Deutsche Bank. They were all from the Sieniawa Palace, a residence of the aristocratic Czartoryski family. Muehlmann said that they were taken by the Germans in full agreement with Count Stefan Zamoyski, the representative of the Czartoryski family in Poland, because he wanted to save the collection from the Russians. The pictures were not considered as confiscated but only removed for safekeeping by the Germans. They were brought to Göring presumably as part of this safekeeping policy, but he refused to keep them with his collection. He told Muehlmann that he intended to suggest to Hitler that they be placed in the Kaiser Friedrich Museum in Berlin. This Göring considered most important in the case of the Leonardo because there were no works by the master in that museum. The three paintings were placed in the Kaiser Friedrich Museum for a few months, after which they were returned to Poland.

Then, in December 1939, Hans Posse, the curator for Hitler's future museum in Linz, visited Poland and wrote: "The inspection confirmed my supposition that except for the higher class of art already known to us in Germany, (e.g., the Veit Stoss Altar and the panels by Hans von Kulmbach from the Marienkirche in Cracow, the Raphael, Leonardo, and Rembrandt from the Czartoryski collection) there is not much that would enlarge the German stock of great art."[3] In other words, the authority on German art had identified the five most priceless pieces of art in Poland and considered the remainder secondhand goods.

After Posse's report, Göring again demanded that the three paintings from the Czartoryski collection be returned to Berlin with the intention that, in the future, they were to be placed in the Führer's Art Museum in Linz. The three paintings remained in Berlin only a few months because the danger from air raids was increasing; they were therefore sent to the Wawel Castle in Cracow, Poland, the residence of Governor General Hans Frank.[4] These paintings were exhibited in the castle along with 511 more works of related art.

The Wawel Castle had been renovated in the early 16th century by King Sigismund, who brought in the best native and foreign artists, including Italian architects and sculptors and German decorators to refurbish the Wawel Castle and transform it into a splendid Renaissance palace. After World War I, the authorities of the newly independent Polish Second Republic decided that Wawel Castle was to become a representative building of the Polish state and would be used by the governor and later by the president himself. In 1921, the Polish Parliament passed a resolution that gave the Wawel Castle official status as the residence of the president of Poland. After the invasion by Germany, the castle became the home of Nazi Governor General Hans Frank.

Frank joined the Nazi Party in 1927. He became a member of the Reichstag in 1930 and the Bavarian state minister of justice in March 1933. When this position was incorporated into the German government in 1934, Frank became Reich minister without portfolio. He was made a Reichsleiter of the Nazi Party in charge of legal affairs in 1933 and in the same year president of the Academy of German Law. Frank was also given the honorary rank of Obergruppenführer. In 1942 Frank became involved in a temporary dispute with Himmler as to the type of legal system that should be in effect in Germany. During the same year he was dismissed as Reichsleiter of the Nazi Party and as president of the Academy of German Law.

In the German occupation of Poland, the invaders followed the policy that church property, state museums, and private collections would be available for confiscation and that the Poles would keep nothing. For the time being, the plan was to keep Polish objects in Poland, under the so-called safeguarding activities of the Germans.

Adolf Hitler gave the order that the Veit Stoss Altar should be removed from St. Mary's Church in Krakow and taken to Germany. This large sacred piece was commissioned by the King of Poland in 1477 and took 10 years to carve. In September 1939, Willy Liebel, the bürgermeister of Nuremberg, came to Krakow with a group of SS men and the Veit Stoss Altar was disassembled. It took several trucks to haul the 12-foot apostolic figures to Nuremberg, the home of Veit Stoss, who had died there in the 15th century at the age of 83. As the war continued, Polish valuables began to pour into Germany. Warsaw's Synagogue Library, one of the richest repositories of Jewish culture, was carted off as well.

In 1944 the Red Army advanced to within about 20 miles of Warsaw on the eastern bank of the Vistula. A revolt broke out in Warsaw under the leadership of Gen. Tadeusz Bor-Komorowski, who led the Warsaw uprising during August and September of 1944. The general contacted the Polish government-in-exile and was instructed to organize a resistance and sabotage movement. On August 1, 1944, with the Red Army only miles away, he ordered the home army to rise in open rebellion in response to Soviet radio broadcasts. His plan was to liberate the capital of Warsaw by the force of Polish arms, thus hoping to secure for Poland a future free of Communist control.

The uprising was brutally put down by the Germans, mainly by SS troops. The Germans totaled 10,000 men and the atrocities they committed during the two months of street fighting were almost beyond belief and even offensive to some SS officers who witnessed them. Finally, High Army Cdr. Heinz Guderian appealed to Hitler to withdraw the troops, which, surprisingly, he did.

Shortly before the withdrawal of German troops, the first-choice items of art were transported from Frank's residence in the Wawel Castle to the Seichau Palace in Silesia, Poland, about 150 miles southwest of Warsaw. Frank had managed to replace Kajetan Muehlmann with Ernst von Palézieux, a Swiss citizen, who had decided to accept a position with Frank as a solution to his marital difficulties. His wife, whom he deeply loved, had left him and he was in a state of shock and despair. His solution, therefore, was to join Frank in war-torn Poland.[5]

The Red Army captured Cracow on January 18, 1945, as Palézieux quickly made his way east to Lower Silesia. Here he found matters in an uproar as the space in the Seichau Palace where the art was to be stored was needed for German army officers and their administrative staff and was no longer available. However, arrangements had already been made to move the art treasure. A large furniture truck arrived at the Wawel Castle and was loaded with 511 paintings; some 10 to 15 cases of antique coins were left behind. This truck then traveled 200 miles west to the Jauer, 35 miles inside the German border, arriving at the Muhrau Palace on January 20, 1945. Palézieux categorically stated that Rembrandt's *Landscape*, Raphael's *Portrait of a Young Man*, and Leonardo's *Girl with an Ermine* were included in the shipment and arrived at the Muhrau Palace in Germany.[6] The possibilities of looting by German troops in these early days of withdrawal were almost unlimited.

The following day on Sunday evening, January 21, Palézieux left the Muhrau Palace for Neuhaus, Bavaria, a southward trip of 350 miles, to prepare the residences and offices for Hans Frank and his large staff. This was Frank's hometown. He stated that he took no art objects with him. A few days later Helmut Pfaffenroth, the adjutant of Hans Frank, arrived in a car with two small chests containing Rembrandt's *Landscape*, Leonardo's *Girl with an Ermine*, valuable manuscripts, sculpture, rare religious items, and other small paintings but not Raphael's *Portrait of a Young Man*. Perhaps the Raphael was slightly too large for the chest or too awkward, as it was painted on wood rather than canvas. On the other hand, some items taken by Pfaffenroth were larger than the Raphael. The possibility also cannot be excluded that the Raphael may have been removed by someone else, including German clerks, during the few days that Palézieux had seen it at the Muhrau Palace and as Pfaffenroth had traveled south with the other expensive paintings. Traveling with Pfaffenroth from the Muhrau Palace to Neuhaus were Walther Bader and August Mohr.

Meanwhile two truckloads of art were removed from the Muhrau Palace under the supervision of Dr. Gunther Grundmann and sent to the Bavarian city of Coburg. They were placed in a storage room in the Tambach Castle, a 10-minute drive from Coburg. The Polish art treasures had been removed from their frames, rolled up, and placed into crates. They filled two rooms

40 feet square. A few days later, on January 29, 1945, Dr. Walter Schüler arrived in Neuhaus. He reported to Frank and Palézieux that he was the last German official to leave the Muhrau Palace and that he had turned the remaining valuables over to the Polish authorities who had traveled with Frank's staff.[7]

This is in sharp contrast to Frank's testimony at Nuremberg:

> I was safeguarding them but not for myself. They were also not in my immediate safekeeping; rather I had taken them along with me from burning Silesia. They could not be safeguarded any other way. They were art treasures which are so widely known that they are Numbers 1 to 10 in the list in the book; no one could have appropriated them. You cannot steal a *Mona Lisa*. [This] one last group of art treasures was handed over to the Americans by me personally.[8]

Frank was lying. When Silesia was burning, the valuables were 200 miles away in the Muhrau Castle, as described above. To summarize, it would seem the Raphael was present in the Muhrau Castle when Palézieux departed on or about January 21, 1945, but it was no longer present when Grundmann evacuated two truckloads of art objects approximately eight days later.

Frank was captured by American troops on May 3, 1945, at Tegernsee in southern Bavaria. Upon his capture, he tried to cut his own throat; two days later, he lacerated his left arm in a second unsuccessful suicide attempt.

On May 18, 1945, the home of Hans Frank was targeted by T Force, the highly secretive task force of the Sixth Army Group. T Force had been organized in the early stages of the war to recover German technology, such as atomic resources, blueprints for heat-seeking missiles, jet aircraft, rocket ships, and other weapons of mass destruction. Maj. Arthur Alter and 2/Lt. Walter Stein and members of their unit removed from Frank's Chalet Bergfrieden, by Lake Schlier, and his larger residence at Schoberhof in Neuhaus, the following; diaries, manuscripts, notebooks, recovered speeches, photographs, newspapers clippings, art books, maps and much more. Many of the books taken by T Force had a bearing on the administration of Poland and German law. Included in the documents were large inventories of works of art seized throughout Poland.

The T Force team interrogated Robert Palmi, driver; Erwin Schafer, chief cook; Walter Schuler, bureau chief; Wilhelm Palézieux, architectural adviser; Helene Kraffczck, personal secretary; Cläre Pfaffenroth, adjutant's wife; and Brigitte Frank, wife of Hans Frank. From the analysis of the files found in Frank's office in the chalet, T Force named the following as having the greater importance in connection with their investigation: Pfaffenroth, SS Strumbannführer and adjutant; Hammerle, counselor of Frank in administrative matters; Dr. Maximilian Meidinger, chief of the chancellery; Schüler, bureau chief and awards and decorations; Ernst Kundt, administrator of the Radom District a town in central Poland; Büchler, state secretary; Dr. Ernst Boepple, counselor for economics; Buchner, director general of Bavarian Art Institutes; Muehlmann, state secretary; Dr. Jänsch, bureau chief of personnel; Nickel, police master and handler of personal affairs; and Meyer, superintendent of Count Potocki's family palace at Kressendorf.[9]

The diary was a set of some 38 volumes detailing the activity of Hans Frank from 1939 to the end of the war in his capacity as governor general of occupied Poland. It is a record of each day's business, hour by hour, appointment by appointment, conference by conference, and speech by speech. Each volume except for the last few is handsomely bound; in those volumes, which deal with the conferences of Frank and his staff in the government general, the name of each person attending the meeting is inscribed in Frank's own handwriting on a page preceding the minutes of the conference. It is shocking that such a neat history of murder, starvation, and extermination should have been maintained by the individual responsible for these deeds, but the Nazi leaders were fond of documenting their exploits.

Frank's law library was taken and loaned to Robert H. Jackson, chief U.S. prosecutor at the Nuremberg Trials, with the understanding that after the trial the books would be sent to the Library of Congress.

The objects of art were removed by T Force to the Reich Finance Building in Munich. On June 14, Lt. Daniel Kern of the MFAA office in Bavaria signed for six cases of paintings and miscellaneous art books from the home of Dr. Frank.[10] One wooden box contained two Rembrandts, one Leonardo de Vinci, one Lucas Cranach, and other paintings. These art items included a collection of original letters written by members of the entourage of Louis XIV, valuable tapestries, and Leonardo's *Girl with an Ermine.* They were taken to the Munich Collection Center on June 19, 1945. These 116 items were catalogued and photographed and fully checked with the list and receipts dated May 19 to June 14, 1945, signed by Officer Stein, who conducted the search. A few weeks later, the 149 items from Tambach Castle near Coburg were brought to the Munich Collection Center. All of the paintings were mounted on new frames. As a result of the rough handling, the paint had flaked off in a few places, but the damage was not serious.[11] Six large pieces of Polish furniture from Frank's residence on 22 Pinzenauer Street in Munich, where he lived with his girlfriend, were also taken to the Collection Center. Most of the antique furniture and tapestries were removed from the Munich residence in 1944 after the neighborhood had suffered Allied bombing attacks and the upper floors of the house were partially destroyed.

In the latter half of 1945, trainloads of Polish museum items were found by U.S. forces and duly returned to Poland, but some were lost, including

Raphael's *Portrait of a Young Man*, the most precious work, oil on wood, 29½ by 23¼ inches.

One man would make it his mission to locate this painting. It would become an obsession. Born in London and educated at University of California Berkeley, Bernard Taper was drafted into the U.S. Army in 1943. He served in intelligence and infantry units before being sent back to Berkeley to learn Chinese in preparation for work as a liaison officer assigned to Chaing Kai-Shek's army in China. But at the last minute the entire class was sent to Germany, where the war in Europe had ended.

Lunching outdoors one day in 1946 at an officers' club in Munich, Taper fell into conversation with a dashing chap named Walter Horn. He started telling Taper marvelous, fascinating stories about his job of searching for lost and stolen art. Horn was desperate to go home but could not leave until he found a successor for his art investigating job. When he met Taper, he found his successor, who told Horn that he was not an art historian and probably was not qualified. Horn said that the MFAA section was "lousy with art historians," but that what was needed was somebody who knew how to ask questions. As a budding journalist, Taper fit the bill. As a further inducement, Horn told him he would have the use of a white BMW roadster, would not have to wear a uniform, could travel freely without orders, and would meet women.

Taper's fascination was searching for the missing Raphael. He questioned many people, including the art advisers to Hans Frank, the Nazi governor of the occupied area of Poland. Taper spent many hours questioning Frank's first art adviser, the "infamous" Kajetan Muehlmann and his successor, Wilhelm Ernest von Palézieux, whom Taper found in the French occupation zone. He got conflicting stories (all of these characters suffered from what Taper called "selective amnesia") and tracked down all the leads but came up empty-handed.[12]

Over the years many clues from Frank's plundering began to reappear. In March 1960, Edward Kneisel, the art restorer used by Frank during the war and now living in the New York, gave testimony that he had seen the missing Raphael painting "lying around" in Ernst von Palézieux's villa in the spring of 1945. Kneisel further stated that in 1953 or 1954, Palézieux wrote him a letter from Switzerland asking about the possibility of selling in New York about 50 or 60 paintings "not including the Raphael." Kneisel replied that there was a good market in New York, but he did not receive a response to his letter. Kneisel's statement was not taken seriously by investigators and it appears that there was no follow-up on his statement.

In 1949, two of the paintings from Hans Frank's plundered art objects surfaced in the possession of Robert F. Emrich of Rogers, Arkansas. Emrich served with the U.S. 101st Airborne Infantry Division during World War II. He reported that he had found the paintings in a house in Austria in which they were billeted in April/May 1945. The 17th-century paintings were Quirijn van Breklenkam's *Old Hermit*, 8¾ by 12 inches, painted on wood, with a frame, and Cornelis van Poelenburg's *Landscape*, 9½ by 12 inches, painted on copper and also with a frame. On the back of the paintings were the gallery inventory numbers of the Lazienki Palace Museum in Warsaw. Edgar Breitenbach, chief of the MFAA section, wrote that he was making attempts to verify the ownership of the two paintings. He further wrote: "With respect to the third picture by Peter Neeffs, *Interior of the Cathedral of Antwerp*, we have asked the present holder ... to provide measurements of the painting, without which identification is exceedingly difficult." The two paintings were shortly identified as being the property of the Lazienki Museum, but the third painting, the Neeffs, remained a mystery.

It is not known how the Department of State ascertained that Emrich had the paintings from the Lazienki Museum. He may have had them appraised by an art dealer or museum who notified the Department of State. The earliest correspondence is September 28, 1949, when the Department of State wrote Mr. Emrich that they had received from the Commissioner of Customs photographs of two paintings in his possession. One paragraph explained that there were other famous paintings from this museum still missing and that "any further information as to the approximately location where these were found or about other paintings you may have mentioned in the house would be appreciated." They asked that the paintings be sent to the National Gallery of Art in Washington, D.C., and enclosed a bill of lading paying for the paintings to be sent by Railway Express. A page of instructions on the proper way to package the valuable paintings was included.[13]

Emrich did not return the paintings and the matter was turned over to the attorney general in Washington, D.C. A year later, on September 14, 1950, R. S. Wilson, a U.S. attorney, drove from Fort Smith, Arkansas, to Rogers for a visit with Emrich. During their conversation Wilson asked for the paintings and a very friendly and cooperative Emrich stated that he would like very much to keep them and would discuss the matter with his wife and attorney, who were present. Afterwards he turned over the paintings to Wilson. Wilson reported that he did so

> in view of the fact that he is a member of the Army Reserves, and is going into active service in a short time.... I asked Mr. Emrich if he could name or describe any of the other paintings that were contained in the old palace where he was billeted and where he obtained possession of the two paintings in question, or if he knew what disposition was made of any of the other paintings, and he stated that he could not give me any information along that line

as he did not remember what the other paintings were or what became of them.[14]

Wilson packed the paintings according to the instruction of the letter of September, 28, 1949, and shipped them to the National Gallery of Art in Washington, D.C. They were given to the Polish Embassy in Washington on January 10, 1951.

The third painting mentioned in Edgar Breitenbach's letter still remains a mystery. It is *Interior of Antwerp Cathedral* by Peter Reeffs, painted in 1651 in oil on canvas, 18 by 24⅛ inches.

Indianapolis native Robert G. Gossett, an American soldier of the 30th Infantry Division, 120 Infantry Regiment, took possession of the Reeffs painting near Hof, Germany, in 1945. He offered it along with five others to Wilbur D. Peat, director of the Indianapolis Museum of Art, reporting that he received the painting by trade with a Russian officer. The painting was purchased by Caroline Marmon Fesler in 1946 and bequeathed to the Indianapolis Museum of Art with the knowledge that it might well be returned to the original owner.

Peat contacted the American Commission for the Protection and Salvage of Artistic and Historic Monuments in War Areas in Washington, D.C. for advice. The Department of State opened a file on this painting: "Objects Imported by Members of the Services Reported to the Commission to date, 30 April 1946." In an effort to trace the former owner, correspondence was conducted by the State Department with several American embassies and archives, none of which proved conclusive. In 2003, research was begun anew at the Indianapolis Museum of Art, enlisting the efforts of Sarah Jackson and her European colleagues at the Art Loss Register, but the former owner remains unidentified.

Another unresolved issue is the art collection taken from the Museums of Prince Czartoryski of Poland. The prince filed several petitions in Federal District Courts asking for the return of priceless art objects that were acquired by the Boston Museum of Fine Arts.[15] The Wildenstein Galleries in New York also were accused by the prince of having two looted paintings from his collection.[16] The two paintings had been purchased from a woman in Berlin in 1940 and were subsequently sold to a Vienna Museum by a Polish citizen. The paintings ended up at the Munich Collection Point with claims filed for them by the Vienna Museum, the Wildenstein Galleries, and Prince Czartoryski himself.

Chapter 26
Clara Elisabeth Hertling

In April 2001, a television and media sensation was created in Germany after a mysterious golden cauldron was found in a Bavarian lake. An amateur diver found the 23-pound solid gold vessel at the bottom of Lake Chiemsee, a tourist destination southeast of Munich.

The gold cauldron was adorned with a relief of mythical Celtic and Indo-Germanic figures. The cauldron, 20 inches across and 12 inches high, based on the weight of the gold alone, was worth some $100,000. The vessel resembled the Gundestrup Cauldron that had been found in a Danish bog in 1891; it was believed to be more than 2,000 years old and is now housed at the National Museum of Denmark in Copenhagen.

As Celtic coins and other Celtic items had previously been found in Lake Chiemsee, it was easily established that the beautiful vessel was of that origin. As required by German law, it was turned over to the Archeological State Museum of Bavaria in Munich. The museum then placed the item on the art market and immediately found a buyer. This made the finder very happy, as he had 50 percent ownership rights of the cauldron, for a value of $50,000.

The acquirer examined the valuable relic and decided not to purchase it, as the cauldron appeared to be a fake. How could this be possible? Dr. Ludwig Wamser, director of the Archaeological State Museum, began a detailed examination of the object, using knowledge from other experts and x-rays. Dr. Wamser linked the cauldron to the Nazis and their ideology, which drew heavily on ancient mythology and hero worship.[1]

A trail led to Munich and art dealer Herbert von der Marwitz as well as master goldsmith Luitpold Pirzl. It was here that Marwitz commissioned Pirzl to make imitations of antique figures. In Pirzl's workshop, he counterfeited numerous artifacts, including ornamental gold items from the Celtic and Viking periods, such as a controversial eagle brooch. Marwitz told Pirzl that these pieces were to be made as stylistic imitations at the order of interested customers, and Pirzl was paid a normal fee for his work. Pirzl would deliver these works fresh from his workshop, perfectly executed, to Marwitz, who then "antiqued" them by damaging them slightly or giving them a patina in order to give them the appearance of genuine antiques found in excavations.

Marwitz then had these items photographed and articles published in scholarly periodicals by prominent archaeologists as treasures found in various excavations. With these articles, which did not mention his name, he would sell the items to unsuspecting art dealers and museums.

Pirzl made a gold eagle brooch in the summer of 1937 upon instruction from Marwitz, and Marwitz furnished the large garnets used in it. Marwitz then loaned the brooch to art historian Frederic Adama van Scheltema, who publicized the brooch by writing about it in *Germanic Heritage,* the official Nazi Party magazine. In the full belief that the brooch had been found in an excavation in Königsberg, Czechoslovakia, it was sold through an art house to the German National Museum in Nuremberg for 42,000 Reichsmarks.

Marwitz's counterfeiting caught up with him, and on March 16, 1940, Herbert von der Marwitz was sentenced to five years' imprisonment for knowingly selling forgeries of ancient gold jewelry. The "valuables" in Marwitz's possession were also confiscated. During the trial, Marwitz denied his malefactions to the last, and, surprisingly, many experts contended that the pieces sold by him were genuine.

The art scholar Scheltema, despite the final solution of the forgery case, believed in the genuineness of the gold eagle brooch and so apparently did the Nazi officials. During the war years, the Munich Police took the notorious eagle brooch, on orders from Heinrich Himmler, from the museum in Nuremberg to Castle Berg at Starnberg, near Munich. At the castle the gold brooch was secretly buried. After the war, the grounds of the castle were searched and the hole in which the case with the brooch had been was now found to be empty. Today the whereabouts of the brooch remain unsettled. Will it show up in the foreign art market, or has it been smelted down for the value of the gold and the garnets?

Marwitz served his time and, after the war, told U.S. Army authorities that the Nazis wrongly prosecuted him. At that point the counterfeit items confiscated from him in 1940 were returned and Marwitz continued to maintain his innocence. It took nine years to fully clear up the matter of his forgeries. In 1949, Luitpold Pirzl, the Munich goldsmith, applied for conservation work with the Bavarian Office for the Care of Monuments. To exhibit his skills, Pirzl submitted photographs of the work that had been done in his shop. Among these were replications in gold that had been made for Marwitz. Upon questioning, Pirzl admitted that he had fashioned the controversial eagle brooch and most of the pieces sold by Marwitz as antiques. Pirzl stated that he could furnish prima facie evidence of his statement by submitting photographs, models, and special tools.² Without question, Marwitz was a master swindler, and he had already found another victim.

In 1939, Clara Hertling, her husband, and Gunter, her nine-year-old son, traveled from Pasadena, California, to Hamburg, Germany, to visit her family. Just before the outbreak of the war on September 1, Gunter's father returned to the United States. There he filed for a divorce and remarried. Gunter and his mother remained in Hamburg through the last week of July 1943, when Allied bombing created one of the greatest firestorms in World War II, killing roughly 50,000 civilians and practically destroying the entire city. Mother and son left the ruins of the city for the southern part of Germany, where she taught music and English in a number of private schools. Then she taught school in the village of Marquartstein, just six miles south of Lake Chiemsee, coincidentally the site of the discovered golden cauldron in the year 2001. Gunter, now a teenager, was one of her pupils. It was here that his mother met and befriended the elderly art dealer Herbert von Marwitz.³

They were in Marquartstein when the war ended and, as Gunter was an American citizen born in Pasadena, he was immediately reissued an American passport. His mother, however, was a German national, whom he was not about to leave alone in war-torn Germany. In order to leave Germany, Clara had to have an American sponsor so that she and her son could return to the United States together. Accordingly she was sponsored by Franz Gutmann, a Methodist minister from Chapel Hill, North Carolina, and Dr. F. S. Chandler from Milwaukee. Gutmann, through contacts with Herbert von der Marwitz, had immigrated to the United States in the 1930s and lectured in economics at the University of North Carolina from 1939 to 1945.

On December 12, 1947, the 47-year-old Clara Elisabeth Hertling and her 17-year-old son returned to the United States from Germany aboard the *Marine Flasher*, which had sailed from Bremen, Germany. Since 1946, this ship had carried many Holocaust survivors and displaced persons seeking better lives in America.

Mrs. Hertling had in her possession 11 pieces of antique gold jewelry that were given to her by Herbert Marwitz. One of their first stops on December 17 was the Metropolitan Museum of Art in New York City, where she left several of the items and presented an affidavit of ownership that read as follows:

> I, Clara Elisabeth Hertling, declare that the pin, which I am offering to the Metropolitan Museum of Art for $500, was originally the property of Dr. Lederer, a collector from Vienna, who died in Switzerland during the war.
>
> Dr. Lederer was befriended by Graf Herbert von der Marwitz and lived in his castle in Switzerland. In gratitude he gave to Marwitz this pin with other gold objects. Mr. Marwitz is a friend of mine and met me at Marquartstein

Clara E. Hertling and Herbert von der Marwitz during a hike in 1946. She may have participated in a deception by master swindler Marwitz.

[near Munich and Rosenheim], where I taught school for eight years during the war, when I was stranded in Germany, where I had gone with my son to visit my mother.

Mr. Marwitz gave me the gold piece, including this pin. I hereby declare that I am the sole owner of these objects, including this pin. Mr. Marwitz is now living in his castle at Marquartstein and hopes to come to this country next year. He was in a concentration camp for a number of years....

/S/ Mrs. Clara E. Hertling[4]

Apparently Clara Hertling wanted to sell only one of the items, as she was in need of cash. James J. Rorimer, curator of the Metropolitan Museum of Art, recognized the jewelry as a modern forgeries. The following day, December 18, 1947, Clara Hertling removed the items from the Met in order to add them to the customs declaration as antique jewelry in her private collection.[5] A couple of days later, she and her son left by train for Los Angeles.

At an early date, Rorimer suggested that the Paul Drey Gallery in New York had purchased four of the pieces, which he considered to be originals. Dr. Drey acquired the jewelry from Mrs. Hertling for $850. These four pieces were prehistoric gold objects consisting of a bowl from the Bronze Age, one Langobarden pin, a bracelet, and a brooch, all supposedly dating from or before 1000 b.c. On October 12, 1948, Dr. Drey wrote Marwitz a letter and stated that three of the four items had been sold and that the remaining one was being offered to an institute. The arrangement for the purchase and sale between Rorimer, Hertling, Drey, and Marwitz indeed sounds out of the ordinary. Did Rorimer purchase them for the museum from Drey so that he could have clear title?

Little more became known about this case until six years later, in the autumn of 1952; Herbert von Marwitz dined in the elegant restaurant in Lago Maggiore, on the Italian-Swiss border. He left a large tip on the tray and retired to his room in the nearby hotel. The next morning, he, identified from his passport, was found dead. The craftiest art forger of the Third Reich had shot himself with a pistol.

Also at this time the jewels brought into the United States by Mrs. Hertling take on a strange twist. Somehow a Mrs. William George became custodian of this jewelry. In 1953, the Bureau of Customs began an investigation of Clara E. Hertling when these seven forged items were introduced into the art market as genuine antiques. Four of the original pieces of jewelry had been previously sold, and during this investigation James J. Rorimer told an agent of the Bureau of Customs that these four were "in his opinion genuine artifacts." He further told the agent the four items had been purchased by a dealer in New York, although he refused to identify the dealer. Rorimer's rationale was "that customs had not lost anything on the transaction inasmuch as the items were genuine antiques."[6]

The purchaser of the antiques, Paul Drey, died on March 18, 1953, and his wife destroyed most of the firm's records just before she set sail on the *Queen Mary* for Europe. Therefore the purchasers of the four items from the Paul Drey Gallery remain unknown.

According to a customs investigation, the entire amount of $850 from the original four items was paid by Mrs. Hertling to Mrs. William George. The remaining seven pieces were known as the Szirach Treasure. According to an article in the periodical *Germania*, these gold treasures, from the people's migration period, were found in Szirak in northern Hungary. In 1937 Marwitz had submitted the article. For these remaining items, Clara Hertling was asking $350,000.

In the summer of 1953, U.S. Customs was hot on the trial of Marwitz's items brought to the United States by Clara Hertling. On August 28, 1953, customs agents in Los Angeles recommended seizure of the jewelry and instituted forfeiture proceedings.

The following seven items were seized from Clara Hertling. On September 21, 1954, they were turned over to the Smithsonian Institution.

    1 gold necklace set with 30 garnets
    1 round-headed fibula [brooch] with garnet inlay
    1 brooch
    1 amethyst ball pendant framed with gold
    1 gold ring studded with 3 garnets
    1 Y-shaped fibula
    1 coin of Constantine II (317–340)

A handwritten note on the receipt of the Smithsonian Institution reads "forgeries with the possible exception of the coin."[7]

On February 1, 2010, after several years of correspondence, Gunter H. Hertling, the son of Clara, wrote a letter to the Smithsonian requesting a release of the seized objects "on ethical and moral grounds."

The papers of James J. Rorimer, museum director and art historian, are today in the Smithsonian. They were donated by Kay Rorimer, his widow, after his death in 1966.

Clara Hertling died in Munich in March 1980.

Part VI

Looting from Hungary in World War II

Chapter 27

Hungary

Early in 1940 the Hungarians had formed an alliance with Germany and furnished 13 divisions to fight against the Russians on the Eastern Front. After the German defeat at Stalingrad, a battle in which Hungarian units suffered tremendous losses, Admiral Miklos Horthy and Prime Minister Miklos Kallay recognized that Germany would likely lose the war. With Horthy's tacit approval, Kallay sought to negotiate a separate armistice for Hungary with the Allies. In order to forestall these efforts, German forces occupied Hungary on March 19, 1944. Horthy was permitted to remain regent. In the 1920s he had restored the monarchial government of the kingdom of Hungary without filling the throne of King Karoly IV, who had been exiled to Austria. Thus Hungary had become an anomaly — a kingdom without a king, governed by an admiral without a navy, who acted as a Protestant representative of a Catholic crown.

Most tragically, Adolf Eichmann, working under the directions of Himmler, would within a few months murder 300,000 Hungarian Jews, 75 percent of the Jewish population in Hungary, as part of a methodical plan to destroy European Jewry. Up to then, because of the alliance with Germany, Hungarian Jews had escaped the horrors of the concentration camps.

In light of the worsening military situation and facing threats, Horthy resumed efforts to reach an armistice with the Soviet Union, whose army was on Hungary's borders. When the Hungarians signed a peace agreement with the Russians on October 11, 1944, the Germans, under Otto Skorzeny's command, attacked with SS tanks and airborne troops. Skorzeny captured Regent Miklos Horthy and his cabinet, and within the hour Budapest radio proclaimed the new Hungarian Nazi regime.

On October 15, 1944, a German officer informed Horthy that the "prime minister" was requesting his presence. Horthy followed the German officer into the next room and to his astonishment, Ferenc Szalasi, an ally of the Nazis, stood before him. Horthy suggested that Szalasi have the Germans appoint him, Horthy, prime minister unless that had already been done. Horthy added, "I am a prisoner here; therefore, I cannot exercise any official function. But in any case you would be the last person I would be willing to appoint."[1] Immediately the Germans, who had been keeping Hungary under military occupation since March 1944, seized Horthy. They issued a recantation in his name together with a declaration that he had abdicated and carried the regent off to Germany.

On November 4 at 1 P.M., an emissary of the Third Reich, the Japanese and Italian ambassadors, and other diplomats assembled in the large hall of the Royal Palace, which was brilliantly illuminated by 20,000 candles. In the middle of the hall was a pulpit covered with red velvet. Before it stood the gold-mounted case containing the Crown of Saint Stephen. At both sides of the pulpit stood the members of the two parliaments. Archduke Josef Ferenc, in a field marshal's uniform, stood between the two chairmen of the house. The crown was removed from the case and placed upon the pulpit and, at the same time, Szalasi was escorted into the massive hall. He swore that he would be loyal to the country, keep its old customs and have others keep them, and that he would do everything he could for the public will and the country's glory.

After taking this oath, Szalasi left the Royal Palace for the prime minister's office. The Hungarian Arrow Cross Party, a motley organization of fanatical extremists endorsed and financed by the Nazis, had seized power. Szalasi, its leader and a former general staff major, proclaimed himself the leader of Hungary and issued orders for the continuance of war on the side of Germany. He organized his own cabinet under the direction of Heinrich Himmler, an action that would cause ill-fated Hungary, even at this late stage of the war, to continue to bleed for Hitler. The Szalasi regime was short-lived. Having done everything he could for the "public will and the country's glory," Szalasi and his associates fled to avoid capture by the Russians; they crossed the Austrian frontier and placed themselves under the protection of the tottering Nazi leaders.

The Hungarians, Axis partners of Nazi Germany, slowly retreated from the advancing Soviet Army. Staying just out of artillery range were the valuables of the Hungarian regime, their gold reserves, silver reserves, coronation regalia, and a trainload of valuables taken primarily from Holocaust victims. Ferenc Szalasi, the Nazi-appointed leader, was waiting for additional weapons promised by Hitler that would supposedly force the reversal of the war and his return to power in a triumphal Hungary. For Szalasi and millions of others under the Axis power, this was only fantasy. The collected valuables, the assets of the Hungarian National Bank, the Hungarian crown jewels, and Jewish valuables carried on a train known as the Hungarian Gold Train would be overrun and seized by U.S. Army forces. Some of these items were returned, while others, such as the Hungarian crown, were used as pawns in the Cold War. Many disappeared in the aftermath of the war.

Chapter 28

The Hungarian National Bank's Gold and Silver Reserves

The end of World War I left a catastrophic situation for the Hungarian economy. The League of Nations solved this by granting credits to Hungary but also insisting that the Hungarian economy be reorganized. In conforming to this demand, the Hungarian National Bank was created in 1924. It had the exclusive right to issue pengoes bank notes (Hungarian money) and transact international banking business for all of Hungary. The bank's activities remained under the financial control of the League of Nations, with an advisor appointed from the Bank of England. This relation continued until the outbreak of World War II.[1]

In 1935 the National Bank of Hungary, fearing the world political situation, built a huge underground office complex so that the bank's activities could continue without disturbance during a war, especially during air raids. In 1944, when air raids against Budapest became a daily occurrence, the underground complex was occupied by the bank and its staff. The bank was free of Hungarian Nazi Party members until the Szalasi régime took control of Hungary. At that time Leopold Baranyai, the president of the bank, was "dragged off by the Germans" and replaced by Laszlo Temesvary. He had been an owner and editor of the weekly newspaper *NEP* and became president of the bank solely because of his connections with Szalasi. With Temesvary's appointment as president, the paper was discontinued owing to a paper shortage and Temesvary's new responsibilities.[2]

In December 1945, as the advancing Red Army began to threaten Budapest, the National Bank of Hungary loaded its assets and gold reserves as well as its staff and their families aboard a train which then began to head westward. The refugees spent the next two months on that unheated train as it sat stalled on a side track of the main railroad, protected by Hungarian guards. Finally the Germans sent a locomotive and connected it to the train, which continued to the village of Spital am Pyhrn, Austria. The plan was to

A German laborer carries a Hungarian silver bar from the vaults of the Foreign Exchange Depository in Frankfurt, Germany. This much-publicized silver was being returned to Hungary by the U.S. government (courtesy National Archives).

move the bank and its staff to Switzerland, but this was opposed by the Germans.³

On the journey from Budapest, the Hungarian Bank's silver reserves were separated from the bank's other assets on January 17, 1945, at Sopron, Hungary. The silver was released to the German minister of finance and then loaded into seven freight cars. The train then proceeded to Vienna, but because of Allied bombing of the railway system, the silver was transferred to nine large trucks. These arrived in Magdeburg on January 29, 1945, but owing to severe air raids, the Magdeburg Reichsbank did not have the personnel or equipment to make a complete inventory. The officials merely signed a receipt for delivery of the silver.

After the capture of Magdeburg, members of the U.S. 30th Division questioned the Reichsbank officials and forced them to open the vault and assist in examining the contents, which included, 769 large silver bars, 5,273 small silver bars, 34 miscellaneous small silver bars, and 536 boxes of silver bars, coins, and records. The Magdeburg Reichsbank officials produced a letter showing that the deposit of silver in the bank was originally a part of Hungary's silver reserve.

The bank officials stated they had no knowledge of the Hungarian gold reserves. Gold had not been discussed during the silver transaction, they said. U.S. intelligence knew that the Soviets had advanced through Hungary and surmised that the Hungarians and Germans had not allowed the Hungarian gold reserves to be seized by the advancing Red Army.

On May 9, the 30th Division shipped 198,000 pounds of the remaining silver to the Foreign Exchange Depository in Frankfurt as shipment number 17.[4]

As the 80th Division of Gen. George Patton's Third Army advanced toward Spital am Pyhrn at the beginning of May 1945, Edgar Tornay and Count Geza Bethlen, two Hungarian bank officials, presented a letter from the National Bank to Col. E. A. Ball, the 80th Division's military governor. The letter stated that the bank was located in Spital am Pyhrn, where the valuables were being guarded by the Hungarian Royal Police, and requested protection from U.S. military authorities for the bank's valuables and its 680 employees and family members.

On May 10, 1945, Sgt. William DeHuszar, U.S. 80th Division, CIC, reached the Austrian town and took into custody the Hungarian Bank's valuables, which had been stored in a monastery adjoining a church. The material consisted of tons of paper pengoes, documents, receipts, coupons, bills, and other paper securities plus about 100 automobiles and various trucks. DeHuszar's first action was to arrest of Laszlo Temesvary, who had full power of attorney concerning the management of the bank. As DeHuszar reported, "Temesvary is considered a strong anti–Semite and believes in Szalasi."[5]

On May 12, the following order was issued in the name of Gen. Omar Bradley:

> It is desired that gold found in Lucky area [Gen. Patton's Headquarters, Third Army] whether or not in Austria be properly transported to Reichsbank at Frankfurt under proper security arrangements and delivered to Currency Section for Germany together with any documentary or other evidence relating

to ownership interest in such treasure. Tally should be made prior to removal and delivered to Currency Section with treasure. Information requested relating to discovery, ownership interest, and contents of such treasures.
By Command of General Bradley

It further stated that the commanding officer of the 317 Infantry Regiment would turn over to Maj. Lionel Perera the gold, currency, jewels, and other valuables at Spital.[6]

Major Perera took control of the more valuable assets of the Hungarian National Bank and on May 14 acknowledged he had the following valuables:

> a. 633 cases said to contain gold bullion and gold coins, net weight, 29,855.0465 kg
> b. 2 cases said to contain foreign bank notes and coins
> c. 19 cases said to contain safekeeping deposits
> d. 3 containers marked I-3048, II-3048, III-3049
> e. 1 package said to belong to Hungarian Military Police and to weigh 3.315 kg
> f. 28 cases to have been deposited by the Trust Company for Orphans of Budapest
> g. 1 sack said to contain: one case of sealed envelopes regarding Jewish properties, one package said to have been deposited by Commercial Bank of Budapest[7]

On May 15, 1945, Company K, 319 Infantry Regiment, loaded 15 trucks with this material. Traveling two days on a 400-mile trip, the U.S. 3805 Quartermaster Truck Company delivered the entire gold reserves of Hungary to the Foreign Exchange Depository in Frankfurt, Germany, as shipment number 20. The receipt for this shipment as described above was signed for by Col. H. D. Cragon. Remaining in Spital am Pyhrn were the staff and family members of the Hungarian National Bank and tons of books, postage stamps, and documents, including Hungarian paper money weighing 105 tons and consisting of about four billion Hungarian pengoes.

Dr. Julius Biber, the manager of the Hungarian National Bank, worried about his valuables and the welfare of his staff, wrote letters to the International Bank Settlement, Switzerland, the Federal Reserve Board, the Bank of England, and the International Red Cross expressing concern that the U.S. Army had taken over the assets of the bank. Biber was justifiably worried about his staff and wrote:

> There remains, however, one more problem to be solved, touching the most vital interest of the bank's employees; that is the question of their eventual delivery to the Russians. The bank and all persons belonging to it immigrated to Austria first of all to be safe from the Russians. The reason for that is to be found in the first rank — beside the generally known conduct of the Russian

28. The Hungarian National Bank's Gold and Silver Reserves

The gold in these boxcars is being checked after crossing the Hungarian border (courtesy National Archives).

occupiers — in the bank's hundred per cent capitalistic policy, incompatible with bolshevism.... It is therefore evident that the delivery to Russians would mean the most intensive danger to life for each and every person belonging to the Bank.[8]

His letters went on to request permission for the bank's staff to be allowed to immigrate to Switzerland and noted that their expenses for transportation, food, and housing could be taken from the bank's foreign credit balances, which at the time included Swiss Francs valued at $72,000.

Biber's letters regarding the Hungarian gold must have had an impact on the Allies, for on November 9, 1945, an international conference opened in Paris involving all the countries that had been at war with Germany. The purpose of the conference was to determine the amount of reparations payable by Germany following World War II. Surprisingly, at this conference the Hungarian gold was specifically exempted from the Allied "gold pot" of 420 tons of tainted Nazi gold recovered in Europe.

The bank's staff was allowed to remain in Spital am Pyhrn for a year. Later, as the remaining items were being readied for shipment back to Hungary, the U.S. Army Displaced Persons Office had no plans to force the separation of the Hungarians bankers at Spital am Pyhrn. The DP officer told Captain William R. Loeffer, who was in charge of sending these remaining items to Budapest, that the employees of the bank were out of favor with the present regime in Hungary and therefore were afraid to return. Loeffer asked for a list of the employees and also a separate list of those who wanted to return with the bank's records. Some 70 to 80 people asked to return.

Meanwhile it was planned that the four freight cars of pengoes would remain in Austria as paper pulp; however, it was then decided that the currency, which was now worthless, would be a more valuable commodity as waste paper in Hungary than it was in Austria.[9] Also the sealed deposits were opened and examined for gold, foreign currency, and securities. Unfortunately there is no record as to what was found.

On the morning of August 30, 1946, a total of 24 freight cars and 4 passenger cars chugged out of Spital am Pyhrn for Budapest, Hungary. The remaining Hungarians were allowed to resettle in Germany.

As inflation in Hungary spiraled and the economy descended into chaos, Imre Nagy, the Hungarian prime minister, traveled to Washington, D.C., and negotiated with the State Department for the release of the gold and silver reserves seized by the American during the last days of the war. On June 14, 1946, the United States informed Nagy that the gold would be returned, and on July 10, a preliminary conference was held between representatives of the Foreign Exchange Depository and the Hungarian Restitution Delegation to discuss procedural matters in this regard. As a result, a Hungarian mission headed by Dr. Nicholas Myaradi, minister of finance, arrived in Frankfurt on July 3 to make arrangements for the return of the gold.

On July 31, Col. William G. Brey gave the order to break the ribbon seal on the door of compartments five and six in the lower main vault of the

Foreign Exchange Depository in Frankfurt, Germany. These compartments contained gold and cloth bags for packing the gold bars. After 1,300 cloth bags were taken, the compartments were immediately resealed. Colonel Brey then gave the order to open compartment seven in the lower vault, the one that contained the Hungarian gold. These compartments had not been opened since the gold was first stored there on May 16, 1945.

A team of seven Americans and six Hungarians then assiduously checked and compared the bars of gold as they were removed from the 90 piles and packed into the bags. A 55-pound weight limit was set for each bag. The bags were numbered, sealed, and removed to compartment nine, which had been emptied previously. The bags containing gold coins were not repacked but just opened and checked. A total of 1,222 bags were used: 1,184 contained gold bars and 38 contained gold coins. The repacking took four days and was completed on Saturday afternoon, August 3.

On Monday, August 5, the removal of the gold from the vault began under guard of the 381st Military Police Battalion. The MPs loaded a small hand truck with five bags of gold and wheeled it to a ventilator opening and from there loaded the bags onto a fleet of 16 trucks. The last bag was loaded at 1:30 P.M. The trip from the Foreign Exchange Depository to the train station was made under tight security and the utmost precautions were taken as the trucks moved through the streets of Frankfurt. Two tanks escorted each truck and no incidents occurred during the transfer to the train station. The gold was then reloaded into three large baggage cars that were locked from the outside with special $3/8$-inch twisted iron bars. Three U.S. Military Police with machine guns were posted in each baggage car. On each car there was a sign in five languages saying that anyone who approached and tried to open the door would be shot without warning. The train consisted of three armed baggage cars, two sleepers, a lounge car, and dining car; the lounge car had been Adolf Hitler's and one magnificent sleeper had belonged to Eva Braun. Now the train was the property of the U.S. Army.

The train left Frankfurt on August 6, 1946, at 6 P.M. with 56 American soldiers as guards, including Col. Brey. Several officials of the Hungarian government also were on board. The 600-mile trip took two days. During that hot August, the heat in the baggage cars became unbearable for the guards, who removed their jackets and shirts. During the journey, the train entered the Soviet Occupation Zone at Bad Enns, Austria, and two Soviet majors boarded the train to escort it through Soviet territory. The U.S. Army proved a gracious host and served Coca-Cola, wine, beer, roast beef, asparagus, and coffee to the Russians and the Hungarian delegation.

At the Austro-Hungarian border, several Hungarian officials, five whom boarded the train, welcomed it. From the border to Budapest, a distance of about 116 miles, crowds who had gathered to watch it pass greeted the train enthusiastically. This train contained the hopes of the Hungarians for an end to the depression caused by the war. The closer the train came to Budapest, the bigger the crowds at the stations and crossroads became.

Thousands of people jammed the railway station at Budapest to greet the train when it arrived at 8 P.M. on August 7, 1946. The station was decorated with Hungarian and American flags and guarded by a great number of Hungarian policemen. Officially welcoming the train was a large reception committee from the Hungarian government. Ambassador Arthur Schoenfold and Gen. Weems represented the American government; also present were representatives from the Soviet Union. After a speech from the minister of finance, Ambassador Schoenfold presented a symbolic bag of gold to Prime Minister Nagy. When the sack was opened, the sparkling yellow gold glittered in the station lights and both statesmen smiled broadly.

Under heavy police security, the sacks of gold were quickly and noiselessly loaded onto trucks by employees of the Hungarian National Bank and taken through the blocked-off street to the bank's vault. By 10 P.M. the last bag was loaded onto the truck and 10 minutes later was in the vault. After a year and eight months, the gold had safely ended its trip and come home.[10]

During January 1947, the Foreign Exchange Depository received a report from the Hungarian National Bank that it had received a surplus of gold coins in the shipment of gold reserves. Originally the gold bars and coins had been placed in compartment seven by Col. Bernard Bernstein and his staff and they had sealed the vault door. It was always assumed that the entire contents of that compartment was the property of the Hungarian National Bank. The bags of coins were weighed and both the Hungarians and Americans agreed that the coins matched the available records.

But when the Hungarians revalidated the actual weights and number of coins, gold coins of Turkey, Japan, and Colombia were discovered. An embarrassed Col. Brey and one security officer returned to Budapest in March 1947 and picked up the coins to return them to the depository even though the men were not sure who the owners were.[11]

Because U.S. forces in Germany recovered the Hungarian silver reserves, there was a controversy among the Allies regarding their return to the Hungarian government. Despite the controversy, the United States made a commitment to the Hungarian government to return the silver reserves. In the middle of March, 1947, the Departments of Defense and State issued a joint directive to return the silver immediately to Hungary.

On March 21, 1947, work began in the Foreign Exchange Depository with an inspection of the vaults by Col. Brey and his staff to prepare the silver for removal. It was necessary to type a full list by number of the location of each silver bar. Since some of the bars did not have their weight stamped on them, they had to be weighed in order to have a complete and accurate record. The vault operation involved the checking of the 6,783 silver bars against the prepared listings, and the final check of the shipment was completed on April 9. The following day a conference on transit problems and other arrangements was held at the depository, attended by Foreign Exchange Depository personnel and Hungarian representatives. Procedures for the loading of the silver, a train schedule, security preparations and publicity were reviewed and final adjustments made.[12]

On April 21 the 198,000 pounds of silver and other valuables were transferred from the vaults at the depository to five freight cars at the main railway station in Frankfurt. Other items were also transferred from the vaults, items seized with the Hungarian gold reserves but not returned with them. They included foreign currency, gold coins, gold bars, platinum, the personal property of former President Ferenc Szalasi, and deposits of the Trust Company for Orphans of Budapest.

Photographers and motion picture cameras recorded various phases of the transfer of the valuables for posterity and documentary proof.

Two additional baggage cars containing jewelry and crated art objects were attached to the train at Regensburg. The art was valued at $20 million and consisted of 51 paintings and 340 drawings. It included works of Da Vinci, Raphael, Rembrandt, Van Gogh, and Dürer. The trip was similar to the gold delivery except that one silver-laden car developed a hot box in the wheel assembly. An additional baggage car had been provided for such an emergency. Colonel Brey, the off-duty MPs, and Hungarian officials then transferred the silver to the extra car.[13]

Karl Kristof of the Hungarian paper *Vilag* was invited to Frankfurt to cover the story of the return of the Hungarian Silver. It follows:

> Frankfurt on the Main, in a small undamaged section of the city and situated on a large square a huge building, the Foreign Exchange Depository. There is no admission to it. The Americans have taken charge of the building and within it they guard the treasury stolen by the Nazis. In the company of the capable chief of the Hungarian Commission, Alexander Ham, I enter the building. At the door leading to the hall of the vault room our papers are checked once more. Now we turn to the immense basement located in the Depository. A heavy steel door is opening and we are within a treasury chamber. In long rows the silver bars are piled up, 50 bars piled on top of each other form one pile. The ordinary bar weighs 30 pounds, the larger ones 66 pounds. We are showed to a place surrounded by iron bars. Here thousands of diamonds, cut and raw ones lie on tables, Pitiful contents are seen in boxes guarded by members of the M.P.s; gold teeth torn from the mouths of victims of Auschwitz.

On Monday morning at eight o'clock the loading of the Hungarian valuables is started. German labor service men place the silver into trucks. On the way to the station one jeep proceeding and another one following every truck. The trucks tore through the town with sirens on full blast. Soon the 97 tons of silver was loaded in the railroad carriages. As the train approached Wiestal, an axel of one of the carriages broke down. The train stops. All of us crowd around the breakdown. We all take part in the reloading of the silver. During the night the train stops at Regensberg. Here two further carriages are attached to the train. In one is loaded the art collection of the Museum of Fine Art. At the frontier of the Russian Zone four Russian army officers board our train. They speak an excellent English and they are most amiable. They accompany the train to Budapest. A great number of American reporters came to Budapest.[14]

Thus ended a second successful mission providing Hungary with another step forward in its struggle for financial and economic rehabilitation from the destruction of World War II.

In this way Hungary's much-needed silver and gold was returned by the United States. Surely there would also be quick resolution for the Crown Treasure and Holocaust era assets.

Chapter 29

The Acquisition of the Hungarian Crown Treasure

The most outstanding objects to cross an international frontier during World War II were the Crown and Coronation Regalia of Saint Stephen, the first king of Hungary, who was crowned in the first year of the 11th century. He became a saint because he led the people of his country to the Christian faith. According to the views and customs prevailing at the time, a request for title of king and for a crown could be directed only to the Holy See. This was rooted in the medieval Christian concept of the divine origin of royal power. According to general opinion and his own belief, only through the granting of such a request could Stephen become equal in rank to the other Catholic monarchs of his time. Thus the royal crown was given to Stephen by Pope Sylvester II.

Saint Stephen died on August 15, 1038. In the year 1090, the tomb of Saint Stephen was opened and his right hand, which rested on a piece of ivory wrapped in silk, was found in a state of perfect preservation. A beaded pearl bracelet of diamonds and rubies set in gold encircled the hand across the fingers. Two identical bracelets encircled the wrist, and between them was another bracelet of gold leaves. The hand was then hermetically sealed in a gold and crystal shrine and remained in the Burg Chapel of the Royal Castle at Budapest. This "holy hand" became a symbol of the first apostolic king and symbolic of the adoption of Christianity by the Hungarians. Every year on August 20, the procession of Saint Stephen is observed; in it, the sacred hand is carried by the first primate of Hungary, followed by the king and the members of the Hungarian Parliament.

During Saint Stephen's reign and for generations thereafter, the royal crown was constantly in the king's immediate vicinity. He was in effect its keeper and guardian, as well as its wearer and supreme representative. Whenever he made a journey to the provinces, which he did several times each year in his capacity as chief justice to hear cases in open court, he had the crown at his side. Sessions were held outdoors so that the people could see their monarch; the crown would be on exhibit near his person, protected by hand-picked guards.[1]

For eight centuries following the reign of Saint Stephen, no Hungarian had any doubt that the relic known as Saint Stephen's Crown had been sent by Pope Sylvester II to the Hungarian leader in the year 1000. Not until 1790 were a few selected art historians and other specialists given the opportunity to examine it. The time allowed was short, but it sufficed for the experts to reach unanimous agreement that the crown had two hemispheric bands of gold, bisected above a gold crown, all highly ornamented with rough-cut jewels on nine enameled paintings of the apostles. The upper half of this exceptional work was of magnificent European workmanship done at the time of Saint Stephen. The lower half of the relic was of Byzantine origin and designed for a female. It was made in Hungary in the last quarter of the 11th century, although its enameled tablets were made between 1074 and 1077 in the Byzantine imperial workshop. The two crowns had been welded together no earlier than 1270.[2]

The gold, enameled, and bejeweled holy crown of Saint Stephen was kept in a velvet-lined box inside the royal chest (courtesy National Archives).

What all this means is not, of course, that the crown is counterfeit; merely that it is not what it had been believed to be. Whatever the case may be, the crown had assumed a mystical, historical, and psychological identity of its own. This is so strong that it renders most Hungarians virtually impervious to scholarly arguments that might throw the slightest doubt upon its genuineness. Few today know much about the true history and archaeological background of the crown; nearly all venerate it in its assumed capacity as literally "Saint Stephen's Crown."[3]

Specific legal provisions were not made for the physical care and safety of the crown until the middle of the 15th century. From the late 19th century onward, the prime minister was given increasing authority to ensure the safety of the crown. In 1928 it was declared: "As authority and responsibility of the Royal Hungarian Council of Ministers also extends to the custody of the Holy Crown and the Coronation Insignia, the Custodian of the Holy Crown exercises his rights and duties under the present law in conjunction with the legally appointed Royal Hungarian Council of Ministers."[4]

The same legislation established the formation of the Royal Hungarian Guards. Their task was to protect faithfully and permanently the Holy Crown and Coronation Regalia in a fortified room designed especially for this purpose within the Royal Castle in Budapest. A score of guards were carefully selected and tested both before their assignments and periodically thereafter. On duty in front of and in the vicinity of the Armor Room, they cut exotic figures, wearing medieval-style headgear and dark-green-braided tunics, yellow morocco boots, and a cloth cloak lined with red silk.

On November 7, 1944, as the Red Army's armored divisions began to encircle Budapest, the relic and other coronation regalia from the Armor Room in the Royal Castle were removed and taken to the branch office of the Hungarian National Bank in the town of Veszprem. On December 5, they were transferred to a monastery at Koszeg and three weeks later to an air-raid shelter built into the slope of a hill at Velem. On March 17, 1945, Col. Ernoe Pajtas, commander of the Crown Guards, accompanied by 12 of the guards, carried the Crown Jewels by truck into Austria. The coronation regalia, consisting of two chests, were taken by Ferenc Szalasi's entourage. The linkage between Saint Stephen's Crown and the coronation regalia during this time is unclear, but it is apparent Pajtas and Szalasi were in close proximity and in constant communication.[5]

In Mattsee, Austria, on the night of March 26, 1944, Pajtas and two of his most trusted sergeants went to the truck containing the large chest holding the crown and other valuables. They opened the large 20th-century iron chest and removed from it the Holy Crown as well as the scepter and sphere, which were in their original leather coverings. Pajtas' hands trembled as he lifted them out and placed them into a military gasoline barrel slit in half. Only the sword remained in the chest, which was then locked again. He and the two sergeants took the half barrel and went to a spot in front of a sheer cliff that had been selected the day before, as there were no houses nearby. They dug a deep hole, inserted the barrel, and covered it up. They left no trace of the digging and no one had noticed the three men engaged in burying the treasure.

On May 2, Pajtas and his men continued toward Zellhof, near Mattsee, with the nearly empty locked chest on the back of a truck. In Zellhof they

The crown treasure and heirlooms that once belonged to Saint Stephen, the first king of Hungary, were in this iron chest. They were taken into custody by the U.S. Seventh Army and sent to Fort Knox, Kentucky, where they remained until President Jimmy Carter arranged for their return 33 years later (courtesy National Archives).

stayed in a Roman Catholic Mission House. On May 6, the Catholic priest of the mission went to Seeham, where an American command had been established; he told the Americans that a Hungarian colonel and 12 enlisted men were at his monastery. At 5 P.M. Lt. Granville, an American officer, drove out to the monastery in a jeep. He told the Hungarians that he wanted them to surrender to him as American prisoners of war. Pajtas agreed to this but told Granville that he could not leave the truck, since it contained valuables that he could not leave unprotected even for one moment. They then agreed that Pajtas and his men would follow the jeep in the truck.

On May 7, 1945, they drove the 70 miles to Augsburg, Germany, and there the ancient chest was delivered to the U.S. Seventh Army Interrogation Center. It was then taken to Maj. Paul Kubala. Col. Pajtas stated that it contained the holy crown of Saint Stephen and further he had remained with the crown inasmuch as he was its official custodian and guardian. The iron chest was locked with three padlocks plus the lock of the chest itself. The front of the chest bore the insignia of the Hungarian state. Upon questioning, the colonel stated that the keys had originally been distributed to three people.

The task of finding the keys went to Lt. Granville of the Seventh Army Interrogation Center, who investigated all Hungarians who might know their location. The colonel and four guards stayed with the chest and the rest of the guards were interned as prisoners of war.

On July 24, Granville located the keys in Salzburg. He took them to the treasure chest and opened it in the presence of Maj. Kubala. Much to everyone's surprise, the chest contained only Saint Stephen's sword. Col. Pajtas was located immediately and asked for an explanation. The colonel replied that he knew all along that the chest was empty since he personally had removed the contents and buried them in accordance with instructions. Pajtas went on to say that during his stay in Augsburg he had reported his actions to the Regent Miklos Horthy, also in custody as an American prisoner, and to his great relief the regent had approved of his action. The regent had insisted that the holy crown and its coronation jewels should never be regarded as spoils of war since they had no connection with military operations. The regent had emphasized to Pajtas that the Hungarian authorities and not the Germans had brought the relics from Hungary.

Regardless, it was pointed out to Col. Pajtas that he had put the U.S. Army in a most embarrassing position, as those involved knew that the box was under the protection of the U.S. Seventh Army. President Harry Truman had been informed of the recovery of the holy crown and Maj. Paul Kubala explained that the historic relic was to have been shown to the president and General Eisenhower.

Under extreme pressure, Col. Pajtas and his accomplices told Kubala that the crown was buried in Mattsee. This area was then under the authority of Patton's Third Army. Therefore the Seventh Army Interrogation Center was not authorized to carry out a search in Mattsee. This greatly annoyed Kubala, since it meant that he would have to go through a lot of red tape to acquire the treasure.[6]

Lt. Worth B. Andrews of Fort Worth, Texas, an imaginative young man, told Kubala that he could simply go and get the crown out of the Third Army area. Kubala declined to take the responsibility for such an illegal step. But Andrews insisted, and that night at 11 P.M. he woke Pajtas and said, "Come on colonel, let's go and get the crown. Bring one of your men and also bring some weapons."[7] Pajtas explained that as a prisoner he had no weapons. Andrews then left and soon returned with a large pistol, which he handed to Pajtas.

Although Kubala remained opposed to Andrews' plans, Andrews was determined to go ahead and motioned for Pajtas and two of his men to follow him. Then they went out into the dark and pushed a jeep quietly down the road so that the major would not hear them. Then they started the engine and cut loose into the night. Of course the four men had loaded the jeep with shovels and pickaxes.

In Munich they reached the demarcation line of the Third Army area. The sleepy guard accepted Andrews' credentials without question and permitted the party to travel on. It was still dark when they reached Mattsee. After two hours of digging, they reached the gasoline barrel containing the holy crown and other items, which were in good condition except for the leather coverings, which had been spoiled by their long underground stay. They all admired the holy crown, which sparkled in the gleam of the jeep's headlights.[8]

The following day at noon, the four men returned with the old mud-covered gasoline drum and brought it to Maj. Kubala's room. Kubala immediately embraced his disobedient officer who had cut through all the military red tape.

The drum was then reopened by Col. Pajtas, who removed three muddy, disintegrating leather-covered boxes. Maj. Kubala and Col. Pajtas washed all the mud and dirt off the items and then placed them on the floor to dry. After the items were thoroughly dry, they were placed back into the original chest. The interior of the chest was lined with leather and the subdivided compartments now contained the following pieces:

> The gold-enameled and jeweled holy crown of Saint Stephen kept in a velvet-lined plywood box. [See Appendix D for a detailed description.]
> The royal scepter, a hollow cylinder of gold plate surmounted by a crystal ball, symbolizing the king's authority as supreme judge. The ball is believed by some experts to be of Egyptian rock crystal from the 9th or 10th century, coming close in both time and place to support the Hungarian belief that the ball was brought from the ancient Asian homeland of the Magyars in an age when magic powers were attributed to rock crystal. The scepter has golden hoops running across it which narrows into 10 short gold chains which end with little balls that hang loose and make an attractive ringing sound when moved. This was possibly intended to signal the king's approach during the coronation procession.
> The golden coronation apple, a 14th-century orb or hollowed sphere of silver gilt with a dual cross mounted on top and two coats of arms engraved in it sides. They represent the Hungarian kingdom and the French-Italian dynasty. It symbolized kingly power and justice and was kept in a velvet-lined plywood box.
> The sword of Saint Stephen, symbolizing the king's authority as supreme warlord. It was a straight sword, double-edged with a regular taper. It was sheathed with red velvet and kept in a leather box.

Upon viewing the holy crown, Andor C. Klay of the United States Office of Strategic Services (OSS) said "It is beautiful, in the way a mummy is, or an ancient painting. It's not a glittering kind of thing, not something that radiates. But when you know its history, there is magic about it." The treasure chest was locked back into the ancient chest and kept at the Seventh Army Interrogation Center until August, 1945.

The holy crown, scepter, golden coronation apple, and sword as well as a small glass tube containing some gold, two Hungarian documents, three padlocks, and a key recovered by the Seventh Army Interrogation Center were shipped to the Foreign Exchange Depository in Frankfurt on August 3, 1945, as shipment number 59.[9]

During his stay at the Seventh Army Interrogation Center, Col. Pajtas did not tell Maj. Kubala that he had stashed more valuables in Mattsee, nor did he tell Kubala why he had buried the holy crown. Kubala also never asked why he had retained the chest and sword. Why did Pajtas not bury the complete chest? Because Ferenc Szalasi had instructed Pajtas in the scheme of hiding the crown and showing up with the locked chest and the sword. Then they had planned on charging the Americans with the responsibility of having stolen the crown. Szalasi had hopes of returning to Hungary in authority after the war. At a time well calculated for his benefit, Szalasi would then "discover" the hiding place of the Holy Crown.[10]

On June 17, 1945, as 2/Lt. James W. Shea of the 242nd Infantry Regiment, 42nd Division, 7th Army, and his unit were conducting an investigation of a group of Hungarian fascists who had occupied high positions in the Szalasi regime. These individuals had systematically looted the Jews of Hungary concurrently with the extermination carried out by the SS. They along with Szalasi had withdrawn from Hungarian territory into Austria.

The trail led to the quiet town of Mattsee, near Salzburg, Austria, where relatives of Szalasi and other high government officials had found refuge after their flight from the Red Army. During the interrogation of these Hungarian officials, two cooks, who had been on the staff of Adm. Horthy, stated that they knew where a large box of Hungarian valuables was hidden in a local carpenter shop on the fringe of Lake Mattsee, which was only 100 yards from an American military rest center for enlisted men. They further stated that Father Anton Strasser, a priest in Mattsee, had the key to the box.

Lt. Shea went to see Father Strasser and learned that the priest had been approached in February 1945 by Col. Ernoe Pajtas, commander of the Hungarian Crown Guard, to take three boxes into safe custody. During this conversation, Father Strasser took Shea and his team to the hut, a carpenter shop, by Lake Mattsee. One treasure chest was hidden in the carpenter shop and was pointed out by Father Strasser, who had the key and unlocked the heavy box with its iron fastenings. The box contained Emperor Franz Joseph's silverware. It was then relocked and put under guard of two members of Lt. Shea's counterintelligence team.

The party went to Father Strasser's home where, in his drawing room, there was an apparent couch, but it was actually two boxes covered and camouflaged as a couch. Removing the cover, Strasser pointed out a large wooden box covered with a rubber casing. The rubber casing and wooden screws from the top of the box were removed. The box contained a large roll of fabric, which was Saint Stephen's coronation robe, and the royal coat and gloves of Charles IV. These items were not removed and, after the lid had been closed, Father Strasser opened a small wooden box that contained the holy right hand of Saint Stephen. The hand was in a hermetically sealed gold and crystal casket with the hand resting palm down on a beige tapestry trimmed with gold lace over a piece of ivory wrapped in silk. A beaded pearl bracelet of diamonds and rubies set in gold encircled the hand across the fingers; two identical bracelets encircled the wrist, one at each side of another bracelet of gold leaf. This priceless relic had been kept in the Hungarian Royal Castle in Budapest in the Burg Chapel. The two boxes containing these sacred items were placed under the guard of four men from Lt. Shea's team. The boxes were then locked and at no time were any of the articles removed from the three boxes.[11]

Immediately Lt. Shea contacted Col. Tom Lewis, commander of the field artillery unit at Mattsee, and requested additional guards for the treasure. That afternoon Shea and Lewis drove to Salzburg and reported the find to Capt. George W. Selke, MFAA archival officer. That same day, June 17, and under orders from Lt. Col. Lewis, the treasure was moved to the Stiftskirche in Mattsee by members of the church and guarded by a U.S. Army detachment. Following standard procedure, Lt. James W. Shea asked for a receipt for the items uncovered by his CIC detachment. At the church an inventory of the valuables was supposedly taken by Charles Brousz, Military Government of Bavaria; but unfortunately Brousz translated and typed the Hungarian inventory into English and did not inventory the actual items. Being unaware of this, Selke signed a receipt for the entire set of 29 items of Hungarian crown treasure, including the holy crown, orb, and scepter, valued at $2.5 million in 1945 and in custody of the U.S. Army at the Seventh Army Interrogation Center.[12]

The holy hand of Saint Stephen, one of the most sacred possessions of the kingdom of Hungary, was removed from the wooden box by Father Strasser and placed on the main altar of the Stiftskirche and exhibited from June 17 at 7 P.M. until 2 P.M. the following afternoon for public adoration. It is ironic that the Stiftskirche had been destroyed by the Hungarians (Magyars) on their retreat from the battle of Lechfeld just 1000 years earlier and that this Stiftskirche, rebuilt about the year 1000, was now protecting the reliquary of Saint Stephen, the son of Geza. At 2 P.M. on June 18, the holy hand and coronation robe were handed over in a festive religious ceremony to Prince Archbishop Andreas Rohracher. On June 19, 1945, George Selke wrote: "The Prince Archbishop was designated as the custodian of the holy hand and dedicated coronation robes, to hold them for the military government until further disposition is determined." As we shall see, Prince Archbishop Rohracher did not have the same understanding as Selke. At this time the Americans and Austrians thought that they had succeeded in securing the treasures of the Hungarian nation after the confusion of World War II.

The prince archbishop signed for the following:

> The case containing the holy hand of Saint Stephen.
> The royal robe — this was in its original form a Roman Catholic chasuble (outer vestment of the celebrant at mass) embroidered by Saint Stephen's wife, Gisella, for the coronation of her husband. She donated it to the parish of Szekesfehervar in the year of Stephen's death (1031). The lining bears a likeness of the royal couple amid Latin inscriptions and the date. Made or oriental silk and embroidered with gold yarn, the robe was originally bell-shaped with a circular opening at the top. A vertical cut from the top to hem transformed it for the occasion of the coronation of Maria Theresia (1740–1780) into the mantle-like garment that it is today.
> A heavy metal chest made in the 1600s with the so-called great crest of the lands of the holy crown on it front. The chest was to serve as the official repository for the coronation regalia.
> A roll of fabric sewed into a cambric covering.
> A pair of gloves worn by King Charles IV at his coronation.
> A leather case containing the Hungarian crown treasure inventory from 1630 to 1920.[13]

In error, the prince archbishop also signed for the silverware of Emperor Franz Joseph. These two chests were taken and kept by the archbishop in his protective custody for the military government until further disposition could be determined. The valuables were stored in the treasury of St. Peter's Abbey in Salzburg, Austria. The chest from the carpenter shop, containing the court silverware of Emperor Franz Joseph was deposited on June 18, in the U.S. Property Control Warehouse in Salzburg under the custody of the commanding officer Col. Homer K. Heller.[14]

The Hungarian government was aware of the recovery of these valuables and contacted the U.S. Department of State in Budapest to request their immediate release, claiming that the holy hand would have to be returned for the impending Saint Stephen's procession on August 20, 1945. The U.S. authorities requested that Archbishop Rohracher release the holy hand. He balked, and prior to Archbishop Rohracher's releasing it to Hungary, U.S. military personnel flew to Rome and obtained the Vatican's approval for its release by Archbishop Rohracher to U.S. authorities. On this trip the Vatican expressed its concern about these relics to Gen. Mark W. Clark and asked that the crown be consigned to the Holy See. According to Vatican officials: "the general kindly expressed his readiness to offer every possible assistance."[15]

On August 20, 1945, Chaplain Ralph J. Diefenbach, a captain in the U.S. Army, in the presence of a considerable number of ecclesiastic, military, and civilian dignitaries, delivered the Holy Hand to the archbishop's Vicar General Custodian Witz Bela in Budapest. In 1083, when Saint Stephen was canonized, his grave was opened in conjunction with traditional ceremonies. All of his body had turned into bones and dust with the exception of his right hand. This governing and blessed right hand gave rise to a cult in Hungary, and every year on Saint Stephen's Day the holy right hand is carried around in a solemn and glittering ceremony in Budapest. The ceremony took place in Budapest at the Convent of the English Sisters and in time for the celebration of St. Stephen's Day on August 20, 1945.

In this act of kindness, Chaplain Diefenbach did not request a signed receipt for delivery of the holy hand. In the political arena, this became a big problem, as charges surfaced that the hand was a substitute and the original hand was still in possession of the Americans. Six months later, the embarrassed Chaplain wrote: "The U.S. authorities need an official statement for their files showing that the holy hand of St. Stephen was returned by me to the proper authorities in Budapest and the U.S. Army is cleared for any responsibility in the matter of the holy relic."[16] Fortunately he received a compassionate and positive response from Witz Bela exonerating the U.S. Army and stating the relic had been received intact in the original relic holder with the seals unbroken.

This left one chest in Archbishop Rohracher's possession, which contained the royal robe and other scared objects. Unbeknownst to the U.S. Army, Rohracher was also holding a treasure of Nazi tainted gold coins.

Chapter 30

The Gold Treasure of Kremsmünster

Part of Hitler's elaborate plan for his "Thousand-Year Reich" was the total transformation of Linz, his hometown, into a cosmopolitan cultural center. Arrays of public buildings were to be designed under Hitler's personal supervision. A cultural superstructure, the Führer Museum, was planned for the town center. The collections for this remarkable center were to be selected by the Linz Commission, which was headed by Martin Bormann. Under his direction Dr. Helmut von Hummel was responsible for the collection of coins and armor. The coins had been acquired from all parts of Europe, but the main part of the collection was acquired from religious foundations in Austria, notably that of Klosterneuburg, which also included coins from the Louis Rothschild collections. The collection was known as the gold treasure of Kremsmünster, as it was confiscated by the Nazi regime and selected by Hitler's art experts to form the nucleus of the coin collection of the projected Führer Museum in Linz.

As the war progressed and owing to Allied bombings, this large collection was stored underground in a salt mine in Alt Aussee, Austria. After Germany's surrender, the Allies recovered the paintings and other art objects at Alt Aussee, but the gold coins were missing.[1]

On April 30, 1945, von Hummel arrived at the Alt Aussee mine; there, he had the case of gold coins delivered to him and placed on a truck. Von Hummel stated that he was delivering the gold coins to Prince Archbishop Andreas Rohracher of Salzburg. But the collection was later found to be missing and the bishop's name was associated with this missing $2 million collection. But the archbishop was above suspicion and of course he would never have cooperated with the Nazi in hiding their ill-gotten gains. Or would he?

Late in October 1945, Walter W. Horn, the overworked art intelligencer officer, was informed by the MFAA branch in Salzburg, Austria, that a collection of gold coins was missing. He was also asked for assistance in tracing and apprehending Dr. Helmut von Hummel, the last person known to have had the valuable treasure in his possession. Von Hummel should not have been difficult to spot; his eyebrows met in the middle without thinning and he had a prominent Heidelberg sword scar on his lower left cheek.

Horn had no trouble in locating von Hummel's associates in the city jail at Zell am See; they denied any knowledge of von Hummel's whereabouts but admitted that the gold coins were taken to meet political ends. Finding von Hummel's wife and mother was also relatively easy, but at first each stated that she did not know the whereabouts of von Hummel. Finally, on the morning of April, 17, 1946, Horn again interrogated the TB-infected Mrs. Helmut von Hummel. He forcefully directed her to swear that she did not know the whereabouts of her husband, which she refused to do. Horn then explained to her that refusing the oath was tantamount to admitting that she knew where her husband was. At this she remained silent and began to weep. Under mounting pressure from Horn, she maintained that she could not be expected to betray her husband. Also, she did not want to betray her church. Horn stated that he was interested only in obtaining the collection of gold coins. After still more discussion, Mrs. von Hummel agreed that the most sensible thing for her husband to do would be to give himself up to the American authorities and that such action could only speed his eventual reunion with his family. In spite of all this, she would not disclose her husband's location. She told Horn to give her a week and she would persuade her husband to give himself up. Horn agreed that he would return to her farmhouse in Mondsee, Austria, a week later, and if her mission was not accomplished with some sort of success, she would be arrested in spite of her illness.[2]

One week later, on April 26, 1946, Horn returned to Mondsee. Mrs. von Hummel told Horn that her husband would turn himself over to Mr. Hoffmann, chief of the CIC Detachment, in Salzburg at 10 A.M. on May 10. Also, Mrs. Hummel had in hand a sheet of paper dated April 24, 1946, written and signed by Prince Archbishop Andreas Rohracher of Salzburg. In a most unexpected turn the signed document stated that von Hummel had appeared before Rohracher with the coins that had been removed from the salt mine of Alt Aussee during the last days of the Third Reich and given them to Rohracher for safekeeping. Rohracher also wrote that at that time he had notified Capt. George Selke and the abbott of the monastery at Kremsmünster that he had the valuables and that both agreed that he should safeguard them.[3]

With this document in hand Horn left immediately for Salzburg. The following day he rechecked the files of the MFAA office in Salzburg and the files of the Austrian officials concerning the lost coins. Selke had returned to the United States and Horn was unable to find any information confirming Rohracher's statement that he had notified the proper authorities regarding the gold coins. He then walked the 300 yards to the archbishop's palace and presented him with the document dated April 24, 1946, and signed by him. After several heated debates, on May 1, 1946, the treasure of Kremsmünster was taken into the custody of the U.S. Army in Austria. Sealed in the presence of Rohracher, it was transferred to the Munich Collection Center.[4]

Later, at the Munich Collection Center, it was established that series 1–300 of the gold coins were missing. Because of this, on July 1, 1946, Veron Kennedy, a property control officer, examined the Hungarian valuables that were in the custody of Archbishop Rohracher and stored in the treasury of St. Peter's Abbey in Salzburg, Austria. The gloves worn by King Charles IV at his coronation, which had been turned over to Rohracher on June 18, 1945, were not included in the chest with the coronation robe. They too had disappeared.

A subsequent three-day investigation by Lt. Horn did not turn up the gloves. During this time, however, he traveled to Lake Mattsee and noted that Father Strasser still had in his possession three pieces of Hungarian glazed pottery and a heavy silver platter that he had received as presents. Also it was the belief of Charles Brousz of the military government of Bavaria that the priest had in his possession valuable personal property of the Hungarian fascists who were staying in Mattsee.[5]

Some of the coins from the treasure of Kremsmünster and the gloves worn by King Charles IV at his coronation are still missing.

Chapter 31
Cardinal Mindszenty

The political balance in Hungary in 1945 was threatening, as the Communist Party was making advancement in the ruling of Hungary. In any case the religious elements seemed to offset the Communist Party's presence in the coalition cabinet. This seemed rather prophetic, since expectations were widespread that the bishop of Vszprem would soon be elevated to the highest position in the country's Roman Catholic history. He was in fact named, on October 2, 1945, the archbishop of Esztergom and prince primate of Hungary. A few months later, he was created cardinal by Pope Pius XII. The new cardinal replaced his old German family name of Pehm with a Hungarian one: Mindszenty. The village of his birth was named Mindszent. The Hungarian Cardinal Jozsef Mindszenty (March 29, 1892–May 6, 1975) became a symbol of political and religious resistance to communism. Ordained a Roman Catholic priest in 1915, he was imprisoned in 1919 by the short-lived Hungarian Communist government of Bela Kun. Mindszenty had been known for his royalist sentiments and some of his pronouncements strongly indicated a desire on his part for the accession of Otto of Habsburg, son of the deceased King Karoly IV, to be the crown ruler.[1]

Shortly after his inauguration as prince primate, Cardinal Mindszenty asserted that as the ranking religious dignitary he also regarded himself as the head of the Hungarian nation. In Mindszenty's *Memories* he writes: "The archbishop of Esztergom held the foremost place among the dignitaries of the state as well as the Church. When the king was absent from the country, the archbishop represented him. The king depended on him for advice. If the king violated the constitution, the archbishop of Esztergon was obligated to rebuke him and demand he obey the law of the land."[2]

This supposition on Mindszenty's part was bad history and worse law. Later it would also turn out to be self-defeating. It appears that Pope Pius XII had selected Mindszenty — a provincial priest of little administrative ability and less scholarship — for the exalted position of primate because of a unique combination of factors. He was a Catholic priest of nationwide popularity in the midst of a bleeding population, a proud man among the ruins, a militant anticommunist who had also been a courageous anti–Nazi and had been imprisoned for his defiance to the Hungarian Nazis. He was an outspoken nationalist with a well-known record of firm adherence to tradition in general and royalist heritage in particular. And he was a man of modest origins, without connections abroad but still part of the backbone of the Hungarian nation: the peasantry. The pope alleged that he would have preferred someone of aristocratic ancestry, cool temperament, profound scholarship, and wide European connections; in other words, someone rather like Pius himself.[3]

Cardinal Mindszenty's first direct approach to the U.S. government in the matter of the crown was made on August 31, 1947, in the form of a letter addressed to the American minister in Budapest. He had recently returned from a widely publicized trip to England, the United States, and Canada, where he had met political and religious leaders as well as émigrés, including Otto of Habsburg. In his letter the cardinal asked that the Hungarian crown and relics be transferred to the Vatican. The U.S. government did not respond to the letter.

After receiving Hungary's gold and silver reserves, the chief of the Hungarian Ministry of Finance filed formal claim number 491 for the restitution of the Hungarian crown treasure from Germany to the government of Hungary. The request specifically mentioned Saint Stephen's crown and its accompanying regalia, which had been placed in the Foreign Exchange Depository but had been removed on September 17, 1945, and sent to the Wiesbaden Collection Center, where it remained until April 17, 1948. The crown was then moved to the Munich Collection Center. This request set off a storm of protest, for both the Hungarian government and the Vatican claimed ownership to the Hungarian crown treasure. The Vatican insisted that the treasure had been in custody of the Hungarian Catholic Church for 1000 years and that the Hungarian Catholic Church only had responsibility for safeguarding it. Vatican radio announced that pursuant to a decision by the State Department in Washington, the Hungarian crown treasure would not be given to the present Budapest government but to the pope for safeguarding.[4]

This broadcast set off a furor of activity, including a secret memo stating that the Department of State's view considered it a bad time to transfer the treasure to the Vatican. The memo further stated that all the coronation regalia should be consolidated in one place in the custody of the United States.

The next step in the request for the return of the crown came as the American representative at the Vatican transmitted to the Department of State a memorandum from Cardinal Mindszenty dated March 15, 1948. In it the cardinal requested that the treasure of the crown be deposited in a place befitting its religious character and made it clear that he considered the Vatican best for this purpose. Not surprisingly, a high official in the Vatican liked this idea. The official at the time was Monsignor Giovanni Battista Montini. Later, on the death of Pope John in 1963, Montini was elected Pope Paul VI.

Monsignor Montini, the Vatican's undersecretary of state, approached the American political advisor in Germany in the summer of 1948 through the Apostolic visitator in Germany. He requested the transfer to the Vatican of the crown, which had come to Hungary as a papal gift. He stressed that Pope Pius XII would be profoundly grateful if the Holy See were made the trustee of the sacred crown of Saint Stephen.

In July 1948, Monsignor Giovanni Battista Montini approached the American political advisor in Germany and requested a transfer to the Vatican of "the crown that came to Hungary as a papal present," thus stressing that it had originated from Rome. Montini further stressed that Pope Pius XII would be profoundly grateful if the Holy See were made trustee of the sacred crown of Saint Stephen until such time as it could be safely returned to Hungary. The U.S. government was fully aware of the historical and symbolic significance of the crown and coronation regalia. Aware that the Vatican to a degree had control of some of the regalia that had been placed in the custody of Archbishop Andreas Rohracher by U.S. forces in 1945, a plan was made to consolidate the treasure completely under U.S. control.[5]

On September 17, 1948, Vernon R. Kennedy, property control officer, met with Archbishop Andreas Rohracher and presented him with letters requesting that the remainder of Hungarian treasure be turned over to him. At the time it was the opinion of Kennedy that Archbishop Rohracher was merely safeguarding the treasure for the U.S. Army, as outlined in George Selke's letter of June 19, 1945. Still resentful owing to the removal of the Kremsmünster treasure, Rohracher refused to turn over the valuables. He told Kennedy that he had written instructions from Cardinal Mindszenty not to release the Hungarian coronation regalia to anyone unless he was instructed to do so by the cardinal himself. Kennedy left and returned with a U.S. Army priest, Father Edward J. Saunders, and then Archbishop Rohracher conceded that he would release the property if ordered by higher authority of the papal nuncio in Vienna.

At that time the responsibility for obtaining the treasure had been given to Maj. Richard P. Weeber, head of Reparations and Restitution. Weeber was highly intelligent and well versed in the German language. That day, September 17, 1948, Weeber and Father Saunders caught the Mozart train from Salzburg to Vienna. A meeting with the papal nuncio had been scheduled for 10:20 on Saturday morning, September 18. Alerted by Rohracher, the papal nuncio was out of town and could not be contacted. Without any success, they then discussed a plan to get Cardinal Mindszenty's approval for the release of the coronation robe through the U.S. legation at Budapest. Relating to this plan and in a secret document dated September 23, 1948, Maj. Weeber wrote: "However, realizing the danger of compromising the Cardinal thru a possible leak at Budapest, it was decided that the undersigned, being fully familiar with the case and the German language, seek a conference with Archbishop Rohracher and attempt to induce him to release the coronation robe at Salzburg."[6]

This course of action was agreed upon and Weeber and Father Saunders returned to Salzburg. Weeber then arranged for a conference with Archbishop Rohracher on Sunday morning at his summer residence in nearby Bischofshofen.

The following day at his summer residence, Archbishop Rohracher continued to maintain his earlier position. Finally, at the suggestion of Weeber, the archbishop agreed that a letter signed by Gen. Geoffrey Keyes, commander in chief of U.S. Forces in Austria, would be sufficient basis and authority to permit him to break his word of honor to Cardinal Mindszenty. Archbishop Rohracher even went so far as to suggest the wording of the letter. Weeber could not guarantee the wording, but finally Rohracher agreed to the letter and also a proper receipt for the treasure. At that time Rohracher stated that he was worried about having signed for the silverware of Emperor Franz Joseph in June 1945, which he had actually not received. He was most pleased when Weeber informed him that the silverware had been returned to Hungary on March 1, 1947, as claim number 184. Rohracher then requested that Weeber obtain a proper receipt for the Kremsmünster coin collection that had been taken from him in 1946. The case of the missing gloves of Charles IV or the missing coins from the Kremsmünster coin collection was not mentioned at this time, but one has to wonder whether Weeber was thinking about it.

The following day, September 20, 1948, Rohracher received a letter from Gen. Keyes thanking him for safeguarding the treasure. The letter also contained the following paragraph: "I have been directed by my government in Washington that it is necessary to remove these coronation regalia and appurtenances from Salzburg for security reasons. In due time they will be returned to the proper representatives of the Hungarian Catholic Church and the Hungarian people."[7]

On that same day Archbishop Rohracher received a receipt for the Kremsmünster coin collection. He also received a copy of Capt. Selke's report of June 19, 1945, stating that Emperor Franz Joseph's silverware was not released to the archbishop but was assigned to the Property Control Warehouse.

On September 20, Vernon Kennedy and Chaplain Edward J. Saunders signed a receipt for two iron cases, empty, and one large wooden box, unlocked, containing a roll of padding sewed in a cambric covering; a royal robe (the coronation robe of Saint Stephen) and a leather case containing old documents. Three days later and under the guard of two soldiers, the valuable were taken to Munich and placed in the custody of Evelyn Tucker, the MFAA officer for the U.S. Army in Austria. She signed for these valuables on September 23 and turned them over to the Munich Collection Center. The receipt was signed by Herbert Stuart Leonard. Also that same day the archbishop noticed that the locks on the two empty cases were taken and, as a last request, sent a message to Vernon Kennedy and stated that he wanted the two lock and keys back as they were property of the palace.[8] He received the lock and keys promptly, but it would be 30 more years before the Hungarian crown treasure made its long return journey back to Budapest.

Not wanting the treasure to fall into the hands of the now communist government in Hungary, Archbishop Rohracher wrote Cardinal Francis Spellman a letter and requested that Spellman meet with Cardinal Josef Mindszenty, who also wanted to see Harry S Truman, president of the United States, in order to effect the transfer of the Hungarian crown treasure to the Vatican. Unable to arrange for this meeting, Spellman wrote to Secretary of War Robert P. Patterson, interceding on behalf of Mindszenty, and requested that the Hungarian crown treasure be safeguarded in the United States or entrusted to the care of His Holiness Pope Pius XII.

During this frenzy of activity it was recalled that in 1919, in the wake of the first Hungarian communist dictator Bela Kun, the crown had been offered to a London antique dealer for £4,000. The dealer rejected the offer, whereupon Kun issued orders that the crown be broken up and the gold, jewels, and precious stones sold. According to one version, the dealer approached was Pierre Cartier, then head of the world-famous Cartier jewelry firm; his wife, born Countess Jacqueline Almassy of Hungary, prevailed upon him to reject the offer and dissuade other important dealers from considering the purchase of the crown. It was only through a miracle that the relic was saved. The communist regime collapsed before the artisans entrusted with the task of dismantling the crown could begin their task.

The church officials repeated this story many times, although none of it was ever substantiated, but the many shady deals in Kun's past lent it credibility. It was Mindszenty's conviction and the church's worry that the Budapest regime would treat the crown disrespectfully on its return and see to it in one way or another that it would disappear.[9]

As Hungary's leading church official, Mindszenty became a target of the postwar communist regime. His self-chosen martyrdom as the head of the Hungarian nation made it easy for the Stalinist regime to take measures against him. A strong opponent of communism, Mindszenty was arrested by the

Hungarian government late in 1948 on charges of treason and illegal monetary transactions. At a sensational public trial, Mindszenty pleaded guilty to most charges. It was widely held that his confession had been obtained by drugging him, because he had said in advance any confession he might make in case of arrest his arrest would be false. In the 1949 trial, the prosecutor thunderously asserted that Mindszenty "not only wished to deprive our state of this precious relic, the crown, but wanted to be sure that it would be ready at hand in case he wanted to put it on the head of Otto Habsburg."[10]

The court sentenced him to life imprisonment. Released from prison because of ill health in 1955, Mindszenty was kept under close watch. During the Hungarian revolution, he was freed by rebel forces. When the revolt was crushed, he took refuge in the U.S. legation and refused to leave Hungary unless the Hungarian government rescinded his conviction and sentence. In 1971, after 15 years and an agreement between the Vatican and the Hungarian government, Mindszenty left Hungary for the Vatican. Shortly afterward, he settled in Vienna.

In November 1949, Robert A. Vogeler, a vice president of the International Telephone and Telegraph Company, had been arrested in Hungary and indicted on charges of espionage and sabotage. He was found guilty and sentenced to 15 years in prison. The Hungarians offered the release of Vogeler in exchange for the crown of Saint Stephen. The Department of State issued a press release saying that the U.S. government was not prepared to discuss the return of the crown as a condition of release of Vogeler.[11]

As the Cold War continued, on November 19, 1951, an unarmed U.S. C-47 transport plane was forced down by Soviet fighters in Hungary after it had lost its course through navigational error. This unfortunate incident brought with it a resurgence of anxiety about the possible exchange of the Saint Stephen crown. After two weeks, the flyers were released by the Soviets to the Hungarians, who asked that the crown be exchanged for the flyers. There was no question regarding the C-47, as it would not be returned. In protest, the United States closed its Hungarian consulates. After a few months, the flyers and Vogeler were released.

In 1953, the sacred crown of Saint Stephen and other relics were removed from Munich, Germany, and sent to the United States, where they were stored at Fort Knox, Kentucky. During the following years, relations with Hungary gradually improved and discussions regarding the return of the Hungarian relics continued. On April 19, 1970, the *New York Times* printed an article referring to the possibility that the crown would be returned to Hungary. This article triggered a furor of protest that cumulated in a meeting at the Department of State. That meeting, held on May 21, 1970, is reported as follows:

Monsignor Bela Varga, President, Hungarian Committee, expressed appreciation for the interview on behalf of himself and all Hungarians who were united in the view that this historic and symbolic object should not be returned to the present government of Hungary. He expressed regret that he was unable to keep an earlier appointment with Mr. Emory C. Swank, deputy assistant secretary, and explained that a colleague, Edward Neumann de Vegar, had become so agitated over the crown that he had suffered a heart attack and died. Lady Malcom Douglas-Hamilton, Citizens for Freedom, interjected that she was a veteran of anticommunist struggles and cofounder in 1947 of the organization Common Cause, of which John Foster Dulles was a director. Monsignor Varga then emphasized that the plea he had come to make was simply "do not give up the Hungarian Crown."[12]

Cardinal Mindszenty furthers the cause by expressing his concern regarding the article. In a December 8, 1970, memorandum for Henry A. Kissinger, Mindszenty asked the president to resist any such step or, alternatively, to send the crown to the Vatican. The Department of State responded by replying that President Richard Nixon believed the Hungarian Crown should eventually be returned to Hungary.

From his self-imposed exile in Vienna, Mindszenty responded: "It was the donation of it and it has been my first suggestion to return it back to the Vatican. The undersigned Primate of Hungary representing the absent king has to act on behalf of it as a national property."[13]

Because of his unbending attitude regarding the Vatican's efforts to normalize relations with Hungary, Pope Paul VI relieved Mindszenty of the primacy of Hungary in 1974. On May 6, 1975, Mindszenty died. (In 1991, Mindszenty was reburied in postcommunist Hungary.)

Chapter 32

The Return of Saint Stephen's Crown

On July 16, 1975, Hungarian Prime Minister Gyorg Lazar made the first official request to the United States for the return of the crown to Hungary. On September 24, 1975, the American embassy in Budapest sent Secretary of State Henry Kissinger a telegram seemingly favoring Lazar's request. It said "The echoes of the vituperative debates in the Unga have died away; the 1956–1971 Mindszenty interludes no longer poisons bilateral relations; and even the cardinal himself has left the scene."[1]

The crown continued to be an outstanding issue, vexing relations between Hungary and the United States, and after 30 years the Hungarian government was putting the United States on notice that they wished to secure the royal property that belonged to them. Washington continued to maintain a stony silence on this question, which was of transcendent importance to all Hungarians.

The Vietnam War entered into the controversy. The International Commission of Control and Supervision (ICCS) had been created after the signing of the Paris Peace Accords, ending the war in Vietnam on January 27, 1973. The ICCS was composed of military and civilian personnel from two communist nations, Hungary and Poland, and two noncommunist nations, Canada and Indonesia. There were continuous disagreements between the communist and noncommunist nations about treaty violations. Hungary's performance on this issue was considered a negative factor, and the U.S. position was that there must be a "substantial improvement"[2] to enable the crown's return. A secret September 1975 letter from the U.S. Ambassador of Budapest stated it more bluntly: "Dashed Hungarian hopes and it was accompanied by their own club-footed performance on the ICCS in Vietnam which transformed dreams into unrelieved gloom."

In the spring of 1977, Congressman Charles A. Vanik began studying ways to extend nondiscriminatory trade status with Hungary and at the same time return the country's crown of Saint Stephen. Vanik wrote to both President Jimmy Carter and Secretary of State Cyrus Vance that it was time to return the crown to Hungary. Carter turned to Zbigniew Brzezinski, assistant to the president for national security, to intervene. As was to be expected, Vanik's suggestion brought a strong counterresponse from Congresswoman Mary Rose Oakar and Congressman Frank Horton, who had large ethnic Hungarian-American constituencies. Oakar went so far as to introduce a bill (H.R. 6634) requiring that the crown not be returned unless Congress authorized such action by law. Not to be outdone, Horton submitted a concurrent resolution (H. Con. Res. 21) requiring that the crown "remain in safekeeping of the United States government until Hungary once again functioned as a constitutional government established by the Hungarian people through free choice." Senator Robert Dole also expressed vocal opposition.

During this time Cyrus Vance wrote a six page undated SECRET/NODIS (no distribution) memorandum to the President Carter that read in part as follows:

> Our relations with Hungary have been improving steadily since Cardinal Mindszenty left asylum at our embassy in Budapest in 1971.... The cardinal primate of the Catholic Church in Hungary has informed us that the church in Hungary would welcome the Crown's return.... For most Americans, return of the crown would not be an issue. It would probably be supported as a moral act, giving back the object which does not belong to us. As Congressman Frenzel said, "It's theirs; it's *right* to return it to them." ... Morally and legally it is indefensible to continue to withhold from the Hungarian people their most important symbol of nationhood.... I strongly support the early return of the crown to the Hungarian people.

In private, the attitude of Congress toward the return of the crown was mixed but chiefly favorable, and Vance intended to return the crown to Hungary by September 15, 1977. Plans were worked out that the crown would be displayed in an appropriate setting in Budapest and there would be no restrictions on foreigners or Hungarians who wished to view it.

On October 1, 1977, Frigyes Puja, the Hungarian minister of foreign affairs, was informed by Philip M. Kaiser, the American ambassador, that the United States was willing to return the crown and other coronation regalia on the following essential conditions:

> That various segments of the Hungarian public, including the Roman Catholic cardinal primate, participate in the ceremonies in which the crown is returned.
>
> That the crown be displayed publicly and appropriately in an historic location not associated with the Communist Party.
>
> That the crown be treated with respect. In addition, arrange a return cer-

emony which will emphasize the national, religious and cultural nature of the crown. The U.S. is seeking to underline the fact that the American people are returning to the Hungarian people a national treasure which rightfully belongs to the Hungarians. The U.S. would plan to secure a public statement from the Hungarian government to the effect that Hungarians from all over the world are welcome to visit Hungary and view the crown.[3]

Puja met with members of the Hungarian parliament and immediately informed the American Embassy that they agreed with the details of the return. Of course, the last sentence would require the Hungarian government to announce that an amnesty had been declared for political prisoners in Hungary and that any Hungarian abroad would be granted a visa to see the crown. This was not an absolute requirement but was not recommended lightly. The Hungarian ambassador assured the United States that there were no political prisoners in Hungary and that Hungarians from all over the world would be welcome to see the crown.

In all of this careful wording and negotiations, what the United States wanted to avoid was the direct involvement of the leader of the Hungarian Communist Party. The Carter administration did not want the return of the crown to be a symbol of legitimacy for the Communist regime. Therefore a simple, quiet, dignified ceremony was planned. But unfortunately the discovery of this aspiration was "leaked" to the *Los Angeles Times* and, based on this now public knowledge, protests from congressional leaders immediately began again, with a letter of objection sent to the Department of State by Senator Robert Dole. All questions pertaining to the return of the crown were ignored by the Department of State. What started out as a simple achievement had now turned into front-page news.

Congresswoman Mary Rose Oakar wrote Jimmy Carter a blistering letter opposing the return of the crown. She had 41 other congressmen cosign her letter. Letters from other members of Congress continued.[4]

Needless to state, the International Relations Committee was pressured into immediately proceeding to retain the crown. On November 9, the subcommittee held hearings on the subject. The three-hour proceedings were frequently interrupted by applause and jeers from a standing-room-only audience of some 200 people. The audience was composed almost solely of Hungarian-Americans opposed to the return of the crown.

A panel of three witnesses testified in favor of return. Their general consensus was that the crown would do more good in Hungary than in the vaults of Fort Knox. Nevertheless, Oakar and Horton urged repeatedly that a full investigation be conducted by Congress before any action was taken by the president to return the crown.

Jeane Dixon, the renowned psychic, wrote President Carter with her solution for this issue. She insisted that her letter concerned a spiritual matter that had become entangled in diplomacy. She wrote that the crown was entrusted to the Americans for safekeeping and that this sacred trust must not be betrayed. In her four-page letter, she suggested that the crown be displayed in Washington at the Smithsonian Institution for the entire world to see and that it be guarded by a triple honor guard, one American, one a member of the papal Swiss Guards, and one a volunteer from among the brave Hungarian freedom fighters who fled their country after the 1956 revolt. She further wrote:

> If the dream is now betrayed by the American government, it will become our nightmare — your nightmare. And your presidency will be haunted by it until your last day in the White House and beyond.... I want to assure you of my prayers as you struggle with this difficult decision, which may well determine not only the fate of the Hungarian people but also the future of your presidency.[5]

On November 30, 1977, U.S. Ambassador Phil Kaiser called on Cardinal Laszlo Lekai, primate of Hungary's Roman Catholic Church. In this moving meeting the cardinal left no doubt of his whole-hearted support for President Carter's decision to return the crown. The cardinal was overcome with joy at the prospect of its return. The cardinal assured Kaiser that he would be an active participant in the Hungarian delegation and said if Kaiser looked at him at the airport, he would see tears running down his cheeks. In response to Kaiser's question as to his communication with the Vatican regarding the return of the crown, Lekai said that the Vatican told him that it was indifferent and neutral (*indifferens es semeges*). The Vatican regarded this matter as one between Hungary and the United States. The cardinal thought this was the correct attitude. At the end of the meeting, Lekai asked Kaiser to report the following to Washington: "I [Cardinal Lekai] support the return of the crown, the Catholic Church supports the return of the crown, and the Hungarian people support the return of the crown."[6]

The following day Cyrus Vance wrote to the president and urged him to set a date for the return of the crown. Vance suggested that the president set the date of return for January 7, 1978. Two days later, on December 3, the Department of State cabled Ambassador Kaiser that he could inform the Hungarian government that the crown would be returned on Friday, January 6, 1978. Needless to say, discontent continued, with Senator Samuel Ichiye Hayakawa and Representative Jack Kemp instituting legal action in the District of Columbia for a temporary restraining order against the president and officers of the Department of State to prevent them from transferring the crown to Hungary. At approximately the same time, Democratic senatorial candidate Anthony Robert Martin-Trigona filed a civil action against Jimmy Carter and Cyrus Vance.

The Department of State continued with it plans, as it was confident of the soundness of its legal position in blocking these motions for a restraining order. As late as December 23, 1977, Senator Robert Dole also filed suit in Kansas City to block the return of the crown.[7]

At the same time, the American Embassy in Budapest, Cardinal Lekai, and the Hungarian government were polishing up the wording for the conditions of the return. Letters governing the transfer of the crown and long boring texts for toasts were drafted, translated into English and Hungarian, and rechecked for accuracy. Also a list of who would participate in the ceremonies was being drawn up. For some reason President Jimmy Carter was never considered, although his wife, Rosalynn, was initially at the top of the list.

As the month of December wore on, the protests and legal actions continued, but plans for the return also endured, with the request for color television transmissions from Budapest to the United States taking priority. Arrangements were worked out with the Hungarian Post Office for direct lines with facilities for American broadcast standards. Another small glitch took place: the Hungarian committee decided that in order to stress the people-to-people concept, the dignitaries would be accompanied by their wives during the various ceremonies. As soon as this was known, the American delegation immediately made plans for the ranking official's wives to attend.

As the time of the transfer of the crown drew closer, Senator Dole asked the Supreme Court to review his blocking order. Also, on December 31, he cabled the president asking him to reconsider his decision and further wrote: "Let us begin 1978 with a renewed commitment to the principles of liberty and freedom upon which our nation was founded and for which the people of Hungary still yearn." In all a total of four suits were brought against the crown's return.

After January 6, 1978, all four suits were dismissed as moot, for on January 5, 1978, the U.S. delegation flew from McGuire Air Force Base in Washington, D.C., to Budapest. Besides the passengers, the aircraft carried two large containers. One was a trunk approximately 56 by 24 by 20 inches weighing 360 pounds. It was tied down on a fork-lift pallet and contained the crown and other regalia. The other was 5 feet in radius, 2 inches thick, and weighed 160 pounds; it contained the coronation robe. The plane arrived in Budapest at 9:30 P.M. The delegation was met at the airport and welcomed by Deputy President of Parliament Janos Peters and other important Hungarian officials. The crown was off-loaded smoothly and taken to the National Assembly, where symbolic custody was maintained until the ceremonies the following day.[8]

On January 7 at 1 P.M., Secretary Vance arrived at the airport. The turnover ceremony began at 4 P.M. in the Central Hall of Parliament and went off flawlessly before an audience of Hungary's parliament, American embassy diplomats, and some 200 representatives of the Hungarian people. Thus, after more than 33 years, the myth, legend, and symbol of Hungarian nationhood, the Saint Stephen crown, had once again returned to its homeland.

Had the United States made final restitution to the Hungarian people? No, it would take another 27 years for this to happen.

Chapter 33

The Hungarian Gold Train

Hungarian Jewry had a rich cultural, religious, and economic history in Hungary. By the 1930s, the Jewish community of Hungary was central to Hungarian life. There was also a deep cultural tradition among Hungarian Jewish families that went back hundreds of years, as they constituted a considerable part of Hungary's commercial and professional middle class. However, with the spread of Nazi power and influence in the 1930s, the Horthy regime in Hungary adopted anti–Semitic policies, both as a means of bartering with Hitler and keeping control of the Nazi party inside Hungary. Even though Hungary was growing closer to the Third Reich, Horthy refused to follow orders from Berlin to deport, starve, and exterminate Jews, and talk of the Nazis' "final solution" disappeared from the agenda of the Hungarian government.

Hungary refused to adopt any further policy of violence toward Jews, ceased deportations, refused to create Jewish ghettos, and did not require Jews to wear the stigmatizing yellow badges. On March 19, 1944, Hitler's troops invaded Hungary, occupied the country, and established a puppet government. Despite the fact that the Nazi cause was assuredly lost, Hitler picked the notorious Adolf Eichmann to oversee the cleansing of Hungary of its Jews and their property. The "final solution to the Jewish problem in Hungary" was to be Eichmann's crowning achievement in Europe.

In early April, the Nazi puppet regime required Hungarian Jews to leave all their valuable property, including wedding rings, in certain financial depositories. Jews were forced to register their assets with the authorities, and the contents of their safe deposit boxes were frozen. Through these decrees, the Nazis confiscated all Jewish personal and real property, including but not limited to Jewish gold, jewelry, silver, currency, securities, diamonds, watches, carpets, furs, china, and paintings. the Hungarian Jews relinquished some of their property to Hungarian officials, banks, and other government installations.

Typically, Hungarian Jews would carefully pack household property in suitcases, envelopes, strongboxes, and other containers; close and secure the containers or seal them in the case of envelopes; place some form of identification on the exterior of the packed container; and deposit the container at the bank or institution authorized to accept Jewish property under the decrees. Upon deposit, the Jewish owner was issued a receipt. Once all the Jewish property had been collected and registered and properly accounted for and documented, the property, still in its original packing, was consolidated in a central location within the larger cities for eventual planned transport to Budapest.[1]

With the Red Army advancing in Hungary and the war assuredly lost, the Nazi government of Hungary gathered the Jewish property from Budapest for transport away from the advancing Red Army in order to safeguard and protect it from confiscation. The train left Budapest on October 14, 1944, and originally consisted of some 18 to 22 boxcars of Jewish property. Heading westward from Budapest through farmlands, vineyards, and orchards, the train set out on a precarious journey with one objective: to protect the property. In the end, over the next several months and over numerous miles, the "gold train" made its way from Hungary into Austria, but it never made it to Switzerland, the intended destination.

The gold train arrived in Zirc, Hungary, on October 16, 1944. Here, the Jewish valuables, gold, currency, jewels, diamonds, and so on were offloaded and taken to the Óbánya Castle of Count Tattenbach. Following the same route, additional property forcibly taken from Jews throughout Hungary and stored in government banks and other installations was brought to Óbánya Castle and added to the collection. In November 1944, after the Nazi Arrowcross Party officially came to power, Dr. Árpád Toldy was appointed commander of the gold train. In this capacity, he arrived at Óbánya and ordered that the valuables be sorted into the following categories: gold; gold watches, jewels, diamonds, coins, and currency.

The sorting of some of the stolen Jewish property lasted until December 7, 1944. Toldy then ordered that the consignment of valuables be reloaded and transported with the remaining stolen Jewish property to Hungary's western border.

On December 13, 1944, the train left Zirc. It arrived in Brennbergbánya — a western border settlement — three days later, where it remained ahead of the advancing Soviet forces. Here Toldy added even more stolen Jewish property to the train. For example, boxcars and trucks transporting valuables and other Jewish property arrived from other Hungarian cities and were added to the consignment on the gold train. The train grew longer and longer by the day. Toldy also placed the stolen Jewish "valuables" in small containers, fir-made miners' cases, and sealed their lids shut with screws.

Then, the case number and its general contents were painted on the lid. Altogether, 105 cases and 2 iron strongboxes were filled with Jewish valuables.[2]

In Brennbergbánya, the German commanders made an agreement with the Hungarian government to allow the train into Germany, take custody of the valuables, and protect escorts and family members for as long as the war went on. After hostilities, the agreement stated, the Hungarian nationals and the contents of the train would be returned to Hungary. In reality, this accord was of little value; George Patton's Third Army would soon storm in from the northeast, followed by Alexander Patch's Seventh Army from the southeast, Mark Clark's Fifth Army from the south through Italy, and the Soviets through Hungary from the west. No longer was the German Army able to save itself, let alone the passengers and cargo of a train. Its offer of protection was a worthless gesture.

At the Brennbergbánya railroad station, greed had begun to set in. Dr. Toldy and his immediate staff began to loot the contents of the train. Boxes, trunks, and other containers were opened and the gold, silver, jewelry, and diamonds removed. The plan was to remove the diamonds from their settings and then smelt the gold and silver jewelry into bars. The gold bars would be most acceptable in Switzerland. If the valuables remained as jewelry, the Swiss or other neutral countries would shy away from them as being Nazi loot. Unfortunately for Dr. Toldy, the rapidly advancing Red Army began shelling Brennbergbánya with artillery, preventing the smelting operation from taking place. The items that had been removed from the train were quickly packed up and brought back on board. During this activity at the station, considerable looting by civilians took place. Prior to the departure of the train, Toldy loaded two trucks with 50 cases of gold and diamonds and fled from Brennbergbánya, presumably headed for Switzerland.[3] Dr. László Avar, the mayor of Ziertz, Hungary, who was a passenger on the train, was then ordered by the Ministry of the Interior to take command. The Soviet infantry was only six miles away as the train left Brennbergbánya.[4]

The train now consisted of 52 railroad cars, of which 29 were freight cars containing items of great value. The cars were sealed, locked with large padlocks, and guarded by Hungarian soldiers and gendarmes. Comprising the rest of the train were the large steam engine, the coal car, the dining car, the galley, passenger cars, and sleeper cars for the 52 guards and approximately 100 men, women, and children who had managed to arrange passage.

The freight cars were heavy-duty top-notch cars, the best that could be found at this late stage of the war. The outsides of the freight cars were marked with such varying points of origin as Dresden 191307, Germany 1533, Mav Hungary G127260, France 207557, and FS Italia FC 1132599. They contained cases of gold, 60 chests of jewelry, and chests of the finest collections of Meissen,

Dresden, and Chinese ivory figurines. There were over 5,000 hand-woven Persian rugs, exceptional works of art, five large trunks full of stamps, over 300 complete sets of silverware, and 28 large boxes of mink and sealskin furs. Other personal effects of the murdered victims included American dollars, Swiss francs, gold coins, small bags of gold dust, watches, rings, Bibles, skis, musical instruments, cameras, typewriters and — for some unknown reason — a solitary box of coal. One freight car contained diamonds; assigned to it was a special three-man guard detail.[5]

The train crossed into Austria and arrived in Wiener Neustadt on March 30, 1945, continuing westward under the command of László Avar. It reached Wilhemsburg on April 1, 1945. Here, Austrian officials held the train up and, unbeknownst to Avar, detached the locomotive, thus leaving the train without an engine. By the time the Austrian officials gave Avar permission to move the train along, he had no locomotive to power it. So Avar bribed the Austrian officials with rum and 500 inexpensive watches to obtain an engine and finally left Wilhemsburg, arriving in St. Polten on April 6, 1945. Here, the Nazi SS attempted to disarm the Hungarian guards and capture the train, but with the aid of Austrian officials, the Hungarians stood their ground and protected the train without losing any of the valuables.

The gold train continued on, reaching Amstetten on April 7 Salzburg on the 8th and stopping in Hopfgarten the same day. Here, at Toldy's request, the train was held up on April 10, 1945. Toldy sent Avar an order commanding him to remove everyone from the train and leave the train unprotected. Avar disobeyed. Over the course of events Avar had become convinced that Toldy simply wished to steal the valuables for his own personal gain. On April 22, 1945, Hungarian Ensign Gyula Galambos arrived in Hopfgarten driving a truck from Toldy's convoy of Gold Train "valuables." Galambos had fallen behind the other part of Toldy's convoy and expected to find him in Hopfgarten with Avar. The next day, Avar loaded the valuables from Galambos' truck onto the gold train, increasing the final consignment to 61 cases. Over the next several days, Avar and his men were able to fend off the SS as well as Toldy and other fellow countrymen and to avoid bombings and skirmishes with Allied soldiers. In short, they succeeded in protecting the valuables by moving the train and hiding wherever possible.

On April 21, 1945, the Hungarian gold train began making final preparations for its 150-mile dash from Hopfgarten to Switzerland. The Americans were unaware of the train or its contents but were still conducting a war against the Third Reich, which meant that they would shoot practically anything that moved. The transportation system was a prime target for the U.S. Army Air Corps. This area of Austria was the target area for 450th Bombardment Group of the Fifteenth Air Force, stationed in northern Italy.

On April 21, the 450th bombed and destroyed the railroad bridge in the small village of Brixlegg and, before it could be repaired, the U.S. Seventh Army joined with the U.S. Fifth Army from Italy at the Brenner Pass. Austria was cut in two by the Allies and the escape route to Switzerland was blocked. As the train began to backtrack from Brixlegg, the Hungarians removed 54 cases of gold (7,937 pounds) and two cases of diamonds from the train and buried them between Brixlegg and the relative safety of the nearby Tauern Tunnel. The train then steamed into the tunnel to protect it from the constant threat of Allied bombings.

Chapter 34

The American Army Takes Custody

After the war ended on May 8, 1945, and because of the precious cargo and the precarious situation, Avar sought out the Americans to turn the train and its contents over to the U.S. Army for protection until it could be safely returned to Hungary. Avar and the gold train were now in the Tauren Tunnel and had been there since May 5, 1945. Avar attempted to make contact with the Red Cross and the Swiss consulate, and through them, the U.S. Army. In the first days, his efforts seemed in vain. However, on May 11, 1945, one of Avar's men succeeded in making contact with an army major in the Kaiserhof Hotel in Badgastein. Around noon on the same day, a U.S. Army detail arrived, spoke to Avar, and inspected two rail cars (numbers 174137 and 136632), and confirmed that the train was transporting a valuable treasure. Avar requested that the Americans take custody of the gold train to protect it and its contents until it could safely be returned to Hungary. The United States agreed to this.

On May 16, 1945, the 3rd Infantry Division, 15th Regiment, A Company, commanded by Lt. Joseph A. Mercer, entered the Tauern Tunnel 60 miles south of Salzburg. To their astonishment, they discovered a partially concealed train crammed with gold and other valuables. The kitchen waste and human filth that had accumulated in the tunnel was sickening. It was decided to quickly move the train from the tunnel to avoid the risk of disease to the crew and its captors. The train chugged from the darkened tunnel and pushed on to the small market town of Werfen, 50 miles to the north.

There, the train was jointly guarded by the Hungarian guards and members of the 15th Infantry Regiment, Third Division. A round-the-clock guard detail was assigned to protect it. The cars containing gold and diamonds were posted with double security and the complete area was off limits to unauthorized personnel. The families remained on the train and continued, despite hardships, with their daily routines.

The train remained in Werfen until July 18, 1945, because of the widespread destruction of the railway system. The army then abandoned the steam locomotive at Werfen and connected an army locomotive to the train for the last 30 miles of its precarious journey. The train finally left the rail siding in Werfen under the tight security of both the 101st Airborne and Hungarian guards, bound for the *Stuberkaserne* army barracks located on 51 Klessheimer Allee in the Marglan suburb of Salzburg. This military camp had been renamed Camp Truscott by the Americans.

The chore of overall security during unloading was placed upon the shoulders of Maj. John F. Back, commander of the highly esteemed but off-the-record Target Force, and four enlisted men under him. As the unloading began, Avar László, who had taken over as trainmaster after Toldy's exit at Brennbergbánya, delivered to Maj. Back two black suitcases packed in a canvas rucksack, apparently a "getaway" bag. The valuables were not included with the material in the train but were in the possession of Avar. The suitcases contained diamonds, jewelry, and currency that had been stolen from the parcels on the train.

During the unloading, it was noted that practically all of the containers had been broken into and then reclosed by nailing boards across them. Seven parcels, numbered V1 through V7, were sealed with sealing wax and displayed the names of the owners on the outside. These were culled out by Maj. Back and Col. Homer K. Heller from the contents of the train during the four days of unloading. Parcel V1 contained currency that included $44,639 in U.S. bills. Included in this stash were six $1,000 bills and two $500 bills. Also found were a packet of diamonds and two lots of gold jewelry. Parcels V2 through V6 contained jewelry, diamonds, rings, and watches, but V7, a canvas bag, contained only diamonds. During the examination of an old steel box, after removing old rags and envelopes, the two men found many papers written in Hungarian. The papers were lists of the owners of the train's contents and were separated and left in the warehouse with Homer Heller for possible future use in determining ownership. It was never made clear what later happened to packages V1 to V7, nor did the papers of ownership ever surface.[1]

It took four days for two U.S. Army trucks to move the valuables from the train to the ground floor of a former Wehrmacht warehouse 100 yards away. The cargo included 850 chests of silverware, 5,000 hand-woven Persian rugs, alarm clocks, watches, cameras, bolts of cloth, underwear, topcoats, typewriters, chinaware, stamp collections, coin collections, cases of diamonds, cases of gold coins, and large amounts of currency. The warehouse was selected because it was considered to be a fire-resistant, dry, burglarproof building. Assigned as guards during the four days of unloading were guards of G Company, 242nd Infantry Regiment, 42nd Infantry Division.

After unloading, and to their complete surprise, the Hungarian guards were disarmed and sent to a prisoner-of-war camp. Their wives and children were separated and sent to Riederburg, Austria, a camp for displaced persons.

The unloading was completed on August 29, 1945. In 1945 terms, the value of the train's contents was estimated at $206 million, which would translate to several billion dollars today.

Chapter 35

The General's Kingdom

Maj. Gen. Harry J. Collins was commander of the 42nd (Rainbow) Division. This division occupied the eastern part of the Tyrol in Austria and, as other divisions were deactivated, the 42nd extended its occupation duties and took over the entire U.S. Zone of Austria.

General Collins, like most conquering generals of the past, lived comfortably. For one of his homes during the occupation, he acquired a castle at Zell Am See. This 15th-century residence, beautifully furnished and immaculately maintained, was the Prielau Castle. A majestic 8- by 10-foot 15th-century French fireplace was built into its entrance hall. Equally imposing were the Greek marble columns and Byzantine *Christ on the Cross* that were the centerpieces of an estate appointed with valuable furniture and furnishings. Numerous assortments of old Austrian peasant furnishings were also mixed in in a most agreeable manner.[1]

Collins also acquired a nearby castle for his command staff. The Fischhorn Castle was at the south end of a small but deep lake at Zell Am See. Most important, Zell Am See had a rail line running through its center. This line would be used by Collins and his immediate staff for their trips to Salzburg. The general had, in effect, acquired a private railroad for his daily trips. As the 42nd Division took over the Fischhorn Castle for a headquarters building, the Fuschl Castle, near Salzburg, considered German property, was also taken over and used as an officers' rest and recuperation center for Collins' 42nd Infantry Division.

Collins needed to supply himself, his private railroad car, the three castles, and his officers with the superior rewards that a conquering army would acquire. It did not take him long to discover and tour the Property Control Warehouse located in Salzburg. After reviewing this large accumulation of wealth, Collins had Maj. R. W. Cutler send a letter to Lt. Col. Homer Heller directing that, without delay, a large quantity of household goods be sent to him for his personal use. The directive demanded that all the items be of "the very best quality and workmanship available."[2] The general specifically told

General Harry J. Collins (right) was the first to appropriate valuables from the Hungarian gold train (courtesy National Archives).

Maj. Cutler that he intended to hold Heller responsible for securing the requested items. The request was initially refused by Heller, whereupon he received the following memo:

> Homer—
> General Collins wants you to be at the warehouse promptly at eight o'clock in the morning to give every assistance to his aides in providing furnishings, etc. for him.
> To say the least he is very displeased with the treatment accorded the aides by you today.
> I have tried to reach you by telephone this evening but couldn't.
> I suggest you do not fail to be of great help to him and the aides.
> Lieutenant Colonel Fredrick Gallagher
> Wednesday evening, 2000 hrs

The letter was written on August 29, 1945. The following morning, under coercion, Heller watched the general's aides take 25 oriental rugs, 8 paintings, 60 sheets, 30 sets of table linen, 45 sets of Rosenthal chinaware, 45 sets of silverware, and 90 highball, cocktail, wine, champagne, and liquor glasses.[3]

The general had his railroad car stripped of all furnishings and two rugs permanently installed by nailing them to the floor. Partitions were then reinstalled, securely fastened by wood screws into the walls and into the floor through the carpets.

Unfortunately this requisition of property by Collins established a precedent for hundreds of U. S. military officers to requisition thousands of items from the Property Control Warehouse for use in households, offices, and clubs.

Collins further let it be known that he was interested in providing proper quarters and house furnishings for families of the military and expected demands to be made upon property in the Property Control Warehouse. In a wild stretch of the imagination, this was interpreted by Collins' staff as meaning that the restitution of the property in the Property Control Warehouse would "jeopardize satisfaction of the minimum requirements of the Austrian economy" and further that the Hungarian property was required for the "essential needs" of the occupation forces. Also, Collins held that the release of the property was justified by a military need that could not be met elsewhere.

Additionally, it was suggested that high-quality solid silverware be acquired by the chest and not separated. Inscribed inside the tops of many of the chests of silver were the names of the owners, such as "Viktor Mayer." Donald W. Brann, William C. McMahon, Charles Saltzmann, and Edwin B. Howard, all U.S. Army generals, were just a few of those who took advantage of this interpretation of the "Supply Procedure for Allowances of Household Furnishings for Dependents, Bachelor Officers and Civilians, Americans and Allies." Gen. Henning Linden received china, silverware, and linen for his Salzburg home; Gen. Hume received 18 rugs, silverware, linen, and glassware; Gen. Holland received nine rugs, one silver set and 12 silver plates to decorate his Vienna apartment; and Brig. Gen. Linden received 10 rugs for his quarters on the Von Trapp estate. Gen. Linden's essential needs included a camera, tripod, and printer. Linden later claimed that the camera and its accessories were taken to the United States by an officer of the 42nd and further stated that he would make every effort to have it returned.

Silverware was also released for the use of the officers of the artillery staff of the 42nd Division, which had taken possession of the von Trapp estate in Salzburg, which included a chest "bearing name of Gergely Henrik." This chest was not returned to his widow, Jolán Gergely, despite its clear labeling. In addition, Gen. Ladue received a silver set for 10, marked with the name and address of "Dr. Otto Arodi, Tokai No 19"; and Brig. Gen. Morrill Ross dined with a silver set marked by the monogram "Emma."[4]

To cover himself, Col. Heller wrote a memo explaining that Gen. Collins had "issued household furnishings of superior quality and workmanship to various general officers for use in their villas." These requisition orders, at his best count from memory, comprised 22 shipments of property totaling "a substantial sum of money." All of this property was drawn from the Hungarian gold train. Less than two weeks after writing this memo, on April 1, 1946, Heller was redeployed and sent home. He would not have another chance to interfere with the unlawful acquisition of Jewish property.

Heller was replaced by Capt. Howard A. Mackenzie, who realized that a detailed inventory of the gold train property had never been made. Understanding that many of the valuables were now in the possession of generals and other U.S. personnel based on his review of Colonel Heller's letters, he immediately ordered that all gold train valuables be identified and an accurate report of their whereabouts be obtained because there was "considerable doubt as to the present location" of the gold train property on "loan." However, the three soldiers he assigned to the task of following up on the whereabouts of the property were almost immediately thereafter redeployed home, and the army failed to appoint anyone to follow through on the inventory.

Mackenzie admitted that

> The officers would requisition one rug, 8 × 12, light color, flower design. The rug taken and signed for would be a priceless hand-woven oriental rug. If the rug was returned, it would be a very sad looking 8 × 12, light color, flower design rug made in Austria. The only difference between the Germans and Americans in looting was [that] the Germans kept very accurate records and with the Americans it was free enterprise unchecked.[5]

Chapter 36

The End of the Gold Train Property

On June 4 and July 13, 1946, Gen. Mark Clark sent telegrams to the War Department and Department of State. The message in both was that "the property now contained at the United States Military Government Warehouse, Salzburg, is of unknown origin and ownership." In an apparent attempt to clarify the situation, on August 23, 1946, the U.S. Department of State issued a telegram (WARX 98112) to Gen. Clark. Its intent was to clarify the terms of the Final Act of the Paris Conference, Article 8D. It clearly stated that property could not be returned if determination of national origin was impractical and that property could not be restored to the lawful owners because they had died or ceased to exist without legal successors. It also stated that property could not be disbursed to the Inter Governmental Committee for Refuges (IGCR) if determination of individual ownership was impractical. Regardless of the claims in the telegram, the truth is that the property in the Property Control Warehouse was known as to its national origins and in many cases was still identifiable as to individual ownership. The telegram further expressed that property turned over to the IGCR must be removed from Austria and Germany and sold in acceptable foreign currency outside these two countries.[1]

Hungarian officials were aware that the Property Control Warehouse had not been guarded adequately and that large-scale looting had further decimated the valuables stored within it. Hungarian museum objects and religious relics were displayed openly in local Salzburg merchants' windows. The black market for items was so lucrative that the Hungarian government protested the lack of security and stressed that while Austria had not won the war with the Allies, it apparently was sharing in the war booty. More valuable items were burglarized from the Property Control Warehouse in Salzburg than in any other place in occupied Europe.

On December 5, 1946, representatives of the Hungarian Restitution

Delegation visited the warehouse. The Hungarian government requested an inventory of all items and demanded that Hungarian experts be allowed to examine the objects to determine which belonged to Hungarian citizens. During the visit, the Hungarians discovered the valuable Kisfaludi collection of crockery and four cases of tobacco seeds. For some inexplicable reason the tobacco seeds were handed over to the Hungarian Ministry of Agriculture, the only property returned by the U.S. Army to the Hungarian government.

The Hungarian Restitution Ministry then filed a claim for the Kisfaludi collection and wrote for permission to inventory the warehouse for additional Hungarian claims. Mr. Nyardi, the Hungarian secretary of finance, insisted that all of the train's contents be returned to his native land for the benefit of the 100,000 remaining Hungarian Jews. Nyardi was informed that because of the terms of the Final Act of the Paris Conference, Article 8D, signed by the United States, England, and France, Hungarian Jews would not receive their confiscated property and that it would be sold for the benefit of Jewish victims from Germany and Austria. Despite protests from Hungary, the valuables from the Budapest train would not be returned.

Based on the previous unsubstantiated telegrams from Mark Clark asserting a lack of proof of ownership, Capt. Howard Mackenzie was notified that all previous instructions concerning the Hungarian valuables were superseded by cable number WX-85682. This cable, sent on November 16, 1946, by the Joint Chiefs of Staff, stated that all valuables in the Property Control Warehouse with the exception of Jewish items of cultural or religious significance would be turned over to the IGCR. Again this directive underscored the fact that national origin or identification of ownership of the property was impractical. Again, this was simply untrue — still remaining in the warehouse and unopened were 2,732 boxes, trunks, suitcases, and other containers of valuables. Proof of ownership lay in Capt. Howard A. Mackenzie's testimony as a witness for the prosecution during the court-martial proceedings of enlisted men on September 27, 1946. The testimony follows:

> Court-martial members:
> Small objects of high value for their size, was there any effort to lock them in boxes or safes to make them secure from people walking through there?
>
> Captain Mackenzie:
> They were kept in the original containers because it was felt if they were removed the means of identification would be lost. A great deal of material the ownership of which has never been determined is in there.... Most of the valuable material is nailed into boxes. Some of the most valuable material is still in the original suitcases and baskets and trunks in which they were found.

But neither the U.S. Army nor the Hungarians had expected the order of November 16, 1946. This order instructed Mackenzie to open the containers and sort the items into categories according to type of merchandise and value. After the sorting process, the determination of individual property would be impractical and the property could be turned over to the IGCR.[2]

The Property Control Officer at Salzburg was delighted by this unexpected turn of events. The army had been investigating the rapid disappearance of property from the warehouse and many officers had returned to the United States with filched property. Additionally, two suitcases of gold dust had disappeared from a vault containing many valuables from the Hungarian gold train. In spite of thorough investigations, no progress was made in the recovery of the gold dust or in identifying the location of property removed from the warehouse. By mixing up the property and rendering it unidentifiable as to ownership, the U.S. Army could be held blameless. Without an adequate inventory list, an owner, even if he or she recovered some items, would have no recourse in claiming that more property was due him or her.

Thus the unproductive investigations of previous missing property fizzled out as large quantities of gold, jewelry and watches, silver, and coins were separated from thousands of hand-woven Persian rugs and thousands of mink, muskrat, rabbit, lamb, and seal coats. As the army engineers opened, sorted, and repacked the gold train valuables during the summer and fall of 1947, additional gold, silver, currency, and diamonds were found hidden in the clothing of the former owners. Several $500 bills were found sewn into the cuffs of dress shirts. This method of hiding money and jewels by concentration camp victims was a common and pitiable practice. Identification of ownership was fast becoming impossible.

On May 19, 1947, the IGCR team, consisting of four people, appeared at the Property Control Warehouse. The team was understaffed and unqualified to inventory, classify, and appraise the Hungarian property and transfer it from Austria to the United States. Furthermore, the Department of State was anxious to have the items shipped to the states as quickly as possible, because the Hungarian Restitution Delegation was anxiously trying to block removal of the valuables from Europe. The U.S. Army was equally anxious, since a transfer would cover its irregular activities.

In the warehouse the IGCR was busy appraising much of the Hungarian property. The remaining gold and silver jewelry was grouped as bulk scrap and appraised on the basis of weight times market prices. The IGCR considered this necessary to avoid having their four "experts" perform endless months of appraisal work. During the packing operation, tons of valuable metals had been discovered. Much of this was gold- and silver-plated jewelry, often encrusted with diamonds and other gems.[3]

The IGCR team at Salzburg made 10 shipments of this immense cargo on railroad cars and trucks to the German port of Bremerhaven. The shipment's final destination was New York City. These valuables were turned over to the IGCR and auctioned by Parke Bernet Galleries in New York for only $1,807,000.

In 1966 the United States filed a claim against Hungary for war damage and debts to American citizens. Much to the surprise of the United States, the Hungarian government filed a counterclaim for $206 million for "property carried to the United States by the U.S. Military after World War II." Approximately $47 million of this claim represented the property of 900 Hungarian citizens.

In defense of the claim, the Department of State contended that liability for the valuables on the Hungarian gold train rested with the German government. It further contended that the German authorities took the property and that, because of this, the U.S. forces had no legal duty to protect the property from theft or deterioration. Finally, it maintained that under Article 30 of the Peace Treaty, the United States had the right to keep the Hungarian property with no legal obligation to return it.

The story of the Hungarian gold train remained untold until the publication of my book *Spoils of World War II*, in 1994. In 1998 the Presidential Advisory Commission on Holocaust Assets visited my home and copied over 10,000 pages of documentation. A year later, the Presidential Advisory Commission on Holocaust Assets found that there was "documentary evidence that American Forces in Austria misappropriated so-called unidentifiable property of Hungarian Jews found on the Gold Train."

On May 7, 2001, Cuneo Waldman & Gilbert, L.L.P., filed *Irving Rosner et al. v. United States of America* in the U.S. District Court in Miami. The suit was a class action against the United States on behalf of Hungarian Holocaust survivors and their heirs. It claimed that the plaintiffs' valuable personal property was loaded on a train by the Hungarian Nazi government during the waning days of World War II. The U.S. Army later seized the train and its contents but never returned the property to its owners or heirs. This was the first suit of its kind brought against the United States.

On Monday, December 20, 2004, in a major breakthrough, the attorneys for the plaintiff Hungarian Holocaust survivors — together with senior attorneys from the U.S. Justice Department — read the following statement to Judge Patricia Seitz in federal court in Miami. "The Government and Plaintiffs' Counsel, after consultation with class members and Jewish organizations, have reached an agreement in principle to settle this litigation. There are still significant issues to be worked out, but we are confident that we can indeed work them out."

36. The End of the Gold Train Property

On September 30, 2005, after more than four years of hard-fought litigation, the Hungarian gold train litigation was finally concluded successfully. The U.S. District Court for the Southern District of Florida gave its final approval to the proposed settlement of $25.5 million paid into the settlement fund. This fund was allocated to pay for social welfare benefits to financially needy Hungarian Holocaust survivors.

On January 31, 2006, the lead counsel wrote:

> There is little question that this whole sorry episode would never have come to light had you [Kenneth D. Alford] not unearthed it. For that and for your generosity in sharing with us your time, your expertise and insights, and your files, I want to express deep gratitude on behalf of the lawyers and plaintiffs. You should be extremely proud of your role in helping to right this historic wrong.[4]

Gen. Harry J. Collins began an affair with Irene Gehmacher, an Austrian actress. The story goes that when his unit returned to the United States, Collins' aide married the actress. Then, upon entry into the United States, the aide divorced her. The general then divorced his wife of many years and married the actress. Being Catholic, he was excommunicated, but he ignored this action and attended mass every Sunday on the military post. He was always late but required the chaplain to delay the service until he arrived. His new wife had quite a reputation and enjoyed her role as "Frau General."

Collins, disliked by his men, was known as "Hollywood Harry." One of his stateside assignments was as commander of the 31st Infantry Division at Fort Carson, Colorado. Of this time, one of his officers wrote:

> His eccentricities were obvious from the start. He required that his soldiers, enlisted and officer alike, wear no neckties but blue infantry branch scarves with our shirt collars over our Ike jackets (class A uniform). At his own expense he outfitted the division band in Confederate uniforms and the stars and bars flew proudly next to the stars and stripes on all occasions. At periodic officer calls in a large auditorium, the band at the back would play "Dixie" and Collins would stride on stage. He would begin by addressing us as "My soldier men." When he was done, he would say "Thank you, my soldier men," the band would play "Dixie" again, and he would leave the stage.
>
> He also organized and outfitted at his own expense a bagpipe band, kilts and all, which he used to wake up the troops in each of the three regimental areas on a rotating basis. I like bagpipes but not so early in the morning. It was a weird experience. It was obvious that General Collins had paid for the unusual band arrangements out of his own pocket.
>
> I last saw the general and his wife at an Officers Club party in Berchtesgaden, Germany, in 1958. They were retired and living in nearby Salzburg, Austria. Collins was in a wheelchair because he had been seriously injured in

an automobile accident. I remember well that the band played "Dixie" for him and we all stood up.

Harry Collins had the ego of George Patton but nowhere near the ability. He was able to get away with unacceptable behavior because of his rank and the times in which he lived.[5]

Gen. Collins died on March 8, 1963, and is buried in St. Peter's Churchyard Cemetery in Salzburg, Austria. The headstone, written in German, states that Gen. Collins was an honorary citizen of both Salzburg and Linz. His wife, Irene, died on December 26, 1987, and is interred with him.

Appendix A
Anton Wiede's Missing Stamps and Paintings

> Inventory from case record EU(13)-55-247,
> Headquarters U.S. Army, National Archives.

Five Albums Each About 40 by 30 cm and About 12 cm Thick (16" × 12" × 5")

Complete sheets with stamps were fastened to cardboard folios by broad cellophane strips. Blocks of four were encased in separate cellophane strips.

1. Complete in whole sheets and blocks of four (not stamped)
    a. German Reich: from first prints (1872) until 1945, including all special stamps, official service, and airmail stamps. All proof prints, misprints, and all experimental issues. Among them, values that were issued in a few copies.
    b. Stamps of German post offices abroad (China, Morocco, Turkey) and in all German colonies.
    c. All stamps issued by German occupation authorities (occupied territories until 1945).
2. Complete sets (and colorings) in individual stamps, stamped and not stamped.
    a. German post offices in the territories occupied from 1914 to 1918, in the German territories where plebiscites were held, and in Danzig, the Memel, and Saar territories.
3. All values and coloring of former German states, including misprints, stamps and to a large extent not used, in individual items (among them many duplicates), all flawless.
    a. Bavarian from 1814
    b. Helgoland from 1867
    c. Prussia from 1850
    d. Saxony from 1850
    e. Thurn und Taxis from 1852
    f. Württemberg from 1851
4. It is impossible to specify the collection of foreign stamps (e.g., England, France, the United States, and Finland) contained in one section of the album. Among

them were some especially rare items (early issues), since in addition to his complete collection of German stamps, my father had specialized only in this type.

Missing Paintings — Descriptions by Frau Else Wiede

Rumänierin, by Franz von Lenbach

Purchased in 1905 by Johannes Wiede, Trebsen, at Arnold's art salon in Dresden, Schlosstrasse (owner Gutbiert). Previously owned by a resident of Vienna. As far as I can recollect, the names or seals of the owner were stated on the back of the painting, and the portrait itself bore the signature of the artist. The certificate of authenticity was kept in the desk and probably disappeared with the painting. Size about 60 by 70 cm, upright.

Painted in oil on canvas (taken away without frame).

Head of a woman (girl) of about 20 years, almost life size. Background in Lenbach brown; no predominant colors.

Half profile, head slightly raised, looking to the right. Delicate profile, intelligent, grave, almost melancholy and remote look, not direct at you but yet fascinating the observer. Thinly laid on color.

Thin lipped, sharp cut nose, the large nostrils almost appear to be vibrating.

Especially remarkable in the auburn hair, with long locks, slightly waved, evenly parted, falling down on the shoulders.

Slender, erect neck, well-marked and narrow neckline, bordered by dark dress, of which not much can be seen. Thus no half-length portrait.

In addition to the *Rumänierin*, Lenbach is said to have painted at the same time the portrait *A Woman of Florence* (Florentinerin).

The painting, packed in a nailed-up wooden crate, was stored in the cellar of the Wiede residence at Trebsen, a.d. Mulde (district of Leipzig).

Abendstimmung am unteren Main by Hans Thoma

Purchased after 1918 but prior to 1924 by Johannes Wiede, Trebsen, at Arnold's art salon in Dresden, Schlosstrasse (owner Gutbiert). Formerly owned by a lady in Frankfurt/ Main. Signed by the artist.

Size about 45 by 60 cm, broadside.

Painted in Oil on impregnated cardboard (taken away with frame).

Impression of peace and quietness (stagnate air). In the foreground the small river between irregular river banks, partly covered by grass and shrubby. On the side of the river, high broad-leaved trees gold colored by the shine of the setting sun (autumnal coloring).

The air, a clear blue sky interspersed with small white clouds, is of special beauty. In the middle of the river, in harmony with the whole picture, a boatman pushing a punt, still emphasizing the solitude of peace.

Small waves in the wake of the boat show its slow movement toward the other bank of the river. The face of the boatman is turned away from the observer.

The whole painting reflects some kind of reverie, similar to the characteristics of

Steinhausen (A religious painter — translation note), but lacking any slurring effects. Clear color and arrangement.

The painting, packed in a nailed-up wooden crate, was stored in the cellar of the Wiede residence at Trebsen, a.d. Mulde (District of Leipzig).

Falkner auf Schimmel by C. van Valens (Netherlands School)

Property of Else Wiede, inherited from her great grandfather Dr. Auf Mothes, Leipzig, who acquired it about 1820 from an estate of inheritance (Querfurth).

The name of the artist and the name Querfurth were written in ink on the back of the frame.

Size about 25 by 30 cm, upright.

Painted in oil on canvas, which is old and yellow. Badly restored, glossy, stained. Gilt frame.

Dutch landscape. By the side of the rider a boy handling over a falcon, the whole painting is somewhat turbid. I remember a blue riding coat.

The painting was in the vestibule of the Wiede residence, which was used as headquarters office.

Conzilium by Idwith

Purchased about 1925 by Johannes Wiede, Trebsen, in Munich. Signed by artist (English?).

Size about 30 by 45 cm, broadside.

Painted in oil on canvas under glass, gilt frame.

Sitting at a table and standing beside it are cardinals in red gowns, vividly gesticulating and conferring.

Overall impression, red in various shades.

The painting was in the vestibule of the Wiede residence, located on the ground floor, which was used as headquarters office.

Appendix B

The Missing Kaltenbrunner Treasure

Inventory from the Foreign Exchange Repository
U.S. Army, National Archives.

Contents of Shipment 21 A

Silver coins

1. 197 Polish zloty at 10: 1,970
2. 500 Polish zloty at 5: 2,500
3. 152 Polish zloty at 10: 1,520
4. 924 Polish zloty at 2: 1,548
5. 28½ Silver bars (6 in. long by ¼ in. diameter)
6. See attached sheet

Gold coins

7. 74 U.S. $20: 1,480; 1 Austria-Hungary ducat
8. 743 British sovereigns; 280 U.S. at $20: 5,600; 12 French francs at 10: 120; 6 Neth. guilders at 5: 30; 72 French francs at 20: 1,440; 97 Brit. half-sovereigns 242 Neth. guilders at 1: 242
9. 31 Silver bars (6 in. × ¼ in. diameter); 1 knife handle — "silver"
10. 318 Rubles at 5: 1,590; 122 Rubles at 10: 1,220; 14 Rubles at 15: 210
11. Miscellaneous gold pieces as follows: 2 Rubles at 50; 1 Eng. sovereign at 1; 1 French franc at 20; 1 French franc at 10; 2 Polish zloty at 20; 1 Polish zloty at 10; 4 Aust-Hun Korona at 20; 1 Napoleon at 40 fr: 40 fr; 1 Napoleon at 50 fr: 50 fr; 1 Austrian kronen: 100 kr; 1 Austrian shilling: 100 s; 21 Austrian goldpieces said to be ducats; 1 Sealed sack labeled "Gold Pd Stig 2500"

Gold coins

12. 475 U.S. at $20: $8,500; 225 U.S. at $10: $2,250; 394 Rus. rubles at 5: 1970 rbls; 51 Rus. rubles at 10: 510 rbls; 16 Rus. rubles at 15: 240 rbls

Currency

13. U.S.: $1,271; Swiss: 9045 fr; English: 220 pounds; Swedish: 655 kronen; Danish: 130 kronen; Norwegian: 50 kronen

Silver coins

14. French 1 at 20 fr: 20 fr; French 1 at 1 fr: 1 fr; German 2 at 1 RM: 2 RM; German 1 at ½ RM: ½ RM; Polish 2 at 5 Zl: 10 Zl; Polish 1 at 1 Zl: 1 Zl; Bulgarian 1 at 5: 5 Lewa; Bulgarian 1 at 100: 100 Lewa; Bulgarian 8 at 1: 8 Lewa; Lithuanian 1 at 10: 10 Der

Gold coins

French 59 at 20 fr: 1180 fr; U.S. 88 at $20: $1760; Peru 1 at ½ : ½; Denmark 1 at 20 kr: 20 kr; Brit. 474 at 1 sov: 474 sov.; Brit. 20 at ½ sov: 10 sov.

15. Silver coins; German 1 at 10 Rm: 10 Rm; French 746 at 20 fr: 14920 fr; Spanish 6 at 5: 30 pesetas; Spanish 3 at 2: 6 pesetas; Spanish 26 at 1: 26 pesetas; Polish 4 at 10 Zl: 40 zloty; Polish 22 at 5 Zl: 110 zloty; Polish 25 at 2 Zl: 50 zloty; Aust 1 at 2: 2 shillings; Italian 1 at 2: 2 lire; Russian 20 at 5 Rbls: 100 rubles; Slovakian 1 at 5 K: 5 korons; Polish: 3 damaged coins, values unknown; Polish: 2 medals
16. Silver coins; Polish 55 at 1 Zl: 55 zloty; Polish 148 at 2 Zl: 296 zloty; Polish 236 at 5 Zl: 1180 zloty; Polish 17 at 10 Zl: 170 zloty; Russian 31 at 5 Rbls: 155 rbls; Unknown 4 pieces
17. Silver coins; Polish 76 at 1 Zl: 76 zloty; Polish 1001 at 2 Zl: 2002 zloty; Polish 13 at 5 Zl: 65 zloty; Polish 1 at 10 Zl: 10 zloty
18. Miscellaneous costume jewelry, small value
19. Miscellaneous unset precious or semiprecious stones and gold medallions, value unknown
20. Large number of precious or semiprecious stones, value unknown
21. Silver bar, weight 30 lbs
22. 4 bracelets, jeweled, gold; 4 rings, jeweled, gold; 2 watch chains, gold; 2 necklaces with jeweled pendant; 1 gold pendant; 1 pr. gold cufflinks; ½ gold locket, jeweled; 1 gold pendant, jeweled; 4 gold bracelets, jeweled; 5 gold pins or pendants; 1 gold ring; 1 gold mesh purse

    In suede purse: 1 broken gold ring; 2 2-ear drops; 2 gold rings, jeweled; 1 pearl and sapphire bracelet, broken; 1 jeweled bracelet; 2 jeweled rings; 1 small piece, silver; 2 compacts, gold
23. 32 silver purses; 1 gold ring; 26 strings of pearls; 145 tableware pieces; 20 silver pieces.
24. Miscellaneous bracelets — mostly broken — scrap gold, 30 pieces
25. 8 small clocks — valueless —1 silver medallion
26. 26 pieces costume jewelry
27. 194 miscellaneous rings
28. Miscellaneous costume jewelry
29. 29 Miscellaneous cigarette and vanity cases
30. Miscellaneous costume jewelry

31. Watch chains, wt. about 5
32. 44 watches
33. Scrap gold and silver, costume jewelry, wt. approx. 2
34. Miscellaneous costume jewelry, wt. approx. 12
35. Miscellaneous fountain pens and pencils, used
36. Miscellaneous costume jewelry, wt. approx. 3
37. 200 watches and/or watch cases, approx. 10
38. 29 pieces of silver (compacts and cigarette cases)
39. Miscellaneous spectacle frames, wt. approx. 1
40. 21 pieces, cigarette and vanity cases, appear to be silver
41. 246 rings, also assorted earrings, wt. approx. 5
42. 17 bottles, approx. 6 ox. cap., silver chips
43. 11 spools of gold thread, also loose gold thread
44. Scrap gold, silver coin bracelet, semiprecious stones, trinkets, total wt. approx. 1
45. Approximately 300 assorted rings

Appendix C
Thefts from the Weimar National Art Collections

Inventory list from the Ardelia Hall
Collection, National Archives.

List of 13 Paintings Stolen from the Schwarzburg Depository

1. & 2. **Dürer, Albrecht** [returned 1982].

    Portraits of the couple Hans Tucher and Felicitas Tucher, née Rieter
    Oil paintings on wood, combined in a folding frame as a diptych. On the reverse side of the man's portrait the coats-of-arms of the Tucher and Rieter families.
    On the man's portrait, upper left, the inscription: Hans Tucher, aged 42, 1499.
    On the woman's portrait, upper right-hand corner, the inscription: Feiltz Hans Tucherin, 33 years old, Salus, 1499.
    Height of each picture, 28 cm. Width 24 cm. Stolen with the frame.
    Both paintings have since 1824 at the latest been Weimar property.

3. **Barbari, Jacopo de.** *Bust of Christ* [returned 2000]

4. **Tischbein, Johann Fredrich August.** *Portrait of Lady Elizabeth Hervey* [returned 1997]

5. **Cranach, Lucas the Elder.** *Venus with Cupid Pursued by the Bees.*

    Youthful nude roman and nude boy with wings in the foreground of a broad wooded landscape.
    Upper left, four lines of a Latin inscription, signature of Cranach (snake with wings) and the year 1530, lower right, on a stone.
    Oil painting on wood, removed from the frame. Height 50 cm, width 35 cm.
    Property of Weimar Museum since prior to 1851.

6. **Fredrich, Caspar David.** *Landscape with Rainbow.*

    Landscape on the Island of Rügen, with view of the sea. Right, on an eminence, a shepherd standing; over the landscape a flat, wide rainbow. No artist's mark.

Most famous painting of the master. Oil painting on canvas, removed from the frame. Height 59 cm, width 84.5 cm. Probably purchased by Goethe from the artist for the Weimar Court around 1810; since 1824 in the Weimar Museum. Colored facsimile reproduction has appeared as a Piper print.

7. Greff, Afton. *Portrait of the Poet Gellert.*

Half-length portrait, facing right. Oil painting, oval in form, on canvas. Removed from the frame. Height 47 cm, width 39 cm. Since the time of Goethe the property of the Weimar Library and in 1869 taken over by the museum.

8. Van de Velde, Willem the Younger. *Beach with Rough Sea.*

A fishing boat lying at the shore; another out at sea. Oil painting on oak, removed from the frame. Height 24.1 cm, width 32 cm. Signature, lower right-hand corner, on a planks W V V 166. Purchased by Duke Carl August of Weimar in 1814 at Frankfurt a. M. Not yet mentioned in the literature on Van de Velde.

9. Lenbach, Franz. *Farmyard with Chickens.*

Oil painting on canvas, removed from the frame. Height, 28 cm, width 32 cm. Signature, lower right-hand corner, F. L. Work of the master's Weimar period from the Weimar School of Art, where Lenbach taught from 1861 to 62.

10. Lenbach, Franz von. Wegkapelle Inventory Number 585.

11. Baum, Paul. *March Landscape at Weimar.*

Meadow landscape with brook, willow trees, and many crows. The church tower of Ehringsdorf, near Weimar, in the background. Marked, lower right-hand corner Paul Baum. Wmr. 1885. Oil painting on wood, removed from the frame. Height, 22 cm, width, 33 cm. Purchased in 1935 for the National Art Collections from a private owner in Weimar. C. Hitzeroth. Paul Baum. Dresden 1437. Cut 7.

12. Seekatz, Johann Conrad. *Young Woman and Wahrsagenrin Zigeunerin.*

Oil on canvas, 24 cm by 22 cm.

13. Dietrich, Christian W. E. *Broom Binder with Child.*

Oil on wood.

*Three Paintings of the National Art Collections
in Weimar Stolen from Other Repository by American Soldiers*

1. Grosvenor, Thomas. *Countryside with Mill on a Stream.*

Oil on canvas, 77 cm by 104 cm.

2. Riess, Paul. *In the Summer.*
   Oil on canvas, 50 cm by 74 cm.

3. Thiele, John Alexander. *Flusslandschaft.*
   Oil on wood, 25 cm by 33 cm.

Appendix D

Otto v. Falke's Description of the Crown of Saint Stephen

> From the report on St. Stephen's Crown
> compiled for the Foreign Exchange
> Repository, National Archives.

I cannot conceal the objections I have in accepting the kind invitation to give an opinion upon the Holy Crown of Hungary. To reliably judge a relic of such a singular historic and national significance from the viewpoint of fine arts requires the most minute examination of its style and technical fashioning. This thorough knowledge of the Crown I do not possess. Solely, the feeling of gratitude for the kindness which was shown to the International Museum Association by the display of the Crown on occasion of its 1928 Budapest Meeting obliges me to herewith submit in writing my impressions on this instructive though short inspection.

The lower part of the Holy Crown, that part resting on the forehead, through the inscribed cloisonné paintings has been verified to be of Byzantine origin dating from approximately 1075 and is no longer a problem. Because the prevailing conditions allowed only a brief inspection, I centered my attention upon the upper part, especially to both of the crossed arcs, and will also confine myself herein to this section. Examination from the standpoint of fine arts must deal mainly with the question: Were the enamel paintings on the arcs, which are regarded as the remaining part of the crown of St. Stephen donated by the Pope, made before the year 1000 or not until after the Géza Crown which means around 1100? Without giving detailed reasons Kondakow, Dayton, Diehl and Molinier have pleaded for the later date, however, as it seems, only on the basis of inadequate illustrations. To mention the essential point first, as a result of the examination, I have been inclined to take the other view which, in its essential points, agrees with that of Franz Bock and of the Hungarian scholars Arnold Ipolyi, Béla Czobor, F. v.Radisics, and Elemér v.Varju whose opinion is derived from a thorough knowledge of the Crown.

Too few Byzantine and western cloisonné relics still exist and their dates can seldom be fixed, so that by merely checking against their styles the enamel paintings on the Crown arcs could be determined as originating from the last years before 1000;

nevertheless, there are relics enough to classify them incontestably in the middle of three style eras which must be distinguished in the development of gold cloisonné. In the early years of cloisonné, which started with the Alexandrian gold cup of the St. Maurice d'Agaune and includes the Syrian Fieschi relic, The Roman Paschalis Cross and the frames of the Milan Palliotto of the Carolingian era, the "painting in enamel" was predominant. In this type, the gold plate was covered with enamel from one edge to the other. The second era emphasizes the "enamel en creux (intaglio)" in which the enamel painting lying in a slight depression is set off against the unenamelled golden background. This flourishing period which approximately covers the 10th century is characterized by the careful and artistically symbolic use of the gold bands for representing the folds of the vestments. The formation of cloisonnés is prompted by the painters artistical intent without disclosing that they have the simultaneous technical task of offering the enamel an adequate foothold. This style era culminates in the Limburg Cross Relic of the emperors Constantine and Romanos II (948–959) which is one of the highest achievements of cloisonné art.

The first reliably dated work of the third period is the Byzantine Monomach Crown of Budapest; its time of origin is limited by the years 1042 and 1054. The hitherto symbolic drawing of folds which was prompted from a plastic standpoint has here been replaced by a conventional method which, by acute angles, straight lines, and spirals arranged close to each other, suggests a schematic drapery and through the numerous paths increases the adhesion of the enamel, thereby facilitating the technical at the expense of artistic design. The enamel paintings of the Géza Crown from around 1075 show this late style fully developed, however these do not yet affect the enamel paintings on the arcs.

On the arcs are found nine enamel paintings in a fine filigree gold mounting: on the top of the crossing a somewhat larger square plate en creux with the enthroned Pantokrator and eight rectangular plates each with the figure of an apostle between ornamental fields. It is generally acknowledged that these nine cloisonné plates are of western origin and this need not be proven again; the Latin inscriptions on the picture of the apostles, the convergently squinting eyes, the open mouth, and especially the very awkward drawing of the clumsy large-headed apostle figures plead clearly enough against Byzantine origin.

The Pantokrator plate on the crossing at first seems superior to the apostle pictures since the goldsmith followed a good Byzantine model very closely, however, the converging squinting and the open mouth prove the identical origin of all nine plates; also the scrolls of the cypresses surrounding the Pantokrator figure are similar to those on the plates representing St. Philippus and St. Thomas. Although the enthroned Christ has been damaged in the center by the hole subsequently made for the little cross, the design of the drapery on the lower part of the body shows clearly the artistic style of the tenth century. Of course, the author of the nine plates — apparently an Italian — is inferior to the artistic technique of the Byzantine court goldsmiths who created the Limburg Cross relic; but his artistic aim was the same and in spite of the awkwardness prevailing in the western cloisonné workshops of the 10th century, he still succeeded in expressively representing the draping of the vestment between the calves, the gathering of the folds above the left knee, and the tension of the cloak above the right one. A comparison of this vigorous design with the delicate, compact, technically masterful but schematic network of the Pantokrator picture of the 1075

Géza Crown, practically decides the question of which parts of the Holy Crown are older and which are more recent. The striking compositional resemblance of both of the Pantokrator painting joined at the Crown can only be explained by the fact that the master designing the square plate used as his model a Byzantine Pantokrator type of the 10th century which still was recognized when the Géza Crown was fashioned.

Among the western cloisonné works, especially the Blessed Virgin image shown in the Munich Uta Codex, a Regensburg work of the years after 1002 (M. Rosenberg: *Zellenschmelz* [Cloisonné] II, 1921, illustr. 69), in so far as the fold design is concerned, seems me to be so similar to the enthroned Christ on the Crown of St. Stephen that the dates of their origin presumably also fall into the same period.

The eight apostle paintings, although undoubtedly created by the same artist as the square plate, look much more like antique because here the Byzantine influence is expressed less by the figures than by the ornaments. The Byzantine models, regarding the arrangement of the ornaments on the sides of the figures, are in somewhat similar to the Monarch Crown plates, but older by half a century, since there is no doubt as to the contemporary origin of the apostle paintings and the square paintings. The different ornamental designs of the apostle paintings do not contradict this: the lion pairs on the St. James and the St. Peter plates facing each other on an enamel background which is decorated with rosettes and circles, are already found in the Alexandrian gold cup of St. Maurice dating from the 7th century (Mr. Rosenberg, *Zellenschmelz* [Cloisonné] III, illustr. 44); on the basis of this fact the creation of the apostle plates must be fixed earlier rather than later. It is true, the stepped lozenge pattern beneath the lions of the se two apostle paintings has accompanied Byzantine enamel paintings throughout the centuries, but in the 10th century, this style has its culmination in the edge of ornamentation of the Limburg staurothek (cross-shaped case) dating from around 950; the same decoration is found as edge pattern on an Italian cloisonné painting, the Chiavenna Pax, which is fixed at around the year 1000. (Rosenberg, elsewhere, II illustr. 90) The scrolls, already mentioned in connection with the cypresses of the square plate, which end in clover leaves and are represented on the Philippus painting, at the right of Johannes and on the Thomas plate, can be found almost in the same design on some small enamel plates of the Andreas relic from the Trier Egbert School (975–993, illustrated by Falke, *Deutsche Schmelzarbeiten des Mittelalters*). Thus, it must be concluded that the Byzantine models from which the master of the apostle paintings and the Trier Egbert School goldsmith borrowed their ornamentation stem from the last quarter of the 10th century. The apostle figures were given only a few Byzantine features of their maker. As a whole, it is difficult to find analogies to these strangely clumsy figures with their cone-shaped outlines still more emphasized by a gold edge; such analogies can only be met in the enamel paintings of heads and relief figures of the Burgund Atheus relic of Sitten, all of which are two centuries older (shortly before 800, illustrated by M. Rosenberg, elsewhere, III illustr.'s 99 and 102). Nevertheless, some details of the apostle figures bespeak clearly their origin from about the year 1000. The exaggerated big hands of Peturs and Jacobus remind of the already mentioned Holy Virgin image of the Uta Codex; also the convergent squinting is especially noticeable on the octofoiled plate of the Uta Codex (Rosenberg, elsewhere, II illustr. 91) and on the Aribert Book cover made in Milan (after 1018, illustrated by Rosenberg, elsewhere, II Table 11). Here, it should be recalled that Marc Rosenberg has proven the dependence of the Regensburg enamel works of the King Stephen era on the Milan School. The reference to the analogies of the Trier and Regensburg works is far from claiming that the apostle plates are of cisalpine origin, but is only made in order to establish and assure the approximate contemporary period of the latter. The technical formation of the apostle plates is very odd. They are worked en creux, but since only the narrow residual tracks of the gold ground are visible which divide every picture into six (Jacobus and Paulus) or four fields (Petrus, Johannes, Philippus, Thomas, Bartolomaus, Andreas), they look rather like full enamel paintings because almost the whole surface is covered with enamel. More probably, such a transition from full enamel painting to en creux painting took place during the second style period of the Ottonic era which followed upon the Carolingian century than during the third one, which had turned away from the full enamel painting, and to which the Géza Crown belongs.

All arguments derived from style and technical constitution of the nine cloisonné paintings on the crown arcs center on the fact that these parts of the Holy Crown originate from the Ottonic style era of the cloisonné arts covering the threshold between the 10th and 11th century. If this has been ascertained, all cause for doubting the account of Pope's donation of the Crown to King Stephen described in Hartwich's Vita Stephani already at the beginning of the 12th century vanishes.

The nine enamel paintings give no clue as to the place where Stephen's Crown was made. There is no visible connection with the Roman full enamel paintings of the early ninth century, nor with the Paschalis Cross, and the Beresford Hope Cross, nor with Venice. In South Italy the Byzantine style was preserved in the bead strings of the 1133 coronation cloak and the mountings on the sword of Mauritius that neither the clumsy apostle figures of the tenth century nor the enamel paintings of the Konrad II imperial crown can be assumed to originate from there. There would remain Milan, where the mentioned Regensburg enamel paintings actually point to. Also the original form of the Stephen's Crown is indefinite. Czobor's and Radisics' assumption that the paintings of Christ and the apostles including the four missing ones, were fixed on a diadem, that means vertically, is obvious since the paintings can be seen only partially when the Crown is being borne and the pictures are lying oblique or horizontal. In contradiction to this, Elmer v. Varju (Arch. Ertesito B. 39) ascertained that the apostle pictures show a slight bend in lengthwise direction in order to follow the curvature of the arcs; therefore he agrees with F. Bock's view saying that the arcs, with the enamel paintings just as they are, were taken from the Stephen's Crown and combined with the Géza Crown. Concerning this point, I have no judgment of my own because I did not notice the curvature of the apostle pictures when inspecting the Crown, neither is it noticeable in the photograph of the whole Crown.

There is still the matter of the series of four triangular and four rounded off gables surmounting the Géza Crown; they deviate technically from the remaining parts of the Holy Crown. They are worked of transparent green enamel, in strong gold cells soldered to each other, without background and *á jour*, that means like windows; this method is extremely rare and is hardly found in enamel paintings of the early middle age. Their golden mounting corresponds to that of the big stones and enamel paintings of the Byzantine Géza Crown. Since crowns with triangular and rounded off gables occur in the eastern pictured manuscripts only in the 12th century (cf. A Weixlgartner, Die weltliche Schatzkammer, im Wiener Jahrb. d. Kunsthist. Sammlungen 1926. S. 24), it must be assumed that they were made for the Byzantine Géza Crown. Where other than in Byzantium could this abnormal and difficult procedure of enamel *à jour* be practiced?

                  Berlin
                  Otto v. Falke

In addition to the above mentioned experts, others (E. Meyer and others) reject the arc enamel paintings as dating from "about 1000" and support their origin at "about 1100."

Chapter Notes

Part I
STEALING A TROVE OF STAMPS

The primary sources for Part I are the National Archives, College Park, MD, U.S. Department of State Records maintained by the Monuments, Fine Arts, and Archives (MFAA) advisor, 1944–1961, Ardelia Hall Collection, Record Group (RG) 59. Box 8 — Wiede Claim Paintings Stamps and Coins.

Chapter 1

1. Martin Collins, e-mail, "I Remember," to Joseph Lipsius, November 9, 2003.
2. Anton J. Wiede, Exhibit K, March 9, 1955, RG 59, box 8.
3. Charles B. McDonald, *The Last Offensive*. Washington DC: U.S. Army, 1984.

Chapter 2

1. Anton J. Wiede, Exhibit K, March 9, 1955, RG 59, box 8.
2. Anton J. Wiede, Annex 6, June 14, 1954, RG 59, box 8.
3. *Ibid.*
4. *Ibid.*
5. *Ibid.*
6. *Ibid.*
7. Hans Unger, Annex 8, June 9, 1954 — The statements contain the following from Unger: "Please excuse the handwriting. There are 3,000 persons In this camp and few quiet places." RG 59, box 8.
8. Anton J. Wiede, Exhibit K, March 9, 1955, RG 59, box 8.
9. Else Wiede, Annex 5, May 24, 1954, RG 59, box 8.

Chapter 3

1. Statement of Edward J. Leary, October 27, 1954, Investigator Adolph Rezendes, RG 59, box 8.
2. Statement of Maxwell A. Snead, October 20, 1954, Investigator Merle E. Stouffer, RG 59, box 8.
3. Statement of Harold Pengelly, December 11, 1954, Investigator Harry Hopkins, RG 59, box 8.
4. Statement of John D. Tower, December 13, 1954, Investigator James J. Zouvas, RG 59, box 8.
5. Lt. Col. Watson E. Neiman, Certificate, December 3, 1954, RG 59, box 8.
6. Merle E. Stouffer, "Report of Investigation," October 28, 1954.
7. Statement of Graham S. McConnell, December 21, 1954, and February 14, 1956, Investigator Robert R. Musselman, RG 59, box 8.
8. Statement of Harry B. Underwood, January 2, 1955, Investigator Oscar F. Wagner, RG 59, box 8.
9. Statement of Edward A. Schlag, March 2, 1955, Investigators Ralph Fienman and Alex Martin, RG 59, box 8.
10. Statement of Doctor Charles A. Owen, May 3, 1955, Investigator William R. Caton, RG 59, box 8.

11. Paul E. Krieger, "Synopsis — Office of the Provost Marshal," Southern Command, January 13, 1956, RG 59, box 8.
12. Burton Hugh Young, February 3, 1956, RG 59, box 8.
13. Statement of Robert S. Anderson, July 5, 1956, Investigator Scott, RG 59, box 8.
14. Post Bulletin Archives, March 5, 2001.

Part II
A Passion for Lucas Cranach Paintings

The primary sources for Part II are the National Archives, College Park, MD, including parts of the 14 rolls of microfiche publication M192, reproduced records relating to monuments, museums, libraries, archives, and fine arts of the Cultural Affairs Branch, Education and Cultural Relations (ECR) Division, Office of Military Government, U.S. Zone (Germany) [OMGUS] during the period 1946–1949. These records are part of the Records of U.S. Occupation Headquarters, World War II, Record Group (RG). Donovan Senter is on roll 14; U.S. Department of State Records maintained by the MFAA advisor, 1944–1961, Ardelia Hall Collection, Record Group 59. Box 2; "Cranach painting returned to Germany." Dale F. Shughart, Recollections of a former U.S. Counter-Intelligence Agent During World War II, 12-page unpublished paper, no date; Al Senter, Donovan Senter's brother, interview, December 1994; Margaret Ann "Gretchen" Obenauf, Donovan Senter's niece, interview, May 25, 2009.

Chapter 4

1. Article, general history, no author, no date, Torrance County, New Mexico, and affidavit document number 1443, Archives, Santa Fe, NM.
2. Interview with Albert J. Senter, Albuquerque; the Fray Angelico Chavez History Library, Santa Fe, NM, and DD Form 398, author's library.
3. Salinas Pueblo Missions, Quarai Trail Guide, National Monuments, National Park Service.
4. Donovan Senter, *El Palacio*, November 21–December 5, 1934.
5. Interview, Albert J. Senter.
6. www.mnsu.edu/museum
7. Florence Hawley Ellis, *Pasatiempo* (Santa Fe), January 6, 1980.
8. Donovan Senter, letter to Dr. Fred Eggan, no date, approximately December 1941.
9. Donovan Senter's military form no. 66-1, author's library.

Chapter 5

1. Donovan Senter's military form no. 66-1, author's library.
2. Joseph P. Lash. *A World of Love*. New York: Doubleday, 1984.
3. James L. Gilbert. *In the Shadow of the Sphinx*. Fort Belvior, VA: U.S. Government Printing Office, and CIC Documents, National Archives.
4. Chief Inspector of Judiciary Police, French Republic, report, St. Avold, France, April 10, 1947.
5. William W. Quinn. *Buffalo Bill Remembers*. Fowlerville, MI: Wilderness Adventure Books, 1991; Allen Dulles. *The Secret Surrender*. New York: Lyons Press, 2006.
6. Emanuel E. Minskoff, "Preliminary Report on External Assets of Ernst Kaltenbrunner, 1945."
7. Dale F. Shughart, "Recollections of a Former U.S. Counter-Intelligence Agent During World War II," unpublished manuscript, Courtesy Dale F. Shughart Jr., Carlisle, PA.

Chapter 6

1. Walter W. Horn, "Illegal Transfer of Works of Art from the Collection of Willy Sachs (supplementary report)," April 2, 1946.
2. Walter W. Horn, "Illegal Sale of Art Works," November 13, 1945.
3. www.historynet.com/world-war-ii-eighth-air-force-raid-on-schweinfurt.htm
4. Walter W. Horn to Captain Edwin Ray, "Illegal Transfer of Art," April 2, 1946.

5. George Mandler. *Interesting Times.* London: Lawrence Erlbaum, 2002.
6. Edwin H Larson and Lieutenant Rolf Watenberg, sworn testimony, no date, summer 1945.
7. Ursula Sachs, copy of translation statement, September 19, 1945.
8. Walter W. Horn, "Illegal Transfer of Art Work from the Collection of Mr. Will Sachs," December 13, 1945.
9. Mandler, op. cit.
10. Emil Henriot, Report, Divisional Commissioner, French Republic, April 15, 1947.
11. William W. Quinn. "Correspondence and Court-Martial of Major Paul Kubala." U.S. Army Military History Institute, Carlisle Barracks, PA.
12. Henriot, op. cit.
13. Walter Horn, "Illegal Transfer of Art Work from Collection of Will Sachs," December 13, 1945.
14. Walter Horn, "Illegal Transfer of Art Work from the Collection of Mr. Will Sachs," April 2, 1946.
15. *Ibid.*
16. *Ibid.*
17. Walter W. Horn to Captain Edwin Ray, "Illegal Transfer of Art," April 2, 1946.
18. Walter Horn, "Illegal Transfer of Art Work from the Collection of Mr. Will Sachs," April 2, 1946.
19. Sergeant Hausemer, hearing, Gendarmery of the Grand Duchy of Luxembourg, March 4, 1948.
20. Elmer Teply, letter, "My Dear Friends," Heidelberg, August 4, 1945.
21. Walter W. Horn, "Illegal Sale of Art," November 19, 1945.
22. William E. Frye, letter, "Report on the Sachs Case," October 29, 1945.
23. *Ibid.*
24. Paul R. Allerup, no title, United States Government (injured party) Criminal Investigation Division, September 18–October 6, 1945.
25. Lieutenant Walter W. Horn, "Synopsis of Fact," December 13, 1945.
26. *Ibid.*

Chapter 7

1. Walter Horn, "Illegal Transfer of Art Work from the Collection of Mr. Will Sachs," December 13, 1945.
2. William G. O'Brien, "Report of Recovery of Three Cranach Paintings Owned by Willy Sachs," December 11, 1945.
3. William G. O'Brien, "Search for Cranach," unpublished manuscript, courtesy of Mrs. Elayne O'Brien, Manlius, New York.
4. *Ibid.*
5. Record of Trial, Donovan Senter, General Court Martial, May 20, 1946.
6. *Ibid.*
7. Lieutenant Senter's statement of May 20, 1946.
8. Lieutenant Colonel Samuel M. Hogan, "Review of Staff Judge Advocate," May 20, 1946.
9. Peter Blos, letter to Mr. Huntington Cairns, September 19, 1946.

Chapter 8

1. Chief Inspector, French Republic, statement of Mr. Jean Victor, 60 years old, April 10, 1947.
2. Emelie Menger, letter, "Dear Mr. Senter," January 15, 1946.
3. The Chief of the Secretariat in Berlin to Director General Justice, subject Lieutenant Donovan C. Senter, June 14, 1948.
4. NA Form 13164, Donovan C. Senter, information releasable under the Freedom of Information Act, National Personnel Records Center, St. Louis, Missouri.
5. *Ibid.*
6. Albert Senter, interview.

Part III
PLUNDERING PRICELESS MANUSCRIPTS

The primary sources for Part III are the U.S. Department of State Records maintained by the MFAA advisor, 1944–1961, Ardelia Hall Collection, Record Group 59. Box 2: Kassel Ivory Diptych — Los Angeles — returned to Germany. Box 3: Rubens painting — Los Angeles, and other paintings from the same source. Box 6: Manuscript of *Hildebrandslied* from Kassel (three folders). Box 9: Paintings from Bad Wildungen

Repository — Koebroek; Paintings by Neeffs of interior of Antwerp Cathedral. Box 19: Bad Wildungen.

Chapter 9

1. Omar N. Bradley. *A Soldier's Story.* New York: Holt, 1951.
2. Thomas Seibel, e-mail, July 25, 2009.
3. Walker Hancock. "A Monuments Officer in Germany," *College Art Journal*, January 1946.
4. Dr. Stuttmann, letter, May 20, 1946.
5. James J. Rorimer. *Survival.* New York: Abelard Press, 1950.
6. Joan A. Holladay. *Illuminating the Epic.* Seattle: University of Washington Press, 1996.
7. Opritsa D. Popa. *Bibliophiles and Bibliothieves.* New York: Walter de Gruyter, 2003.

Chapter 10

1. Electronic army serial number merged file, www.archives.gov, & Application for Social Security Account Number, Baltimore MD.
2. T/Sgt. Chartrand. *History of the 6th Signal Center Liaison Team.* Printed by the International Telephone and Telegraph Corporation, no date; U.S. Army Military History Institute, Carlisle, PA.
3. *Ibid.*
4. C. A. Harrison. *Cross Channel Attack.* Washington, DC: U.S. Government Printing Office, 1951.
5. National Archives, "Guide to Foreign Military Studies 1945–54" B-656 (Pemsel): MS B-637 (Blumentritt); MS B636 (Ziegelmann). B-782 (Oberst Anton Staubwasser G-2 Army Group B). Cf. MS B-901, in which Zimmermann (G-3 of OB WEST) says that the large number of Allied units estimated to be still in England after the Normandy assault made it impossible for the Germans to rule out the probability of a second landing.
6. Harrison, op. cit.
7. David Brinkley. *Washington Goes to War.* New York: Knopf, 1988.
8. Final pay voucher of Bud Berman, National Personnel Records Center, St. Louis, MO.
9. Chartrand, op. cit.
10. New York passenger list, U.S.S. *Monticello* (AP61), www.ancestry.com

Chapter 11

1. Ardelia R. Hall, memorandum of conversation; January 27 and July 12, 1961.
2. Bud Berman, letter, "Dear Mr. Rosenbach," no date; Rosenbach Museum & Library, Philadelphia, PA.
3. The Rosenbach Company, signed by John Fleming, also signed by Meyer Kahn for Bud Berman, two dates: July 6, 1945, and October 8, 1945.
4. Meyer Kahn, information releasable under the Freedom of Information Act, National Archives and Records Administration.
5. Berman, op cit.
6. Ardelia R. Hall, op cit.
7. U.S. Treasury Department, registered letter, commissioner of customs; June 13, 1952.
8. Lawrence S. Morris, letter to customs, August 22, 1950.
9. Edwin Wolf II. *Rosenbach.* New York: World Publishing, 1960.
10. Unsigned memo, commissioner of customs, June 13, 1952.

Chapter 12

1. Carrie Estelle Doheny Foundation and Robert O. Schad, "The Estelle Doheny Collection," *The New Colophon* 3 no. 9, 1950.
2. Ardelia Hall, memorandum of conversation, January 16, 1952.
3. Archbishop of Los Angeles, letter, "My Dear Miss Hall," April 7, 1953.
4. Ardelia Hall, letter, "My Dear Cardinal McIntyre" May 5, 1953.
5. Carl P. White, "Subject Return of Looted Objects," August 14, 1953.
6. Ardelia R. Hall, memorandum of conversation, January 27 and July 12, 1961.
7. Ardelia R. Hall, letter to Mr. Schwenk, October 26, 1953.
8. John S. Baky, Director of Libraries, Connelly Library, La Salle University, e-mail, 08/17/2009.

Chapter 13

1. Records of Museums and Fine Art, RG260, National Archives.

2. Edith Standen, diary, The National Gallery of Art, Washington, DC.
3. Sworn testimony of Dr. Albert Rapp, Charles McLean, inspector general, August 27, 1945.
4. Herbert Steward Leonard, letter, August 13, 1946.
5. Bernard Taper, investigation of missing paintings, July 27, 1946.
6. Diebstahl von Gemälden, printed by the U.S. Army, no date but printed in August 1946.
7. Hans Joachim Zienke, letter to the author, November 20, 1990.
8. LeRoy B. Powers, received from Howard F. Travis, November 21, 1946.
9. Theodore Heinrich, letter, "Dear Dr. Helsinger," June 27, 1950.
10. James B. Byrnes, letter to Thomas Carr Howe, March 1, 1951.
11. Shirley Stephens to Miss Ardelia Hall, "This receipt is acknowledgment of your letter of April 15, in regard to the seizure of two paintings from Laventine Lavin, 4806 Cleveland Avenue, Canton, OH," April 22, 1952.
12. Bill of lading for two paintings, January, 16, 1952.

Part IV
THE SCHWARZBURG CASTLE

In the early 1990s the primary sources for Part 4 were the U.S. Department of State records maintained by the MFAA advisor, 1944–1961, Ardelia Hall Collection, Record Group 59. The documents have since been removed. The author has a copy of these documents.

Chapter 14

1. Shelby l. Stanton. *World War II Order of Battle*. New York: Galahad Books, 1984.
2. After Action Report, 102nd Infantry Division, June 9, 1945.
3. After Action Report, 102nd Infantry Division, June 9, 1945.
4. 102nd Infantry Journal, May 14, 1945.
5. Ralph W. Anderson, Field Director, ARC, 406 Infantry, June 30, 1945.
6. Sworn statement of Clinton R. Walters, Waco, TX, August 18, 1954.
7. Sworn statement of Cecil Wooten, Metuchen, NJ, September 9, 1954.
8. Sworn statement of Clinton R. Walters, Waco, TX, August 18, 1954.
9. Affidavit, Paul N. Estes, state of Florida, December 1979.
10. *Ibid.*
11. "Staatliche Kunstsammlunger, über Diebstahl von Kunstwerke...," January 28, 1961.
12. Walter Scheidig, "Direktion der Staatliche Kunstsammlungen in Weimar," July 25, 1945.
13. Walter Scheidig, registered airmail to Ardelia Hall, October 21, 1953.
14. Affidavit, Paul N. Estes, state of Florida, December 1979.
15. I.A. Gatlin, affidavit, November 24, 1954.

Chapter 15

1. *New York Times*, May 30, 1966.
2. Ardelia Hall to Walter Scheidig, July 1966.
3. cases.justia.com *Kunstsammlungen zu Weimar, Plaintiff-appellant, v. Edward Elicofon*. On January 27, 1969, the Federal Republic of Germany brought suit in the district court for the Eastern District of New York against Edward Elicofon, U.S. Court of Appeals.
4. *Ibid.*
5. *Ibid.*
6. *Ibid.*
7. F. E. Sheehan, "Report on Discovery and Transportation from Eschwegge to Frankfurt/Main of Property Belonging to House of Saxe-Weimar," October 10, 1946, Parkley Lesley papers, National Art Gallery.
8. Affidavit, Paul N. Estes, state of Florida, December 1979.

Chapter 16

1. Affidavit, Churchill J. Brazelton, state of New York [illegible], 1979.

2. *Princeton Alumni Weekly*, November, 17, 1944; June 8, 1945; May 2, 1947; November 19, 1948; and Fifteenth Year Book.
3. Churchill Brazelton, letter, "Dearest Mother," March 3, 1945. The Harry Ransom Center, University of Texas at Austin.
4. Churchill Brazelton, letter, "Dearest Mother," March 2, 1945. The Harry Ransom Center, University of Texas at Austin.
5. Churchill Brazelton, letter, "Dearest Mother," March 3, 1945. The Harry Ransom Center, University of Texas at Austin.
6. Churchill Brazelton, letter, "Dearest Mother," March 16, 1945. The Harry Ransom Center, University of Texas at Austin.
7. *Ibid.*, April 13, 1945.
8. *Ibid.*, May 3, 1945.
9. Churchill Brazelton, letter, "Dearest Mother," May 6, 1945. The Harry Ransom Center, University of Texas at Austin.
10. Omar Bradley. *A Soldier's Story*. New York: Holt, 1951.
11. Churchill Brazelton, letter, "Dearest Mother," July 20, 1945. The Harry Ransom Center, University of Texas at Austin.
12. Churchill Brazelton, letter, "Dearest Mother," June 27, 1945. The Harry Ransom Center, University of Texas at Austin.
13. Churchill Brazelton's letters were donated to the Harry Ransom Center, University of Texas at Austin, by Mrs. T. Berry Brazelton, 2005 Austin Avenue, Waco, Texas, on April 3, 1974. There are approximately 200 letters or about 1,000 pages. Letter from/ to mother and Churchill are consecutively numbered. Both refer to letters, such as #74, and state a subject related to the number. All letters except one are from Churchill (Chuck) to mother. That one letter is to mother from son T. Berry Brazelton, November 23, 1945, at U.S. Naval Receiving Barracks, Naval Training Center, Long Island, NY.

Chapter 17

1. *New York Times*, November 10, 1999; *Thuringer Allgemeine*, December 5, 2000; *Star-Ledger*, December 6, 2000.

Part V
VIGNETTES OF LOOTING

Chapter 18

1. John J. Butler letter to Kenneth D. Alford, National Archives, June 28, 1990, and historical data.
2. Dr. Bernard V. Limburger, commanding officer, June 2, 1945.
3. *Ibid.*
4. *Ibid.*
5. James J. Rorimer, memorandum, August 21, 1945.
6. Bernard V. Limburger, letter to military government, July 2, 1945.
7. Company history: 603, Quartermaster Graves Registration Company, page 53.
8. Captain Francis E. Ewing, Headquarters, 4460th QM Service Company, certificate, December 4, 1945.
9. Lt. Col. Harvey M. Coverley, "Looted Art Treasures at Reutte," July 17, 1945.
10. James J. Rorimer. *Survival: The Salvage and Protection of Art in War*. New York: Abelard Press, 1950.

Chapter 19

1. Lt. Walter Horn, "Paintings Missing from Art Repository of Staedtische Galerie and Lenbach Galerie at Castle Hohenaschau," September 4, 1946.
2. *Ibid.*
3. Lieutenant Jonathan T. Morey, "Paintings Missing from Schloss Hohenaschau," October 17, 1945.
4. Walter Horn, report, September 4, 1946.
5. Lieutenant Walter Horn, "Paintings Missing from Art Repository of Staedtische Galerie and Lenbach Galerie at Castle Hohenaschau," September 4, 1946.

Chapter 20

The primary sources for this chapter are the U.S. Department of State Records maintained by the MFAA advisor, 1944–1961, Ardelia

Hall Collection, Record Group 59, Box 3. "Egyptian Gold Ring from Meroe (M&A Boston) returned to Germany."

1. Konstantin Akinsha and Grigorii Kazlov. *Beautiful Loot.* New York: Random House, 1995.
2. Rabbi Joseph S. Shubow, letter to James F. Malons, U.S. Customs, November 12, 1951.
3. *Ibid.*
4. Dows Dunham, "Dear Ardelia," no date (about August 26, 1951).
5. Dows Dunhill, letter to Ardelia Hall, about August 26, 1951).
6. Rabbi Joseph S. Shubow, letter to James F. Malons, U.S. Customs, November 12, 1951.
7. Lee M. Freedman, letter to Mr. J. H. Burke, November 19, 1951.
8. Lee M. Friedman, letters to several politicians, November 20, 1951.

Chapter 21

The primary informational sources for this chapter are the U.S. Department of State Records maintained by the MFAA advisor, 1944–1961, Ardelia Hall Collection, Record Group 59, Box 3. "MS of Political Testament of Frederick the Great — Returned to Germany."

1. John Henry Murphy, commissioner of customs, August 20, 1951.
2. Extract from *The Montgomery Advisor,* May 27, 1951.
3. *Ibid.*
4. John Henry Murphy, Dr. Ernest Pozener, August, 15, 1951.
5. John Henry Murphy, Dr. Ernest Pozener, August, 15, 1951.
6. John Henry Murphy, letter to commissioner of customs, August, 18, 1951.

Chapter 22

The primary informational sources for this chapter are the U.S. Department of State Records maintained by the MFAA advisor, 1944–1961, Ardelia Hall Collection, Record Group 59, Boxes 14–15. Scalzo and Scalzo Case location: 250/52/9/02.

1. Main Archives, Berlin-Dahlem, September 4, 1959.
2. Dr. Hans Bellee, letter, "Dear Dr. von Tieschowitz," November 5, 1952.
3. Hans Bellee, letter to Custodial Administration of Cultural Property, November 5, 1952.
4. Capt. John A. Bacher, from the Annual Report of the 66th Field Hospital, and Col. John Hodges, "Dear Miss Hall," June 23, 1959.
5. Ardelia Hall, letter, Dear Mr. Shapiro, March 17, 1960.
6. *Buffalo Evening News,* June 2, 1960.
7. Dr. Scheidig, letter to Miss Ardelia Hall, April 11, 1961.
8. *Niagara Gazette,* Niagara Falls, NY, September 22, 1976.

Chapter 23

The primary sources for this chapter are the U.S. Department of State Records maintained by the MFAA advisor, 1944–1961, Ardelia Hall Collection, Record Group 59, Box 10. "Saarbrucken 'Golden Book' and Werner Theis, Landeshauptstadt Saarbrücken."

1. *Deutschen Saar,* September, 6, 1960.
2. *Deutschen Saar,* September 4, 1956.
3. Louis J. Link, Foreign Service Dispatch, September 18, 1956.
4. *Des Moines Register,* September 12, 1956.
5. Robert C. Creel, Officer in Charge of German Political Affairs, letter to Mr. Walter E. Clark, May 8, 1957.
6. *Deutchen Saar,* September 4, 1956.

Chapter 24

The primary sources for this chapter are the U.S. Department of State Records maintained by the MFAA advisor, 1944–1961, Ardelia Hall Collection, Record Group 59. Box 2. "1457 Mainz Psalter from Dresden Landes Bibliothek."

1. Wm. A. Jackson, memo, "The State Department and the 1457 Psalter," no date, NAS.
2. "Memorandum on the Recovery of the 1457 Mainz Psalter by the Department of State," top secret, no date.

Chapter 25

The sources for this chapter are the U.S. Department of State Records Maintained by the MFAA advisor, 1944–1961, Ardelia Hall Collection, Record Group 59, Box 2: Two paintings in Arkansas returned to Poland location: 250/52/9/01. Box 9: Index set of photos and documents for each Czartoryski Collection.

1. Nuremberg Military Tribunals, 1945/1946, International Military Accession Number: AC-94x-05472.
2. Czartoryski Collection, references Charles Estreicher, "Cultural Losses of Poland."
3. Hans Posse, report on the trip to Cracow and Warsaw, December 14, 1939.
4. OSS, Consolidated Interrogation Report No. 2, Theodore Rousseau Jr., September 25, 1945.
5. Vera Münch, written statement, Bad Wiessee, August 8, 1947.
6. Interrogation of Ernst Wilhelm von Palézieux, Bernard Taper, June 17, 1947.
7. Ardelia Hall, letter, "Dear Count Zamoyski," December 15, 1960.
8. Nuremberg Military Tribunals, 1945/1946.
9. Bernard Taper, interrogation of Helene Kraffcyck, former secretary to Hans Frank, June 27, 1947.
10. Lieutenant Daniel J. Kearns, certificate of receipt, June 14, 1945.
11. Howe, Thomas Carr Jr. *Salt Mines and Castles*. New York: Bobbs-Merrill, 1946.
12. *San Francisco Chronicle,* Jesse Hamlin, May 4, 2007.

13. R. S. Wilson, letter to Mr. Lawrence S. Morris, October 9, 1950.
14. R. S. Wilson: letter to attorney general, September 15, 1950.
15. *New York Times*, September 14, 1952.
16. Department of State Memo, January 12, 1949.

Chapter 26

The main sources for this chapter are the U.S. Department of State Records maintained by the MFAA advisor, 1944–1961, Ardelia Hall Collection, Record Group 59, Box 7. "The Hertling fake German antique jewelry."

1. Nuggett, Der Gral, "Geheimnisvoll — der Goldkessel vom Chiemsee," November, 2003.
2. Articles from *Weltkunst,* November 1, 1949; Nugget 53, November, 2003.
3. Gunter Hertling, letter, "Dear Ken," July 25, 2007.
4. Mrs. Clara E. Hertling, affidavit of ownership, no date.
5. Ardelia R. Hall, ICS, March 7, 1953.
6. Stanley P. Spinola, commissioner of customs, September 17, 1953.
7. Thomas M. Beggs, director, Smithsonian Institute, National Collection of Fine Art, September 21, 1954.

Part VI
LOOTING FROM HUNGARY IN WORLD WAR II

Chapter 27

1. Miklos Horthy. *My Memoirs*. New York: R. Speller, 1957.

Chapter 28

1. Dr. Julius Torzsay Biber, letter to the International Red Cross, May 30, 1945.
2. Dr. Julius Torzsay Biber, letter to Colonel Ball, May 29, 1945.
3. Dr. Julius Torzsay Biber, letter to the International Red Cross, May 30, 1945.
4. SHAFE, telegram to G5 Gen. F. J. McSherry, April 1945. OMGUS: Telegram — Economics Division, Restitution Branch, March 1945.

5. William I. DeHuszar, 80th Counter Intelligence Corps, "Memorandum for the Officer in Charge," May 14, 1945.
6. Paul D. Harkins, "Tally, Transport and Delivery of Treasure," May 12, 1945.
7. Major Lionel C. Perera, receipt for valuables, May 14, 1945.
8. Juilis Biber, letter to the International Red Cross, may 30, 1945.
9. W. R. Loeffler, letter to Hungarian National Bank, July 30, 1946.
10. *Vilag*, August 8, 1946, *Magyar Nemzet*, August 8, 1946, *Szabad Szo*, evening edition, August 8, 1946 and from a four-page document titled "Background," no date, no signature.
11. Bank of Hungary, letter, April 24, 1947.

12. Jack Bennett, "Restitution of Hungarian Gold," July 25, 1946.
13. Walter L. Kluss, "Plans for Movement of Hungarian Silver and other Valuables," April 2, 1947.
14. Karl Kristof, Vilag, April 24, 1947.

Chapter 29

The primary sources for information about the travails of the Hungarian Crown Treasure were obtained in response to a Freedom of Information request (9104455); this material was received by the author on October 26, 1993, and November 28, 1994.

1. "Outline of Origin and History, Department of State Study," Secret/Limdis, drafted by Andor C. Klay, 1971.
2. Tamas Bogyay, "Problems around Saint Stephen and his Crown," Munich, April 15, 1970.
3. "Outline of Origin and History," Department of State Study, Secret/Limdis, drafted by Andor C. Klay, 1971.
4. Statute XXV, 1928.
5. "Outline," op. cit.
6. Ibid.
7. *Hungarian Weekly*, Munich, July 7, 1950.
8. Paul Kabala, statement, August 2, 1945, and *The Crown in World War II and Since*, Department of State Study, Secret/Limdis, drafted by Andor C. Klay, 1971.
9. Captain B. S. Schelling, Reference shipment no. 59, August 3, 1945.
10. Martin Himler, *Igy Neztek ki magyar nemzet sirasoi*, New York 1958.
11. Capt. George A. Selke, "Discovery of Holy Hand of Hungarian Court Collection at Mattsee," June 19, 1945, and Lt. James J. Shea, "Discovery of Parts of Hungarian Crown," July 3, 1946.
12. Capt. George A. Selke, received from Lt. James W. Shea, June 18, 1945.
13. Captain George A. Selke, "Material Entrusted to Custody of the Prince-Archbishop of Salzburg," June 18, 1945
14. Capt. George A. Selke, Report to Colonel Janzan, June 19, 1945.
15. Segreteria Di Stato, letter, December 22, 1945.
16. Ralph J. Diefenbach, the Rev. Stephen Komenes, January 11, 1946.

Chapter 30

1. Robert Scholz, [illegible] to the Einsatzstab Rosenberg, May 19, 1945.

2. Lieutenant Walter W. Horn, "The Gold Treasure of Kremsmünster," May 11, 1946.
3. Rohracher, letter of April, 24, 1946.
4. Edgar Breitenback, receipt of one case of gold coins, May 1, 1946.
5. Walter W. Horn, interrogation of Charles Brousz, July 2, 1946.

Chapter 31

1. "Outline of Origin and History," Department of State Study, Secret/Limdis, drafted by Andor C. Klay, 1971.
2. Jozsef Mindszenty. *Memoirs*. New York: Macmillan, 1974.
3. "Outline of Origin and History," Department of State Study, Secret/Limdis, drafted by Andor C. Klay, 1971.
4. *Ibid*.
5. Department of State Telegram T-182, Berlin, July 29, 1948, SECRET.
6. Major Richard P. Weeber, "Hungarian Coronation Regalia," September 23, 1948.
7. General Geoffrey Keyes, Your Excellency, September 20, 1948.
8. Herbert Stuart Leonard, Evelyn Tucker, receipt of the objects listed, September 23, 1948.
9. "Outline of Origin and History," Department of State Study, Secret/Limdis, drafted by Andor C. Klay, 1971.
10. Quoted in The Trial of Jozsef Mindszenty, Budapest, 1949.
11. Department of State Telegram T-182, Berlin, July 29, 1948, SECRET.
12. "Subject: Hungarian Crown of St. Stevens," Department of State, May 21, 1970.
13. Cardinal Mindszenty: letter to Richard Nixon, October 26, 1972.

Chapter 32

1. FM AMEMBASSY BUDAPEST TO SECSTATE WASHDC, September 24, 1975.
2. John A. Baker Jr., Department of State, September 19, 1973.
3. Telegram, Budapest to Dept. of State, October 6, 1977, Secret/NODIS
4. 42 signatures, the President, November 4, 1977.
5. Jeane Dixon, letter to President of United States, November 8, 1977.
6. FM AMEMBASSY BUDAPEST TO SECSTATE WASHDC, November 30, 1977.

7. FM SECSTATE TO AMEMBASSY BUDAPEST, December 26, 1977.
8. FM SECSTATE WASHOC TO AMEMBASSY BUDAPEST, December 24, 1977.

Chapter 33

Primary source are the National Archives, RG 338, E. Hung Jewels, File S4. 8007/3 and Case No. 01-1859-CIV-SETZ, First Amended Complaint.

1. Signature illegible, Hungarian document, April 13, 1946, and Szoke Bela, "Mr. Mayor," July 23, 1948.
2. Unsigned, "Hungarian Train Bearing Civilians," May 16, 1945.
3. John F. Back, "Report on the Werfen Train," September 17, 1945.
4. Dr. Steffan Mingovits, "Sworn Protocol," July, 28, 1945.
5. Maj. F. D. Gallagher, "Property Control," May 21, 1945.

Chapter 34

1. Capt. John S. Back, "Inventory of Werfen Train," September 1945.

Chapter 35

1. OSS Art Investigation Unit, "At present Gen. Collins Lives in Schloss Prilau," September 10, 1945.
2. Maj. R.W. Cutler, Lt. Col. Heller, August 28, 1945.
3. "List of Property Released from Property Control Warehouse Salzburg to War Department Personnel and Agencies in Land Salzburg."
4. *Ibid.*
5. Interview with Howard A. Mackenzie, age 80, December 10, 1983.

Chapter 36

1. From Commanding General U.S. Forces Austria, to War Department, June 4, 1946.
2. AGWAR FROM JCS, November 16, 1946.
3. Abba P. Schwartz, General Jesmond D. Balmer, May 23, 1947, and Walker M. Treece, inventory of movable property, May 23, 1947.
4. Jonathan W. Cuneo, letter to Kenneth D. Alford, January 31, 2006.
5. William H. Fischer, letter, "Dear Mr. Alford," January 10, 2005.

Bibliography

The source material used to prepare this study was largely obtained from manuscript documents, which are listed under the notes for each specific chapter. The titles listed below were used primarily for general background information.

Akinsha, Konstantin, and Grigorii Kozlov. *Beautiful Loot: The Soviet Plunder of Europe's Art Treasures.* New York: Random House, 1995.
Alford, Kenneth D. *The Spoils of World War II.* New York: Birch Lane Press, 1994.
———. *Great Treasure Stories of World War II.* Mason City, IA: Savas, 2000.
———. *Nazi Millionaires.* Haverty, PA: Casemate, 2002.
Bradley, Omar N. *A Soldier's Story.* New York: Holt, 1951.
Bradley, Omar N., and Clay Blair. *A General's Life: An Autobiography by General of the Army Omar N. Bradley.* New York: Simon & Schuster, 1983.
Butcher, Harry C. *My Three Years with Eisenhower: The Personal Diary of Captain Harry C. Butcher, USNR, Naval Aide to General Eisenhower, 1942–1945.* New York: Simon & Schuster, 1946.
D'Este, Carlo. *Patton: A Genius for War.* New York: HarperCollins, 1995.
———. *Eisenhower: A Soldier's Life.* New York: Holt, 2002.
Duberman, Martin. *The Worlds of Lincoln Kirstein.* New York: Knopf, 2007.
Dulles, Allen. *The Secret Surrender.* New York: Lyons Press, 2006.
Edsel, Robert M. *Rescuing Da Vinci: Hitler and the Nazis Stole Europe's Great Art, America and Her Allies Recovered It.* Dallas: Laurel, 2006.
Eisenhower, Dwight D. *Crusade in Europe.* New York: Doubleday, 1948.
Flanner, Janet. *Men and Monuments.* New York: Harper & Brothers, 1957.
Harrison, C. A. *Cross Channel Attack.* Washington, DC: U.S. Government Printing Office, 1951.
Hitler, Adolf. *Mein Kampf.* Translated by Ralph Manheim. New York: Houghton Mifflin, 1943.
Holladay, Joan A. *Illuminating the Epic.* Seattle: University of Washington Press, 1996.
Horthy, Miklos. *My Memoirs.* New York: R. Speller, 1957.
Howe, Thomas Carr, Jr. *Salt Mines and Castles.* New York: Bobbs-Merrill, 1946.
Kurtz, Michael J. *America and the Return of Nazi Contraband: The Recovery of Europe's Cultural Treasures.* Cambridge, UK: Cambridge University Press, 2006.
Lash, Joseph P. *A World of Love.* New York: Doubleday, 1984.
Mandler, George. *Interesting Times.* London: Lawrence Erlbaum, 2002.
McDonald, Charles B. *The Last Offensive.* Washington DC: U.S. Army, 1984.
Mindszenty, Jozsef. *Memoirs.* New York: Macmillan, 1974.

Nazi Conspiracy and Aggression. Washington, DC: U.S. Government Printing Office, 1946.
Nicholas, Lynn. *The Rape of Europa.* New York: Vintage, 1995.
Popa, Opritsa D. *Bibliophiles and Bibliothieves.* New York: Walter de Gruyter, 2003.
Quinn, William W. *Buffalo Bill Remembers.* Fowlerville, MI: Wilderness Adventure Books, 1991.
Report of the American Commission for the Protection and Salvage of Artistic and Historic Monuments in War Areas. Washington, DC: U.S. Government Printing Office, 1946.
Rorimer, James J. *Survival: The Salvage and Protection of Art in War.* New York: Abelard Press, 1950.
Sereny, Gitta. *Albert Speer: His Battle with Truth.* New York: Knopf, 1995.
Shirer, William L. *Berlin Diary: The Journal of a Foreign Correspondent: 1934–1941.* Norwalk, CT: Easton Press, 1991.
_____. *The Rise and Fall of the Third Reich: A History of Nazi Germany.* Norwalk, CT: Easton Press, 1991.
Smyth, Craig Hugh. *Repatriation of Art from the Collecting Point in Munich After World War II.* Montclair, NJ: Abner Schram, 1988.
Speer, Albert. *Inside the Third Reich.* New York: Macmillan, 1970.
Stanton, Shelby l. *World War II Order of Battle.* New York: Galahad Books, 1984.
Trial of the Major War Criminals Before the International Military Tribunal: Nuremberg, November 14, 1945–October 1, 1946. Nuremberg: International Military Tribunal, 1947.
Wolf, Edwin II. *Rosenbach.* New York: World, 1960.

Correspondence and Interviews

The author has retained all correspondence and a copy of all documents used in this work. They can be viewed and copied from his library.

Robert S. Anderson, Wilkes Barre, PA
Arthur W. Bergeron, Jr., Ph.D., Carlisle, PA
Dr. Rolf Bothe, Kunstsammlungen zu Weimar, Germany
Dr. T. Berry Brazelton, Cambridge, MA
Dr. Barbara Eschenburg, Städtische Galerie im Lenbachhaus, Munich, Germany
Professor G. H. Hertling, Lake Forest Park, WA
Robert Kudelski, Warsaw, Poland
Marc Masurovsky, Falls Church, VA
Elayne O'Brien, Manlius, NY
Gretchen Obenauf, Albuquerque, NM
Opritsa D. Popa, Elk Grove, CA
Al Regensberg, Senior Archivist, Records Center and Archives, Santa Fe, NM
Dr. Thomas Seibel, Bad Wildungen, Germany
Albert J. Senter, Albuquerque, NM
Dale F. Shuggart, Jr., Attorney at Law, Carlisle, PA
Robert M. Weisz, Lindenhurst, IL
Stephan Wiede, Rosenheim, Germany
Dr. Konrad Wiedemann, Kassel, Germany
Ralph Williams, St. Joseph, MI

Index

Aachen, Germany 123–124
Accursed Salt lakes 35
Achernar, USS 86–88
Adams, Ansel 38
Albrecht, Gustav 60
Albuquerque, New Mexico 33, 37
Alter, Maj. Arthur 175
Alvarado, Texas 33
Amaker, Mrs. Arrie 145
Amaker, P.F.C. John 145
Anderson, Lt. Col. Robert S. 20, 23, 26, 28
Andrews, Lt. Worth B. 205–206
Apostle, Christopher 137
Apster, Harry S. 105
Archdiocese of Los Angeles 98, 100
Archduke Josef Ferenc 190
Ardennes 42, 62–63
Associated Press 126
Avar, László 229–230, 232–233

Baber, Walther 174
Back, Maj. John F. 233
Bad Wildungen 79–81, 83–84, 89, 98, 102–105, 127–128, 130
Baierle, Hildegard 72
Baierle, Phillis 72
Baranyai, Leopold 191
Barbari, Jacopo de 135
Battle of the Bulge 1, 42, 62, 89, 123
Beauregard, Lt. Joseph 85
Behn, Lt. William C. 88
Bela, Witz 210
Bellee, Dr. Hans 157, 159
Beltz, Erich 72
Benavides, Fray Alonso de 34
Berman, Lt. Bud 4, 85–86, 88–89, 91–93, 100–101
Berman, Irwin 85
Berman, Hyman 85
Bernal, Fray Juan 35

Bernstein, Col. Bernard 45, 198
Bethlen, Count Geza 193
Betzold, Carrie Estelle 96
Bevans, Gen. James 154
Biber, Dr. Julius 194–196
Biever, Aloys 51, 55, 59, 61–62, 64, 71–73
Blaul, Richard 148
Bleibaum, Dr. Frederick 81
Blessing Christ 49–51, 55, 57–58, 61, 65
Blos, Peter 69–70
Blue Network 123
Bol, Ferdinand 56
Bonaparte, Josephine 161
Bonat, Sgt. Leno V. 147–148
Bor-Komorowski, Gen. Tadeusz 173
Bormann, Martin 211
Born, Maj. Lester K. 158–59
Boston Museum 150–151
Boswell, Chaplain 111
Bothe, Ralph 136
Bothmer, Bernard V. 150
Bradley, Gen. Omar 79, 127–128, 130, 193
Brann, Gen. Donald W. 237
Braun, Eva 162, 197
Brazelton, Lt. Churchill 4, 115, 122–134
Brazelton, Pauline Battle (Mrs. T. Berry) 122, 125
Brazelton, T. Berry 122
Brazil 144
Breitenbach, Edgar 98–99, 178–179
Breklenkam, Quirijn van 178
Brennbergbánya 229, 233
Brey, Col. William G. 196, 198
Bristol Harbor 86–87
Brooklyn College 69
Brousz, Charles 208, 213
Brückner, Dr. 18–20
Brzezinski, Zbigniew 222
Bühler, Dr. Curt F. 93–94, 99
Burke, J.H. 151
Burns, Robert 87

271

Burton, G.C. 41
Burton, Hugh Young 26
Bust of Christ 135, 137
Byrnes, James B. 105

Caldwell, Gen. Charles H. 154
Camp Barkeley, Texas 40–41
Camp Crowder 85
Camp Poke, Louisiana 42
Camp Shanks, New York 85
Campbell, Msgr. Thomas 135
Cananea, Mexico 36
Canton, William R. 24
Capron, Doris 74
Carter, Jimmy 222–225
Carter, Rosalyn 225
Carthage, Missouri 33
Castle Berg 181
CBS 123, 126
Chandler, Dr. F.S. 182
Charlemagne 84
Charles IV (king) 208, 213
Cherbourg, France 88
Christie's 104
Churchill, Winston 129–130
City College of New York 40
Civilian Conservation Corps 35
Clark, Gen. Mark W. 210, 229, 239
Clark, Sgt. Walter E. 163
Collins, Gen. Harry J. 235–237, 243–244
Colmar Pocket 42
Columbia University 40, 92
Conner, Martin 7
Conte Grande 88–89
Council 13–14
Cragon, Col. H.D. 194
Cramer-Klett, Baron 146
Cranach, Lucas 4, 47, 49, 51, 57, 64, 70, 112
Creel, Robert C. 165
Cronkite, Walter 126
Crown of Hesse 69
Cuneo Waldman & Gilbert 242
Cutler, Maj. R.W. 235–236
Czartoryski Museum 170

Daine, Col. Henry W. 56
Danto, Lillian 85
D-Day 87
Deane, Silas 94–95
Declaration of Independence 94–95
Degerndorf, Germany 43
DeHuszar, Sgt. William 193
Deming, Capt. E.G. 56
Des Moines Register 164
Deutsche Bank 14–15, 23, 172
de Vegar, Edward Neumann 220

Diebstahl von Genmälden 104
Diefenbach, Chaplain Ralph J. 210
Diessel, Rudolf 47, 54
Dionne, Fran 7
Dixon, Jean 223–224
Doheny, Carrie Estelle 91, 95–98, 100
Doheny, Edward L. 96
Doheny Museum 4
Dole, Robert 4, 222–223, 225
Donovan, Gen. William 51
Downs, Bill 126
Duerbech, Otto 17
Dulles, Allen 43
Dulles, John Foster 220
Dunham, Dows 150–151
Durant, Col. Jack 18
Dürer, Albrecht 112, 119

Edward Laurence Doheny Memorial Library 97, 100
Edwards, Sgt. Norman 147
Ehle, Herr 114
Eichmann, Adolf 189
Eisenhower, Gen. Dwight 205
Elbe River 7, 11, 109, 128–129
Elfvin, John T. 160
Elicofon, Edward I. 117–120, 137
Elko, Lt. Francis C. 142
Ellis, Bruce 75
Empire State Building 92
Emrich, Robert F. 177–178
English Channel 42
Erft Canal 123–124
Eschenbach, Wolfram von 83–84
Estancia, New Mexico 33–34
Estes, Capt. Paul N. 111–112, 114–116, 120–121, 133
Even Mood on the Lower Main River 13–14
Ewing, Capt. Francis E. 143–145

Fabritius, B. 81
Fahrenkamp, Julia 25
Falconer on a White Horse 13–14
Farmer, Capt. Walter 102
Fassbender, Herr 112, 114, 116, 119, 120
Federal Republic of Germany 118, 156, 164–165
Fenstermacher, Edward B. 98
Ferdinand II 160
Ferlini, Giuseppe 4
Fesler, Caroline Marmon 179
Fischer, Ludwig 170
Fish Market at Leydeu 81
Fishblatt, Isabella 95
Flank, Lt. 52
Fleming, John F. 91, 95

Foehl, Thomas 115, 137
Foreign Exchange Depository 44, 120, 193–194, 196, 198–199, 207, 215
Forest Hill, New York 85
Fort Bragg, North Carolina 74
Fort Knox 219, 223
Fort Sam Houston, Texas 74
Fort Sill, Oklahoma 122
Frank, Brigitte 175
Frank, Hans 170, 172–177
Frank, Mr. 142
Franklin, Benjamin 94–95
Franks, Eman S. 94
Franz Joseph (emperor) 208–209, 217
Frary, Capt. Jerry P. 104
Frary, Michael G. 105
Frazer, Gordon 126
Frederick the Great 4, 94, 153, 155–158, 160
Frederick the Magnanimous 49–52, 55, 58, 64
Friedman (lawyer) 151
Friedrich, Caspar David 114
Friedrichshain Flakturm 149
Frye, Lt. William E. 56

Galambos, Ensing Gyula 230
Gallagher, Col. Fredrick 236
Gardiev, Col. Alexander 11
Gatlin, Lt. Col. Isaac A. 112, 116
Gehmacher, Irene 243
George, Mrs. William 184–185
George II (king) 159
Germanic Heritage 181, 185
Germany Army forces: Seventh Army 88; 914th Regiment 88; Army Group B 79
Geschwind 21
Ghost Ranch 75
Girl with an Ermine 171–172, 174, 176
Giuseppe Ferlini Treasure 151
Glanegg Castle, Austria 44
Goebbels, Josef 162
Goebbels, Magda 162
Goecke Hotel 79–81, 89, 102, 104
Goldblatt, Bonnie 136
Golden Book of Saarbrücken 4, 162–165
Goldweigher 56
Göring, Hermann 47, 49–50, 53, 55, 67, 70, 74, 171–172
Göser, Fridolin 146
Gossett, Robert G. 179
Gott, Col. R.C. 56
Graf, Ferencz 60
Granville, Lt. 204–205
Grundmann, Dr. Gunther 174–175
G'Schwend, Walter 85

Guderian, Heinz 173
Gundestrup Caldron 180
Gustke, Anneliese 50
Gutenberg Bible 166
Gutierrez, Juan 34–35
Gutmann, Franz 182

Hall, Ardelia R. 98–99, 115–116, 118, 120, 151, 161, 168
Ham, Alexander 199
Hamilton, Col. Fred L. 130
Hammond, John G. 43–44
Handwerker, Michael 136
Hans Tucher and Felicitas 112, 117, 119
Harvard University 37, 68, 126
Hawley, Florence 36–38, 73–74
Hayakawa, Samuel Ichiye 224
Head of a Girl 147
Heinrich (kaiser) 47, 52–54, 56
Helberg, Paul 69–70
Heller, Col. Homer K. 209, 233, 235–236, 238
Henriot, Emil 72
Hertling, Clara Elisabeth 182–185
Hertling, Gunter 182
Hildebrandslied 4, 81, 92, 94, 99
Hill, Gladwin 126
Himmler, Heinrich 181, 190
Hindenburg, Gen. Paul von 88
Hitler, Adolf 87, 112, 153, 155, 162, 173, 197
Hodges, Gen. Courtney H. 87
Hogan, Judge Samuel M. 68–69
Hohenaschau Castle 146–147
Holsinger, Capt. Joseph Samuel 71–72
Holy Crown *see* Saint Stephen's Crown
Holy See 201, 210, 216
Holy Virgin 51
Hoover, J. Edgar 41
Hopkins, Harry 41
Horn, Lt. Walter W. 57–59, 67, 147–148, 177, 211–213
Horthy, Adm. Miklos 189–190, 205, 207, 227
Horton, Frank 222–223
Hotel Balmoral 88
Hotel Elephantine 112
Houghton, Arthur Amory, Jr. 169
Houghton Library 91, 167, 168
Howard, Gen. Edwin B. 237
Hummel, Dr. Helmut von 211–213
Hummel, Mrs. Helmut von 212
Hungarian National Bank 190–191, 194, 198, 203

Indianapolis Museum of Art 179
Isabel Czartoryski (princess) 170

Index

Jackson, Robert J. 176
Jackson, Sarah 179
Jackson, William J. 167–169
Janetis, Michael 19
John (pope) 216
John the Constant 49–52, 57–58, 65
Josephus (emperor) 160

Kahn, Meyer 92–93
Kaiser, Philip M. 222, 224
Kaiser Frederick Museum 172
Kallay, Miklos 189
Kaltenbrunner, Ernst 44
Karoly IV (king) 189, 214
Kassel Library 83, 84, 91–92, 94, 100
Kassel State Museum 104
Kelly, Raymond W. 137
Kemp, Jack 224
Kennedy, Veron 213, 216
Kern, Lt. Daniel 176
Keyes, Gen. Geoffrey 217
Kibler, Harold R. 41
Kirkpatrick, Sidney D. 1
Kissinger, Henry A. 220
Klay, Andor C. 207
Klein, Thomas 136
Kneisel, Edward 177
Koekkoek, B.C. 105
Konev, Soviet Marshal Ivan Stepanovich 128, 130
König House Archives 153, 156
Kotzebue, Lt. Albert 10–11,
Kowalski, Tec/5 Stephen 11
Kraffczck, Helene 175
Kremsmünster Treasure 211
Kristof, Karl 199
Kronberg Castle 69
Kubala, Maj. Paul x, 49–51, 204–207
Kuhlmann, Henry 26
Kulmbach, Hans von 172
Kun, Bela 214, 218
Kup, Karl 98

La Farge, Maj. Bancel 59
Landgrave of Hess 84
Landscape 171, 174
Landscape with a Rainbow 114
Lash, Joseph P. 40–41
Lawrence, Paul A. 160
Lazar, Gyorg 221
Lazienki Palace Museum 178
Leary, Col. Edward J. 19
Lebel, Hans 146
Lebel, Stephanie 146–147
Le Havre, France 42
Leipzig, Germany 9–10, 13–14, 23
Lekai, Laszlo 224–225

Lenbach, Franz von 13–14, 147
Lenbachhaus Galerie 146–147
Leonard, Herbert Stuart 218
Leonardo da Vinci 170
Lewis, Col. Tom 208
Ley, Robert 162
Liber Sapientiae 81, 83, 91–93, 95, 97–98
Library of Congress 99, 166, 177
Liebel, Willy 173
Liesborn Gospels 97
Life 155
Limburger, Dr. Bernhard V. 141, 143–144
Limburger, Mrs. Bernhard V. 142
Lincoln, Mary Todd 155
Liverpool, England 85
Loeffer, Capt. William R. 196
Long, Long, Ago 125
Los Angeles County Museum 104
Los Angeles Times 223
Louis XIV 176
Löwith, Wilhelm 13–14
Luther, Martin 7
Lüttgens, Mrs. 147

Mackenzie, Capt. Howard A. 238, 240–241
Maes, Nicolaes 105
Magyars 206
Mainberg Castle 47–48, 56
Mainz Psalter 4, 166, 168, 169
Mandler, George 50
Manteau, Louis 55, 62, 64–65
Maraist, Gen. Robert V. 20
Marine Flasher 150, 182
Mark, William 43–44
Marr, K.A. 94
Marwitz, Herbert von der 180–184
Mattsee, Austria 203, 205–208
Maxwell, CIC Agent 60
Maxwell Air Force Base 155
Mayer-Caputo, Jolanda 47, 49, 51, 57–58, 62, 67, 73
Mayo Clinic 23–25
McConnell, Graham S. 21, 26
McIntyre, Cardinal 98
McMahon, Gen. William C. 237
McNarney, Gen. James J. 41
McVane, John 126
Menger, Albert 42, 50–51, 55, 61, 64–65, 69, 71–73
Menger, Amelie 42, 50, 55, 59, 61, 65, 69, 71–72
Mercer, Lt. Joseph A. 232
Metropolitan Museum of Art 70, 117, 150, 182
Meyer, Gretel 91, 98–99
Miami, New Mexico 36

Michels, an art appraiser 51
Milatovic, Maria 25
Miller, Lucille 97
Mindszenty, Cardinal 214, 218–220, 222
Model, Field Marshal Walther 79
Mohr, August 174
Mona Lisa 175
Monticello, USS 88–89
Montini, Monsignor Giovanni Battista 216
Morey, Lt. Jonathan 147
Morgan, J.P. 91
Morgan Library 93, 167
Muehlmann, Kajetan 171, 172, 174, 177
Muhrau Castle 174–175
Mulde River, Germany 7, 10, 17, 21, 25, 28
Munich Collection Center 66, 102, 176, 213, 215, 218
Municipal Art Gallery, Düsseldorf 105
Murphy, John 153–155
Murrow, Edward R. 126
Murry, Jenny E. 144
Murry, W.H. 144
Museum of Ulm 142, 144–145
Musselman, Robert R. 21–22
Myaradi, Dr. Nicholas 196

Nagy, Imre 196, 198
Nash, Capt. Kathleen 18
National Bank of Hungary *see* Hungarian National Bank
National Gallery of Art 179
NBC 123, 126
Neuhaus, Germany 174, 175
New Colophon 95, 97
New York Times 117, 126, 219
Nixon, Richard 220
Normandy 87, 89

Oakar, Mary Rose 222–223
O'Brien, Capt. William G. 59–66, 68
Office of War Information 38
Ohringer, Capt. F.K. Siegfried John 17–18, 20, 26
Old Hermit 178
Old Quarai Spanish Mission 34–35
Omaha Beach 87
Opel, Elinor 47
Operation Overlord 87
Oshima, Baron Huroshi 45–46
Otto of Hapsburg 214–215, 219
Owens, Maj. Charles A. 4, 21–23, 25–26, 28, 29

Pajtas, Col. Ernoe 203, 204–207
Palézieux, Ernst von 174–175, 177
Palmi, Robert 175
Papen, Franz von 162

Parke Bernet Galleries 242
Parma, Mr. 128
Patch, Gen Alexander 51, 229
Patterson, Robert P. 218
Patton, Gen. George 46, 59, 87–88, 229
Paul Drey Gallery 184–185
Paul VI (pope) 216, 220
Pavlovich, Zarko 146–148
Peacock, Maj. J.H. 67
Pearl Harbor 38
Peat, Wilbur D. 179
Pengelly, Harold 20
Perera, Maj. Lionel 194
Peters, Janos 225
Pfaffenroth, Cläre 175
Pfaffenroth, Helmut 174
Philip Melanchton and Dragon 53, 56, 70
Philippot, M. 65
Phillips Academy 126
Pierre Cartier 218
Pirzl, Luitpold 180–182
Pius XII (pope) 96–97, 214, 216, 218
Plymouth Harbor 87
Poelenburg, Cornelis van 178
Pohl, Sister Rose Mary 135–137
Portrait of a Doctor 103
Portrait of a Man in Armor 105
Portrait of a Young Man 4 171–172, 174, 177
Portrait of Lady Elizabeth Hervey 137
Posner, Dr. Ernest 155, 160
Posse, Hans 172
Post, Claude E. 19
Pratt, Trude 41
Priam (king) 149
Princeton University 115, 122
Property Control Warehouse 209, 235, 237, 239
Prussian State Archives 94, 157
Puja, Frigyes 222–223
Pusch, Felix 80

Queen Amanishakhto 151
Queen Carolina 159
Queen Elizabeth, HMS 42
Queen Louise of Prussia 158
Queen Mary, HMS 42, 185
Queen Victoria 159
Quinn, Col. William 51

Rae, Capt. Edwin C. 56, 58, 67
Raphael 4, 171
Rapp, Dr. Albert 103
Rechenau, Oberaudorf, Bavaria 47, 49–50, 57
Red Cross 111
Rembrandt 171
René 47

Renoir 80
Reutti, Germany 141, 144–145
Rhine River 60, 66, 71, 79, 89, 126–127
Ringhotel Rheinhotel Dreesen 127
Ripley, P.F.C. Delbert 147
Robertson, Lt. Sinclair 103–104
Robertson, Lt. William 12
Rohracher, Prince Archbishop Andreas 209–213, 216–218
Roosevelt, Eleanor 40–41
Roosevelt, Franklin D. 35, 50–51, 129–130
Rorimer, Capt. James J. 81, 145, 184
Rosenbach, Dr. A.S.W. 91, 93, 97
Rosenbach, Phillip 91, 94–95
Rosenwald, Lessing 99
Rothschild, Sigmond 155
Royal Castle of Budapest 203, 208
Royal Hungarian Guards 203
Rumanian Head 13–14
Ruoff 60

Saal VIII 149
Saarbrücken 43, 162, 164, 165
Saarland 162, 165
Sachs, Ursula 47, 49–54, 56–58, 62, 67, 73
Sachs, Willy 47–48, 52–53, 56, 59, 75
St. Catherine 104–105
St. John's Seminary 96–97
Saint-Lô, France 88
Saint Stephen 201–202
Saint Stephen's Crown 202–204, 206, 215–216, 219–220, 222, 226
Saltzmann, Gen. Charles 237
Samaria, HMS 85
Satyr and Three Nymphs Frightened by a Thunderstorm 104
Saunders, Father Edward J. 216–217
Saxony-Weimar (grand duchess) 119
Scalzo, Richard H. 160–161
Schafer, Erwin 175
Schaible, Mayor 142
Schatzki, Walter 155
Scheidig, Dr. Walther 112, 114–118, 120–122, 132–134
Scheltema, Frederic Adama van 181
Schlag, Tec/3 Edward 22–24
Schliemann, Heinrich 149
Schmick, Gen. Peter 165
Schoenfold, Arthur 198
Schroeder, J. 26
Schüler, Dr. Walter 175
Schulz, Dr. Fritz T. 52, 55
Schwarzburg Castle, Germany 111, 112, 114–115, 117–118, 133, 135, 137
Scott, George 18
Seichau Palace 174

Seitz, Judge Patricia 242
Selke, Capt. George W. 208–209, 211, 217
Senter, Albert 33–34
Senter, Cedric 33
Senter, Lt. Donovan 4, 33–41, 47–70, 72–75
Senter, Doris 74
Senter, Florence 33
Senter, Florence Anita 37
Senter, Martin Hale 33
Shea 2/Lt. James W. 207–208
Shields, James 146–148
Shubow, Rabbi Joseph S. 149–152
Shughart, Dale 43–46
Sieniawa Castle 170–172
Sigaba 43
Sigismund 172
Simpendörfer, Michel 50
Simpendörfer, Otto 50
Sistine Madonna 166
Skorzeny, Otto 189
Smith, Col. William 92
Smithsonian Institution 185, 224
Snead, Maxwell A. 19
Sotheby's 137
Southampton, England 42, 89
Spa, Belgium 88, 123, 125
Spellman, Cardinal Francis 218
The Spoils of World War II 103
Staatliche Kunstsammlungen zu Weimar 112, 117, 120, 137
Städel Museum 103
Städelsches Kunstinstitute 103
Städtische Galerie 146
Stalin, Joseph 129–130
Stamp Auction Services 26
Standen, Capt. Edith 102–103
Steen, Jan 81
Stein, 2/Lt. Walter 175–176
Stephen Austin 130
Stern, Gerard 117
Still Life 80
Stonter, Edna 29
Strasser, Father Anton 207–208, 213
Survival 145
Swank, Emory C. 220
Sylvester II (pope) 201–202
Szalasi, Ferenc 189–191, 193, 199, 203, 207
Szirach Treasure 185

Tambach Castle 174, 176
Taos, New Mexico 37
Taper, Lt. Bernard B. 103, 177
Temesvary, Laszlo 191, 193
Temptation of St. Anthony 56
Teniers, David 56
Teply, Elmer 55, 72

Index

Thoma, Hans 13–14
Thuringia State Museum 112, 119
Tiergarten Flakturm 149
Tieschowitz, Dr. von 158
Tischbein, Johann Heinrich 137
Toldy, Dr. Árpád 228–229
Torgau, Germany 12, 128
Tornay, Edgar 193
Towers, Maj. John O. 16–18, 20–21
Travis Howard B. 104
Treaty of Versailles 162
Trebsen, Germany 7, 13, 17, 20, 22, 24–25, 28
Truman, Harry 51, 205, 218
Tryhard 13
Tucker, Evelyn 218
Tyler, William R. 167, 168

Underwood, Harry, M.D. 21–23
Unger, Hans 17
USSR Army forces: 175th Rifle Regiment 11; Ukrainian Army Group 128
United Press 126
U.S. Army forces: First Army 7, 10, 79, 86–89, 122–123, 131; First Army Group 87; First Army Press Unit 127; 3rd Armored Division 123–124; Third Army 193, 229; Third Military Government Regiment 59; Third Reinforcement Depot 51, 55; Fifth Army 229, 231; V Corps 88; Sixth Army Group 175; 6th Signal Center Liaison Team 85–86, 88–89; 7th Armored Division 79; Seventh Army 42–43, 229, 231; Seventh Army Interrogation Center 44–45, 49–50, 204–205, 207–208; Seventh Army Special Service Center 60; VII Corps 87; 8th Army Air Force 47; 9th Armored Division 7, 79; Ninth Army 10, 111; 11th Armored Division 40; 12th Armored Division 40; Twelfth Army Group 79, 127, 130; 15th American Infantry Division 114–115; 15th Army Air Force 230; 15th Infantry Regiment 232; XVI Corps 150; 17th Signal Operations Battalion 85, 88; XXI Corps 42–44, 46–48, 50; 28th Infantry Division 43; 30th Infantry Division 179, 193; 31st Infantry Division 243; 36th CIC Detachment 44; 36th Infantry Division 44; 39th Infantry Division, 1st Battalion, Company A 147; 42nd Infantry Division 235; 45th Infantry Division 40; 46th Quartermaster Graves Registration Company 141; 58th Armored Field Artillery, Battery C 146, 147; 64th Field Hospital 160; 69th Infantry Division 19–21, 26; 79th Infantry Division Artillery 56; 80th Infantry Division 193; 89th Infantry Division 110; 90th Infantry Division 40; 97th General Hospital, Frankfurt, Germany 74; 101st Airborne Division 53, 62, 178, 233; 102nd Infantry Division 109–111, 114, 116; 111th Cavalry, Troop A 33; 120 Infantry Regiment 179; 132 Evacuation Hospital 56–57, 66; 221 CIC Detachment 45, 48, 55; 242nd Infantry Regiment 207, 233; 273rd Infantry Regiment 7, 9–10, 12–14, 19, 21–23; 287th Engineer Combat Battalion 66; 317 Infantry Regiment 194; 319 Infantry Regiment Company K 194; 327 Medical Battalion 111; 369 Medical Battalion; 381st Military police Battalion 196; 406th Infantry Regiment, F Company 111–112; 450th Bombardment Group 230; 2756 Engineer Combat Battalion 102; 3805 Quartermaster Truck Company 194; 4460 Quartermaster Service Company 141, 143–144; 6103 Army Hospital, Camp Cook, California 74; Brooks Army Medical Center 74; CIC Border Control Detachment 56; Military Government Detachment G-221 56; Prisoner of War Interrogation Team 145 17, 26; T Force 175–176, 233
University of Arizona 36
University of Chicago 33, 36–37, 39, 68
University of New Mexico 33, 36, 68, 75

Vaccaro, Frank J. 135–136
Valena, C. van 13–14
Valentine, Lavin 105
Valentiner, William R. 104
Vance, Cyrus 222, 224–226
Vanik, Charles A. 221
Varga, Monsignor Bela 220
Vatican 210, 215, 218–219, 224
VE Day 110
Venus with Cupid 112, 137
Victor, Jean 72
Viet Stoss Altar 172–173
Vietnam War 221
Vilag 199
Vincentia Fathers 96
Vogeler, Robert A. 219
Voltaire 158
Vonhoff, Frau Huber 79–80
Vos, Marcus de 132

Waco, Texas 115, 122, 125, 127
Walters, Lt. Clinton R. 111–112, 134
Wamser, Dr. Ludwig 180
Wawel Castle 172, 174
Weeber, Maj. Richard P. 216–217

Weems, Gen. 198
Weimar Museum 4
Weinert, Fritz Otto 161
White, Lt. 111
Wiede, Anton 7–8, 13–19, 21, 23–25, 28
Wiede, Else 13–14, 17, 20, 26, 28
Wiede, Julia 25
Wiesbaden Collection Center 102–103, 169, 215
Wilhelm, Frederick 88, 160
Wilhelm Ernst (grand duke) 119
Wilhelm II (kaiser) 164
Willehalm Codex 81, 83, 89, 92–93, 95, 99

Wilson R.S. 178–179
Wolf, Edwin, II 99
Woolcott, Alexander 125
Wooten, 2/Lt. Cecil A. 111, 134
World Trade Center 41
Wünnenberg, Alfred 162, 164

Young Christ and Saint John 51
Youth in Red Cloak 81

Zamoyski, Count Stefan 172
Zikes, Vladimir 166, 167

www.ingramcontent.com/pod-product-compliance
Ingram Content Group UK Ltd.
Pitfield, Milton Keynes, MK11 3LW, UK
UKHW041929140426
5217IPUK00014B/378